The Complete Book of
FURNITURE REPAIR AND REFINISHING

New Revised Edition

by the staff of
The *FAMILY HANDYMAN*® Magazine

The Complete Book of
FURNITURE REPAIR
AND REFINISHING

RALPH PARSONS KINNEY

CHARLES SCRIBNER'S SONS / NEW YORK

Copyright 1950, © 1971, 1981 Charles Scribner's Sons

Library of Congress Cataloging in Publication Data

Kinney, Ralph Parsons.
  The complete book of furniture repair and
refinishing.

  Includes index.
  1. Furniture—Repairing. 2. Furniture finishing.
I. Family handyman. II. Title.
TT199.K5 1981   684.1′044   80-29616
ISBN 0-684-16839-1

Printed in the United States of America

CONTENTS

one

Furniture Restoration

WHY RESTORE FURNITURE?

There are lots of good reasons for restoring furniture. It's fun to take an old piece and give it new life. By shopping carefully you can often find furniture made with the kinds of woods and craftsmanship that are just about nonexistent in today's factory-made pieces. By working carefully you can improve the good old woods and craftsmanship of years gone by with the vastly superior finishes of today. The end result combines the best of both worlds and can fill you with a feeling of pride few factory pieces could ever evoke.

Restoring furniture can also save you money. It's no secret that secondhand furniture costs a lot less than something fresh off the showroom floor. True, restoration does cost money, but in most cases not much. Often, little more than a can of stripper and another of varnish will do the job. Sometimes you can even get by with a good scrubbing.

Best of all, furniture restoration is not difficult. Modern tools and materials make the work easy, even for a beginner. Time, patience, and care are far more important than highly developed skills.

FINDING FURNITURE TO RESTORE

The first place to look is in your own home. Good candidates for restoration may be hidden away in your attic or in some dark corner of the basement. They may be staring you in the face every day, tired old pieces sitting unnoticed in living room or den, waiting for you to bring them back to life.

Friends and relatives are another good source of used furniture. Furniture from

1-1. Once a sturdy work desk in a mercantile establishment, this large, handsome piece bears the scars of its long years of service. Some surfaces are distressed, and the front edge of the top shows nail holes where there once must have been fastened a small lip that prevented ledgers from sliding to the floor. The finish is a rich, deep mahogany with a high-gloss surface that gleams in the light.

relatives can often be your best find; it's especially rewarding to revitalize a piece that has been in the family for generations.

After exhausting your own supplies, and those of neighbors and relatives, comb tag sales, swap shops, mover's storage houses, Goodwill and other thrift shops, and auctions. Read want ads in the local papers. Really good pieces are becoming harder and harder to find, but they are still out there if you take the time to locate them.

ASSESSING USED FURNITURE

It's not too hard to get caught up in the spirit of shopping for used furniture. When that happens you can find yourself loaded down with a lot of pieces you have no real use for. So think carefully before you buy anything, keeping the following considerations in mind:

Is it functional? How will the piece be used? Where will it go in your home? Will it fit the space, or is it too large?

Is it well designed, with pleasing lines and proportions? Will its style fit in with your furnishings, or will it look out of place?

Is the construction sturdy, or will the piece need repairs? A piece needn't be in perfect condition, but if it does need rebuilding, can you handle it yourself? If not, it might pay to consult a pro, but only if the piece has enough value to offset the cost of repairs.

Are any parts missing? If so, would they be difficult or expensive to replace? Can you do the work yourself?

Is the piece made of well-matched attractive woods, or are a lot of mismatched boards glued together? Furniture made of mismatched boards (light sapwood and darker heartwood, for example) can be stained to a fairly uniform tone with care, but the work takes skill, so avoid the problem unless the piece appeals to you strongly in other ways.

If the piece is poorly constructed or has bad design features, could it be remodeled? With a little imagination, some seemingly worthless pieces can be effectively remade.

Finally, will the restored piece cost less than a new one? If not, it may be wiser to buy a new piece, unless the old one has value as an antique.

Using this checklist to evaluate a piece of furniture, be sure to make your inspection carefully. If the piece is tucked away in a dark corner, move it out into the open where you can get a good look at it. Direct sunlight is your best aid in detecting faults and virtues. Wipe off as much dust and grime as possible. Then proceed as follows:
- Look for missing parts.
- If the piece has drawers, examine the joints where drawer sides meet fronts. Well-fitted dovetail or fingerlap joints are a sign of good workmanship and an indication that other joints in the rest of the piece are most likely well made. (See pages 34–48 for further information on wood joints.)

1-2. *This is a lovely old dining room table that reflects all the charm and simplicity of Shaker construction. It's an extremely graceful design,* *made around 1880. This piece was finished in a light color to show all the natural wood.*

• Check for loose joints by wobbling the piece. This test will also help reveal legs of uneven length.
• Examine the wood closely and try to determine its species. If you are not especially good at identifying woods, bring along a friend who is. Another good idea is to carry a copy of a wood supply house mail order catalog, which usually contains full-color photos of the most common wood species, labeled to help you make identifications. (Such catalogs are available from Constantine's, 2050 Eastchester Rd., Bronx, N.Y. 10461, and Craftsman Wood Service Co., 2729 South Mary St., Chicago, Ill. 60608.) These catalogs may

also prove useful as sources of supply for the various woods, veneers, hardware, and upholstering supplies you will need later on.

• If the piece is covered with old paint, try to find an unpainted area—often the bottoms of surfaces—so you can examine the wood beneath. If you can't find an unpainted area, ask for permission to scrape off a small patch. If the piece is very old and the base coat is red, black, or green, this paint—called refractory paint—may be very difficult to remove because of its resistance to chemical removers and its tendency to penetrate deeply into wood pores. (More information about these paints can be found on page 92.)

• Once bare wood is exposed, you can easily check to see approximately what color it will be when varnished. Just dampen the bare area with water or a small amount of saliva. If the wood takes on a deep, warm glow, you know it will finish nicely. If the wood stays dull and muddy, expect it to do the same when finished.

• Turn the piece over and look at it from its underside. This view will often reveal more about the condition of a piece of furniture than the view from the top. Weak joints, splits and cracks, and faulty repairs are often clearly visible when a piece is inverted. Checking the underside of a piece can also reveal whether it is made of solid lumber or has been veneered. While solid lumber is usually better than veneered stock, that is not always the case. Veneering allows the furniture maker to achieve matching grain patterns and other attractive effects that are not possible with solid lumber. Well-executed veneers can add to the value of a piece. On the other hand, stay away from veneers that are blistering, cracking, or peeling away or are chipping around edges and corners—unless you have the skill and inclination to make the necessary repairs.

PLANNING THE RESTORATION

While evaluating a piece you plan to buy, you may also be working out the rough details of how you want to handle the restoration. Some decisions are easy. For example, if you like the lines and design of a particular piece, but not the wood it is made of, you will probably decide to paint it. Many a dark, dingy fumed-oak dresser has found a happy home in a child's room after being brightened with several coats of colorful enamel.

Most of your other decisions will be a little harder to make, and you won't be able to complete them until you have the piece at home where you can examine it carefully. And, in fact, some decisions are just impossible to make until you have stripped the old piece of its existing finish. Only then will you be able to determine exactly the condition of the wood and the refinishing procedure that suits it best.

Here's a good sequence to follow in evaluating a piece once you get it home:

1. First examine the existing finish. If it is in good condition you may not have to remove it. Don't expect perfection, and don't try to achieve it. While it may be possible to remove an old finish and apply a mirror-smooth replacement finish, doing

so may not be particularly appropriate. In most cases, a piece of old furniture may look better with a time-worn finish than with a brand-new one. As long as the old finish is sound and still able to protect the piece it covers, you are better off leaving it alone.

What's a sound finish? Usually, a few scratches, an occasional burn mark or white ring here and there, even a faded, foggy appearance are all acceptable. Such minor defects can usually be repaired without much trouble. But if the finish shows signs of alligatoring or checking (finishes that have dried out, leaving shallow or deep grooves that resemble the skin of a snake or alligator), or if it has darkened so much that you can't see the wood beneath it, you will probably have to remove it.

Don't be fooled by overly dark finishes, however. Some are merely covered with years and years of dirt, wax, smoke fumes, and other accumulations that can be removed, leaving a good finish behind. So if a particular piece seems dark and dingy, try cleaning it before you strip it.

If you are in doubt about a finish, try saving it (see Chapter Three on reviving old finishes); if you fail, you can always go ahead and strip it off. All you will have lost is a little time. If you succeed, you'll have saved yourself a lot of work and also have achieved a more authentic restoration than you would get from total refinishing. Remember, the less you do to an old piece, the better. Overrestoration will remove a lot of character the piece has picked up over the years.

If you come across a piece that needs

1-3. An antique dry sink can be easily converted into a planter, as seen here. Such units can often be found at antique auctions.

repairs, yet has a good finish (one that needs a small touch-up), do the repairs first, then the touching up. By saving the touch-ups for last, it will be easy to correct any damage the repairs may cause (clamp marks, new nail or screw holes) and to blend in any new pieces of wood you may have added.

2. If you decide an old finish can't be saved, go ahead and strip it. Then make any necessary repairs. Then refinish. Stripping before repairing is the only logical sequence. Why? For one thing, stripping may loosen old joints or raise bits of veneer, which will have to be repaired. Stripping may also reveal mismatched or unsightly pieces of wood you may decide to replace.

After a piece is stripped, look it over carefully, evaluating the type and attractiveness of the wood. Now is the time to decide on the finish most appropriate to the wood and to the style. If the wood is dull and without much character, paint is probably the best choice. If the wood has eye appeal, a natural clear finish is best.

If you decide to use stain, use it wisely. Avoid the temptation to try making one wood look like another. Pine looks best stained to look like old pine; efforts to make it look like mahogany or walnut invariably fail. In some cases you can make one wood look like another, but only when the two species have similar grain structures. Staining can change only the color of wood, not its grain patterns.

Now that you have planned the restoration, the following chapters will tell you how to make that restoration a success.

two

Furniture Repairs

Repair is the most difficult phase of restoration. If you lack the necessary tools or if you doubt your ability to accomplish fine work, take the job to a professional. However, don't avoid repair work entirely. An honest try may surprise you by uncovering a skill and aptitude you had no idea you possessed.

Comprehensive directions for furniture repair will be found in the detailed procedures of this chapter. The steps are easy to follow. Even if you are unaccustomed to using tools, you will not find their use too difficult. Actually, it's the purpose of this chapter to describe the various methods and uses of materials for making GENERAL repairs on ALL kinds of furniture, rather than to dwell on SPECIAL repairs or replacement of parts for PARTICULAR types of furniture.

INSPECTING FURNITURE

The first step in furniture repair is to locate all the areas of the piece that need repair. Work carefully, to avoid the possibility that you may overlook a defect requiring repair after the piece is completed. The following are some things to look for:

1. Examine all surfaces for cracks, bruises, small holes, or dents and for evidence of dry rot, which may have to be cut out and patched. Check veneer for loose edges, blisters, waves, cracks, dents, or bruises. Look for missing parts that must be replaced and for damaged or broken parts that may need repair or replacement, depending on their condition. Place the piece on a level surface and see that it is in balance; if not, one or more legs

may be of unequal length, which must be corrected. Long usage may have shortened all the legs so much that you may wish to lengthen them to restore the piece to its correct height.

Check drawers and doors for loose fit or bind. Make sure the hardware, such as handles, escutcheons, bolts and nuts, and hinges, is in place; if missing, it should be replaced. Check surfaces for board warps; if you find any, decide whether they are bad enough to warrant repair.

2. Rock the frame to locate any loose joints. Remove drawers, doors, and the top of the piece, when feasible or necessary.

3. Examine drawers and doors for loose joints in their construction and for any repairs or replacements that may be necessary. Keep all the hardware and fastenings, if removed, in a separate container.

4. Once you have pinpointed all possible problem areas, plan your work from the repair to the final finish. Select the procedures necessary and read and understand them thoroughly. Every step is important, for a step in one procedure may often be worked in with that in another. There are often optional procedures for achieving the same result, but do not deviate from the method you have selected unless unforeseen conditions arise.

TOOLS AND SUPPLIES FOR REPAIRING FURNITURE

Furniture most often comes apart when the glue bond at the joints is loosened. Animal glues, generally used in old furniture, are subject to attack by fungus organisms. They also dry out and become brittle, or they may be weakened by moisture. All these changes in the glue weaken the joints, and looseness in any one joint puts extra strain on the other ones until they too become loosened.

To repair a broken glue joint permanently, take it apart, clean off the glue, and reassemble and reglue the joints. To do this, you should have the following tools and supplies available:

Glue (See the chart on pages 14–15 for the right glue for the job.)
Clamps (rope tourniquets, C clamps, parallel jaw clamps, bar clamps)
A vise
A claw hammer, or a leather or wooden mallet
A brace and bit, and a hand drill
A small saw
A sharp jackknife
Dowel sticks (the same size as missing or broken rungs)
Dowel pins (grooved pins, ⅜ inch or ⅝ inch in diameter, to mend dowel joints)
Abrasive paper and smoothing block
Newspapers
Rags
Shears
Vinegar (half pint)
Blocks of wood (to use as pads under clamps)
Masking tape and pencil

Some repair jobs don't require all the materials in this list; others need supplies that are not listed.

ADHESIVES

The old animal glues mentioned above were made from hides, horns, and hooves of animals, boiled down to a jelly and then allowed to harden. This dried mass was broken into flakes or ground into coarse powder. When used, it was mixed with water and gently heated in an iron glue pot. This glue was hard, brittle, and brown in color, was not waterproof, and often left a stain on wood.

Today animal glues are used only in special applications. They have been largely replaced by newer glues that are much easier to use and give much better results. By using these new glues you will be able to make repairs at least as strong as and usually stronger than the original joints. But even the best glues will give poor results if you use them improperly. Here are some of the basic rules of good gluing:

• Choose the right glue. (See below and the chart on pages 14–15.)
• Surfaces to be glued must fit well. A poor fit will give a weak joint no matter what glue is used.
• Mating surfaces should be clean and in most cases dry. Dirt, wax, grease, oil, and even old glue must be removed or they will interfere with the absorption of the new glue.
• You must follow the manufacturer's instructions.
• Parts must be held immobile and in firm contact with screws, clamps, weights, etc., until the glue has had time to set.

Choosing Adhesives

There are dozens of different glues on the market today, but you can do almost all your work with just a few. Following are the basic types you should know about:

WHITE GLUE   Glues of this type (Elmer's is the best known) are made of a milky white polyvinyl acetate resin that dries quickly. It will not stain, and dries almost clear, but it is not waterproof and can be softened by heat (even heat caused by direct sunlight). It's a good all-around woodworking glue if you don't need water or heat resistance.

YELLOW GLUE   An excellent woodworking glue, this adhesive looks and handles as if it were a yellow version of white glue. It is an entirely different formula, however, with a few advantages over white glue. It gives stronger bonds and has what is called quick grab, meaning that if one holds parts together for a few seconds, they will "grab" quickly. You can then apply clamps with much less danger of the parts sliding out of alignment. Yellow glue is not waterproof but has better heat resistance than white. Titebond and Elmer's Carpenters Glue are two common brands. An excellent woodworking glue.

PLASTIC RESIN   This is a urea-formula glue consisting of a powder that must be mixed with water. It is not as popular as it was before white and yellow glues came on the market. First, it must be mixed. Second, its brown color makes it more visible than white or yellow glue, which both dry nearly clear. Third, it takes longer to set and thus slows down your work. While not really waterproof, it is highly water resistant. If you need a truly waterproof glue, you are better off with an epoxy or resorcinol formula.

RESORCINOL This is an extremely strong waterproof glue that will bond almost any material with at least some degree of porosity. It's a two-part formula—one can of powder, one of liquid—that sets slowly and has a deep reddish-brown color, a color that is a disadvantage if you want inconspicuous joints in light-colored woods.

EPOXY This is a glue that can do just about anything. It's the strongest glue there is, completely waterproof and usually colorless. It will glue just about anything to anything else, and it doesn't shrink as it sets. That makes it the best choice for loose joints; it fills in the gaps and still retains a fair degree of strength. Except for three things, epoxy could just about replace all other glues.

1. It must be mixed from two parts, and that's a bit time consuming and messy.

2. It is quite expensive compared to most other glues.

3. It can cause severe allergic reactions in some people.

NOTE: The best epoxies are the slow-setting formulas. The "five-minute" types tend to produce weaker, more brittle bonds.

URETHANE Here's another super-strong glue that will bond almost anything. Unlike epoxies, urethane is a one-part glue, ready to use. But it requires an almost perfect fit between the parts being joined or its strength falls off rapidly. Dow Urethane Bond is the common brand.

CONTACT CEMENT This is an air-drying adhesive that is used exclusively for bonding sheet materials such as Formica, laminates, and leather, etc., over relatively large areas. Unlike other glues, it is not used to bond joints. The newest types are water based and are much safer and easier to use than the older solvent cements with their strong fumes and the ever-present fire hazard. Both types are used the same way: brush or roll them onto both surfaces to be bonded, let them dry until no longer tacky, then press together. Parts bond instantly and cannot be moved once pressed into contact.

ANIMAL GLUES These may be made from hooves, animal hides, or fish. Some come ready to use; others are in flake form that must be heated before they can be used. The hot glues have the advantage of setting quickly as they cool, and for this reason are sometimes used for rapid bonding of veneers. Because of their inability to resist heat and water, animal glues are seldom used today except where those weaknesses can be exploited. For example, instrument makers often use them to attach parts that may later require removal to permit maintenance and repair of that instrument. Careful application of heat and moisture will release the part without causing any damage.

OTHER TYPES There are other glues commonly available that are of little or no use to the furniture restorer. Cyanoacrylates such as Super Glue, Krazy Glue, and Eastman 910 are fast setting and incredibly strong, but they work only on non-porous surfaces. That excludes woods. Hot-melt glues that are squeezed from a heated gun offer good strength, but they set so fast that they are tricky to use. Silicone rubber glues (often called sealants) have too little strength to be of much use in furniture work. See the table on pages 14 and 15.

2-1. *Accurate measuring is important when mixing synthetic thermosetting resin glues. Mix the activating powder into the resin, using disposable implements.*

Above: *This type of glue has a working life of about 4 hours. Don't mix too much, and, unless you can throw away containers, wash them out quickly, within the 4-hour limit.*

CLAMPS AND TOURNIQUETS

Clamps and tourniquets are used to hold glue joints firmly together and in alignment while the glue is hardening.

Before clamps or tourniquets are tightened, joints to be glued should be checked to see that they are in the proper position. Once the glue has hardened, it becomes impossible to change the position without damage.

Clamps

The most common types of clamps used in applying pressure to glue joints are as follows:

Wood clamps (the technical name) are more commonly called "hand screw clamps." These clamps come in various sizes, with jaws from about 5 to 20 inches long and with maximum openings from about 2 to 15 inches. These clamps are important shop equipment.

The quickest and easiest way to open or close the jaws is to grip a handle in each hand and swing the clamp around. This keeps the jaws parallel as they move on the screw threads. Clamp the jaws evenly and firmly against the pieces to be held together, then tighten the outer screw to give extra tension. If necessary, you can adjust the jaws out of parallel to fit the shape of your work.

c *clamps* are excellent multipurpose tools. You can use them singly to secure small joints or in groups to exert heavy, even pressure over a large area. A nicely

2-2. Wood clamps in use

GLUE SELECTION GUIDE

	WHITE GLUE	YELLOW GLUE	PLASTIC RESIN	RESORCINOL
Advantages	Easy to use Dries clear Strong Fast setting Inexpensive Won't stain	Easy to use Dries clear Strong Quick grab Fast setting Won't stain Inexpensive	Strong Water resistant	Strong Waterproof

Disadvantages	Vulnerable to
	  heat and
	  wetness
	May creep
	  under
	  strain
		Not water-
		  proof
			Needs
			  mixing
			Dries brown
			Sets slowly
				Needs
				  mixing
				Dries very
				  dark
				  brown
				Sets slowly
				Expensive

Water Resistance	Poor	Fair	Good	Excellent
Preparation	Ready to use	Ready to use	Mix with water	Mix

Working Temperature	Room
	  temper-
	  ature or
	  higher
		Room
		  temper-
		  ature or
		  higher
			Room
			  temper-
			  ature or
			  higher
				Room
				  temper-
				  ature or
				  higher
				Heat speeds
				  setting

Application	Coat both
	  surfaces
	  and clamp
		Coat both
		  surfaces
		  and clamp
			Coat both
			  surfaces
			  and clamp
				Coat both
				  surfaces
				  and clamp

Clamping Time **Hardwood** **Softwood**	1 hour 1½ hours	½ hour ½ hour	16 hours 16 hours	16 hours 16 hours

EPOXY	URETHANE	CONTACT CEMENT	ANIMAL GLUES

Clear
Very strong
Waterproof
Won't shrink
Fills gaps
Glues most surfaces
	Very strong
	No mixing
	Clear
	Glues most
	  surfaces
	Waterproof
	Flexible
		Waterproof
		Requires no
		  clamping
			Hot types set fast
			Easy to
			  disassemble
			Fairly strong

Requires mixing
Expensive
Allergenic
	Requires good
	  fit between
	  parts
	Sets slowly
		Solvent types have
		  noxious fumes
		Parts can't be
		  moved after
		  contact
			Brittle
			Vulnerable to
			  heat, moisture,
			  molds
			Hot types require
			  mixing and
			  heating

Excellent	Excellent	Excellent	Poor
Mix	Ready to use	Ready to use	Depends on type

Depends on formula,
  but most types need
  room temperature
Heat speeds set
	Room temper-
	  ature or higher
		75 or higher	Room temperature
			  or higher; hot
			  types require
			  heating of parts
			  in some cases to
			  slow setting time

Coat both surfaces and
  clamp
	Coat both surfaces
	  and clamp
		Coat both
		  surfaces, let set
		  until no longer
		  tacky, bond by
		  pressing
		  together
			Depends on type

Depending on formula,
  5 minutes to 12 or
  more hours
	2 hours
	2 hours
		—	Depends on type;
			  2 to 3 hours for
			  liquid types, ½
			  hour for hot types

equipped shop should have at least four medium C clamps (of around 4-inch capacity), several small ones for delicate work, and a pair of large ones with extra-deep throats for those projects that require a wide reach. It's best to buy the large clamps—and the bar and pipe clamps described next—only as you need them. They are fairly expensive, and there's no sense investing in them unless you really need them.

The *bar clamp* comes in various lengths and is used for clamping extra-wide work. You will note in the illustration that there are pieces of wood under the jaws of the bar clamp holding the back slats of the chair in place. The wood strips are placed

there to distribute the pressure of the clamp and prevent the jaws from injuring the chair surface. A well-equipped shop should include this type of clamp, but it is not essential, as a tourniquet may often be used as a substitute.

A *pipe clamp* is often used by the handyman in place of a bar clamp. This type of clamp is available to fit either ½- or ¾-inch-diameter iron pipe. One end of the pipe is threaded to accept the fixed jaw. The movable jaw slides freely on the pipe and can be locked in place wherever you want it. The handyman should have several different lengths of pipe to use with his clamps. While you can use a long pipe for all jobs, the excess pipe might get in

2-3. Bar and pipe clamps in use

your way. It's always best to use pipe clamps, like bar clamps, in pairs.

Special clamps are made to hold pieces of wood at right angles while they are being joined. Many of these have openings in their sides through which nails or screws can be inserted.

It is possible to make your own clamps for securing work. For instance, a home-made *wedge clamp* is excellent for binding boards that are to be glued together, edge to edge. It is easy to make and use, as shown in the drawing below. Here is how it is done:

1. Construct this clamp from scrap lumber ¾ to 1 inch in thickness, 6 to 8 inches wide, and about one-half as long as the boards to be glued. On the wide side of the clamp material, mark each end at the midpoint from the sides. Now measure up and mark a point ½ inch above the center on one end and on the other end ½ inch below. Connect these two points by a diagonal line and saw through the material lengthwise along the line. This will give you two wedge-shaped pieces of the required angle, regardless of the length of the material.

2. Apply glue to both contact edges of the boards to be glued and place these edges in the correct permanent position on a level wood surface, over waxed paper, and against a backboard or butt.

3. Drive a nail that is about one and one-half times longer than the thickness of the wedges into, but not through, one of the wedges *only*, on the flat surface near each end, as shown in the drawing.

4. Put the wedges together as sawed, having on the outside and near the middle of the board the one into which the nails were driven, the other one against the outside edge of the board to be clamped.

5. Then drive the nails partly through into the surface below, deeply enough to hold the outer wedge firmly in place but leaving the nail heads above the surface in order that they may be pulled out easily later.

6. Pound the inner wedge tightly in place from the wider end, creating a strong tension against the glued boards. If the boards to be glued are thin, it will be necessary to place a weight on them to keep them from buckling.

7. Using a damp cloth, wipe off any ex-

2-4. An easy-to-make wedge clamp

2-5. The single-tourniquet method of furniture clamping

cess glue squeezed out on the upper surface and keep the boards clamped for 48 hours. A knife may be used later to clear the bottom side of any excess glue.

When using wedge clamps, remember that the work must be done on a level, clean surface, such as a workbench with a back or wall to butt against. A section of a wood floor adjoining a wall is an excellent spot, provided you don't object to nail holes in the flooring.

Tourniquets

The use of a tourniquet is often more satisfactory than a mechanical clamp when properly applied, as it distributes the pressure more evenly. You make a tourniquet by looping a rope once around a furniture piece. The ends of the rope are tied together (a bowknot is good) and a

stick (a short dowel or large spike is good) is twisted in the rope until the desired tension is obtained. Then the stick can be lodged behind some portion of the furniture to maintain the tension.

The best rope to use is a heavy cotton clothesline, because it is soft, strong, and closely woven. There is no need to cut the rope to the size needed. When two tourniquets are needed on a single job, each end of the rope may be used.

GLUING FURNITURE

There are many pieces of very old furniture that should never be dismantled at all the joints. This is particularly true of some of the old chair rungs. The reason for this is that, in the days before glue was used for joints, a chair rung may have been shaped or turned out of dry wood, with a bulb on the end. This was fitted closely into the hole of a green or unseasoned leg. As the wood in the leg dried, it shrank and the joint became tight around the bulb. Such a joint may become loose with wear, but it cannot be taken apart without damage. Many fine old pieces were put together with wooden pins or wedges and can't be taken apart without damage to the pin, wedge, or the surrounding wood.

Shaky and rickety joints in such furniture may be reglued, if clean, without taking the piece apart. When joints fit fairly closely, apply glue with a toothpick and work or rock the piece to and fro, to get the glue well into the joint. Whenever possible, turn the piece so the joint opening is in a vertical position, so the glue can flow downward into the joint. The best glue to use for this kind of work is epoxy, since it will fill gaps well and will not shrink.

Glue may also be introduced into these joints by using a small oil can, plastic squeeze bottle, or a special tool called a glue injector. Drill a small hole (1/16 inch) in an inconspicuous spot at an angle to, or alongside, one part of the loose joint. Insert the tip of the injector into the hole and force glue into the joint. Glue should be forced out around the joint. When this "squeeze-out" appears, clamp the joint, wipe off the excess glue, and let it dry.

For satisfactory results in furniture repair work, follow these general rules for gluing:

1. It is impossible to glue loose or rickety furniture properly if the joints are filled with old glue and dirt. In such cases, if possible, dismantle the piece and clean all the joints thoroughly. To do this, pull all the loose joints apart. Use a hammer or mallet to loosen the joints that don't pull apart easily. Protect the furniture from dents with a block of wood or a thick pad of folded newspaper. Be careful that you don't break parts if you have to force them out of position during this operation.

2. Joints that are firm and tight should be left undisturbed. If such a joint *must* be loosened, soak it with warm vinegar to soften the glue.

3. Scrape or otherwise remove from surfaces to be glued all old glue, paint, dust, oil, wax, grease, old finish, etc. Materials to be glued must be thoroughly clean and dry.

4. When scraping or chipping off the old glue, be careful not to remove any wood. If you can't remove the glue by chipping or scraping, or if there is danger of damaging the wood, soften the old glue with warm vinegar. This is a very sticky process that saturates the wood, so you must wait for the wood to dry before you can continue. Where possible, scrub with an old toothbrush.

5. You need *not* remove all the glue from the end grain of the joint; simply chip off the thickest lumps. Joints are usually constructed with clearance between the end of the dowel, or round, and the bottom of the hole so that the joint will fit snugly at the shoulder.

6. Uneven surfaces must be planed, sanded, or scraped to make perfect, well-fitted contact surfaces.

7. Avoid roughening the surfaces to be

joined. United States Forest Products laboratory tests have shown that smooth, close-fitting parts give the best bonds.

8. When dismantling, it is best to take out, clean, and replace one piece at a time, unless it is obvious how to assemble and there are no similar parts. Otherwise, mark the ends of the parts as they come out and the inside of the joints from which they were removed, so you may reassemble properly. This is particularly important since in many cases a joint would not be loose unless there has been wear, and these worn parts must be returned to the places from which they were taken.

9. When marking dismantled pieces, it is good to make small grooves with a three-cornered file or a chisel on such similar pieces as chair rungs, back slats, etc., because pencil marks may be obliterated in removing dirt, old glue, or paint. However, it is usually sufficient to mark the side wall of the hole with a pencil, as these marks are not apt to be lost in cleaning.

10. Open the pores of the wood to allow the glue to enter freely, either by dipping the parts to be glued in warm water and letting them dry thoroughly, or by laying them on top of a warm radiator or stove, or in the sunshine, until they are warm.

11. When the parts are clean and thoroughly dry, put all of them together again to test them for proper fit. If they fit closely, they're ready to be glued. If an end that goes into a hole fits a little loosely, then follow one of the methods described for "Tightening Round or Square Furniture Joints," page 45.

12. Before gluing, be sure that all materials, tools, and glue are ready to be used. Have the furniture and the glue at room temperature, since cold glue and cold wood won't bond properly. No type of glue will function properly if it or the piece to be glued is too cold. For best results, gluing and drying of glue should be done in room temperatures of 70 to 75 degrees F. Forcing a glue to dry too rapidly will also bring bad results.

13. A thin layer of glue, correctly applied, will hold better than a thick layer poorly applied.

14. Apply glue to both surfaces of the joints and assemble the parts, checking the marks you made earlier to be sure of getting each part in the right place. Place the piece to be glued on old newspapers to catch any glue that might drop.

15. Apply pressure with clamps or tourniquet, placing thin pieces of wood or folded pads of newspaper under the jaws of the clamps or contact points of the tourniquet, so as not to injure the surfaces. Use waxed paper under the wood pieces or pads when it is likely that glue will run out under them from the pressure applied, as this type of paper will not stick to the glue.

16. Immediately after all of the parts have been glued and clamped, and while the glue is still soft, wipe the glue from the finish. Use a stick cut to a smooth chisel-edge to clean around the joints and small places, and then wipe the rest of the surface with a clean, damp cloth. Let the piece remain until the glue is dry (about 24 hours, unless a fast-setting glue has been used).

17. To prevent the glue from running

out of a newly glued joint when the piece is turned to a different position to glue another joint, wipe off the excess glue and wind a piece of string around the joint several times and knot it. Before the glue becomes hard, remove the string. Any excess glue remaining may be removed later after the glue has become crystal hard, with a knife, without damage to the surface.

18. Test on a flat surface all pieces that have many glued joints (chairs, tables, etc.) for perfect alignment. Should this not be done and the piece be out of alignment, it would be impossible to rectify the trouble after the glue has dried.

19. Allow to dry for at least 24 hours in a warm room before releasing clamps or tourniquet and 48 hours before doing further work or using a piece thus glued.

20. When the clamps or tourniquets have been released, clean off all glue that was squeezed out from joints and not reached previously. Often the glue may not be crystal hard. Remove carefully with a knife blade, taking care not to injure the surface. Any glue remaining on a surface will cause spots to show through a clear finish.

Special Techniques

Sometimes it is necessary to use two clamps or to tie two pieces of rope, one on either side of the part being glued, to get enough pressure to draw the parts together. To hold a chair rung tight, place the clamp on the legs directly over the place where the rung enters, or if rope is used, pass it around the two legs at the point where the rung enters. If a rung is being glued on the other side of the chair at the same time, place a second clamp or rope in the same way.

When a loose chair back or the top of a chair is being glued, pass one end of the rope down the front and under the seat and tie it to the other end that comes over and down the back. Make the tourniquet at the front of the chair. Two ropes, one at each side of the back and tied in the same way, are better than one. If the two ropes slip off the top of the back after they are tied, hold them together with a cord.

BROKEN PARTS Simple breaks on legs, rungs, spindles, and arms that are diagonal or lengthwise of the piece may be glued; those broken straight across the short way or across the grain, and tabletops, need special tools and skill to repair them.

A new break may be ready to glue and brace together immediately. An old break that has been glued before must first be washed out to remove the glue and then reglued as directed. Because there is likely to be great strain where the back legs are fastened to a chair seat, those places may need to be made more secure. After the glue has dried, put a long slim screw through the leg and the seat. Countersink this screw, cover the head with matching wood or water putty, and paint it, or apply matching shellac stick (page 30), so that the place will not show.

GLUING CRACKS A large percentage of cracks in wood furniture may be glued and clamped together, resulting in a permanent repair. In every case, the accumulated dirt, old glue, and paint must be removed or the new glue will not hold. Usually, this may be done with the point of a narrow-bladed knife, a pin, or any other thin tool. If the crack is straight, it may often be well cleaned by dragging an old hacksaw blade through the crack, with the teeth down and pointing toward the worker. The loose material can then be dumped or blown out.

The procedures for this work are as follows:

For a crack near an edge, when possible or necessary, widen the crack with several small and thin softwood wedges. Gently drive in one wedge at a time until the crack is wide enough to insert glue. Remove the wedges and apply clamps. Place over waxed paper and put flat sticks under the jaws of the clamps, so as not to injure the wood surface. A tourniquet may often be used on wide surfaces, should you not own bar clamps.

Brads may be used, if preferred, to draw the crack together after gluing. With care and using a small hammer, drive the brad into the board edge, sink the head below the surface with a nail-set, and fill the hole left with stick shellac or wood putty or dough of the same color as the finish. Smooth off carefully with a knife or fine abrasive paper.

For a crack a distance from an edge, after the crack has been thoroughly cleaned, test with a strong bar clamp (with blocks of wood under the jaws so as not to injure the surface) to see if it is possible to draw the crack together. If this can be done, apply glue and clamp.

If the crack runs to the end of thick boards, in crude pieces, it is sometimes good to give added strength on the end by toenailing with finishing nails. (See "Repairs with Nails," page 41.) The head of the nail may be driven below the wood surface and filled, in the way described for a crack near an edge.

If the crack is wide and long, it may be best to reinforce it on the underside of the board with mending plates, provided such a repair cannot be seen.

When it is not possible to draw the crack together with clamps, it will have to be filled. (See "Stick Shellac," page 30.) RE-MEMBER: Don't confuse a space between two boards, caused by shrinkage, with a crack. (See "Repairing Cracks Due to Shrinkage," page 32.)

USING WOOD SCREWS

When using screws to hold together two pieces of *hardwood,* drill holes of two sizes, the larger in the upper piece of wood and the smaller in the lower. A screw driven in hardwood without the proper-sized holes is apt to crack or split the wood, and the screw may refuse to enter it or may break off.

The upper or clearance hole (also called a pilot hole) should be sufficiently large so that the screw can be inserted with the fingers, while the lower or anchor hole, drilled for the threaded part of the screw, must be small enough to give adequate holding power. In using a flat-headed screw, countersink the mouth of the upper hole to accommodate the screw head, so it will be flush with or below the surface.

When working with *softwood*, holes of different sizes are not necessary unless near an edge. However, it will help to drill a small hole in both pieces of wood, smaller in size than the diameter of the screw thread, to serve as a guide for the screw.

As a general rule, a screw should be about three times as long as the thickness of the top piece being joined. Sometimes it is necessary to use a shorter screw to prevent the tip from passing all the way through the bottom piece.

Use of Tables

Table 1 (page 24) gives the lengths (column 1) in which wood screws are made and the number of the screw in both *steel* and *brass* (columns 2 and 3). The sizes of holes needed per screw number is explained later under Table 2.

Example 1: Screws ¼ inch long are made of steel or brass in numbers from 0 to 4 inclusive.

Example 2: Screws 1 inch long are made of steel in numbers from 3 to 16 and of brass in numbers from 4 to 14.

Example 3: Screws 4 inches long are made of steel only, in numbers from 12 to 24, 3½ inches being the longest brass screw made.

Table 2 gives the screw number (column 1), followed by the diameter of the shaft in inches, just below the head. The screw number designates the size of the screw, according to the Standard Screw Gauge. Table 2 also gives the size (diameter) of the drill to use in hardwoods for both clearance holes (column 3) and anchor holes (column 4).

Example 1: No. 0 screws (column 1) are ⅟₁₆ inch in diameter of shaft, so you should use a ⅟₁₆-inch drill for the clearance hole and a ⅟₃₂-inch drill for the anchor hole.

Example 2: No. 8 screws (column 1) have a shaft ¹¹⁄₆₄ inch in diameter, so you should use a ³⁄₁₆-inch drill for the clearance hole and a ³⁄₃₂-inch drill for the anchor hole.

Driving Screws

When driving a screw, keep the following tips in mind:

1. Before drilling a hole or using a screw, mark a small x with a pencil at the exact spot where the hole or screw is to be located, using for this purpose, if possible, a try square. At the intersection of the diagonals of the x, make a small dent by hitting a center punch lightly.

2. If the boards are not already fastened together, remove the upper one and place a flat piece of scrap wood under the board where you wish to drill, to prevent the lower side of the board from tearing or splintering as the drill comes through. Drill the clearance hole, using the proper size twist drill. Power hand drills are excellent for drilling screw holes in hardwoods, provided they are handled with care.

3. Replace the upper board in the proper position over the lower, change the twist drill to the size for the anchor hole, and drill, through the clearance hole into the lower board, the full length of the screw.

TABLES OF WOOD SCREW SIZES

1. LENGTH OF SCREWS **2. SIZES FOR SCREW NUMBERS**

SCREW LENGTH (INCHES)	MADE IN SCREW NOS. (NOS. INCLUSIVE) STEEL	BRASS	SCREW NO.	DIAM. OF SHAFT (INCHES)	SIZE DRILL CLEARANCE HOLE (INCHES)	SIZE DRILL, ANCHOR HOLE (FOR HARDWOODS) (INCHES)
¼	0 to 4	0 to 4	0	1/16	1/16	1/32
⅜	0 to 8	0 to 6	1	5/64	3/32	1/32
½	1 to 10	1 to 8	2	3/32	3/32	1/32
⅝	2 to 12	2 to 10	3	7/64	1/8	1/16
¾	2 to 14	2 to 12	4	1/8	1/8	1/16
⅞	3 to 14	4 to 12	5	1/8	1/8	1/16
1	3 to 16	4 to 14	6	9/64	5/32	3/32
1¼	4 to 18	6 to 14	7	5/32	5/32	3/32
1½	4 to 20	6 to 14	8	11/64	3/16	3/32
1¾	6 to 20	8 to 14	9	3/16	3/16	3/32
2	6 to 20	8 to 18	10	13/64	7/32	1/8
2¼	6 to 20	10 to 18	11	13/64	7/32	1/8
2½	6 to 20	10 to 18	12	7/32	7/32	1/8
2¾	8 to 20	None	14	¼	¼	1/8
3	8 to 24	12 to 18	16	9/32	5/16	5/32
3½	10 to 24	12 to 18	18	5/16	5/16	3/16
4	12 to 24	None	20	21/64	⅜	3/16
4½	14 to 24	None	24	⅜	⅜	7/32
5	14 to 24	None				

NOTE: Should an anchor hole be desired for softwoods, use a size smaller than designated. *Example:* For a no. 10 screw, use a 3/32-inch drill in place of a ⅛-inch drill.

4. Insert the screw and turn it down to its full length, taking care that the screwdriver does not slip from the slot and injure the wood. A small amount of beeswax applied to the thread of the screw will make it go in more easily.

5. The tip of the screwdriver should fit closely into the screw slot and be as wide as the screw head. This prevents slipping and tearing the slot. It is best to use an ordinary screwdriver for furniture, particularly on fine woods. An automatic screwdriver is apt to slip from the slot and mar the wood. Phillips-head screws are easier to drive than slotted screws, since the screwdriver is less likely to slip out of the crossed slots of a Phillips screw.

6. When using steel screws, a screwdriver bit in a brace is good for the final tightening of the screws. Use it for the full drive with large screws, but never use a bit with a brace for brass screws. Brass is weak and will break off easily, usually in the threaded section, causing much trouble.

7. When there are a number of screws in a surface, leave the slots of the screws in a line with the grain of the wood for better appearance. If the screws are on a vertical surface, have the slots parallel with the floor.

REMOVING WOOD SCREWS

A wood screw is often difficult to remove, particularly a steel one that has become rusted in wood or a deeply buried flat-headed screw with a damaged slot.

Methods for removing stubborn screws follow:

1. Use a screwdriver whose blade tip is as wide as the screw head and fits snugly into the slot. If the tip is too narrow and the screw is stubborn, you are apt to tear and damage the slot, making your work more difficult.

2. If unable to remove the screw with a hand screwdriver, try a brace with a screwdriver bit. Press down firmly on the brace, so as not to injure the slot by slippage of the bit, and give a quick turn to the left (counterclockwise) to unthread the screw. If the screw will not move, follow with a quick thrust to the right (tightening the screw) and quickly reverse the motion, to the left, again. This action will often start the screw. If not, try heating the screw by applying a soldering iron or gun to the head. Be careful not to char the wood.

3. Finally, try to jar the screw loose from its hole in the wood (particularly if the screw is rusted) by pounding it sharply on the head. To do this, place the tip of the screwdriver in the slot and strike a fairly heavy blow with a hammer. (For a flatheaded screw, a round, short steel bar not larger than the screw head may be used in place of the screwdriver.) Then try to move the screw with a hand screwdriver. If not successful, use a brace with a screwdriver bit.

A Round-headed Screw
with a Damaged Slot

The slot can often be widened or deepened with a hacksaw, since the screw head is above the surface. If necessary, remove the saw blade from the frame. Then follow the general rules given.

A Flat-headed Screw with a Damaged Slot

A flat-headed screw with a damaged slot is difficult to remove, since the head is flush with, or buried below, the wood surface. Use the following procedures *in the order given:*

1. Place the point of a nail-set in the extreme right-hand end of the screw slot and at right angles to the slot. Slant it as nearly as possible toward the surface of the board (with the point still in the slot) and strike the nail-set with a hammer. If this will start the screw unthreading, repeat until the screw can be removed with a screwdriver, or until the head is raised enough to grip it in the jaws of diagonal cutters. It may then be worked out with that tool.

2. When the first method fails, try this one: Drill a shallow hole (with a twist drill about one-half the diameter of the screw head) down through the center of the head (taking care not to let the drill go so deep that it will go through the head). Select a screwdriver with a point that is *slightly wider* than the width of the hole and pound it down into the hole, thus cutting slots on each side of the hole. Continue pounding, to loosen the grip of the screw threads in the wood. Press down firmly on the screwdriver and apply a quick, jerky motion to turn it toward the left (counterclockwise). Should greater leverage be required, tighten an adjustable wrench over

the flattened lower part of the screwdriver blade and push the wrench as you would a brace, while pressing down firmly on the screwdriver so it will not be torn from the screw top.

3. If both of these methods fail, drill the hole deeper until the head of the screw is cut off from its stem. The upper board may then be lifted off from the lower, the head of the screw picked out from the upper board (or driven out from the underside with a nail-set), and the protruding shaft of the screw may be unscrewed from the lower board with a pair of pliers. A little kerosene put on the screw head and allowed to soak well into the wood will often help loosen a rusted screw. However, since this may darken the wood, particularly softwood, it should be avoided unless the wood is to be painted or stained with a dark stain.

REMOVING NAILS

Many old pieces of crude furniture were fastened with nails. It is often difficult to extract such nails, particularly the old iron cut nails, if rusted. Before attempting to remove a nail having a large head, especially if embedded, attempt to break its bind against the side of the hole. To do this, strike the head a sharp blow, but take care that the force is not such that the nail is driven deeper into the wood. For this, hold a spike with the point sawed off, or a blunt tool of the proper size, against the head and strike one sharp blow with a hammer. Then use the following procedures *in the order given.* The first is less drastic.

1. If the nail is situated where it can be raised by pounding from the underside of the board, as in the case of a nail holding a tabletop to the frame, place a block of wood 6 to 8 inches in length under the top, as nearly as possible below the nail, strike against the block with a hammer, and then pound the board back.

If this raises the nail sufficiently, draw it out a short way with a claw hammer, having first placed a thin piece of metal—a flat scraper is good—under the hammer head to prevent injury to the wood surface. Next, place a block of wood, about an inch thick, under the head of the hammer and continue to draw the nail upward. The block under the hammer head gives a more nearly perpendicular pull.

If it is possible to raise the nail only slightly by the blow, insert a hacksaw blade (removed from the frame) between the two pieces nailed together, saw the nail through, and punch it out from the underside of the top board with a nail-set.

2. As a last resort, remove the nail with diagonal cutters. The points of the jaws will leave a slightly larger hole in the wood surface, but this can be filled with stick shellac, wood dough, or wood putty. To remove a nail by this method, force the jaw points under the nail head, squeeze the handles firmly, and push down. As the jaws are set at a slight angle from the handles, this downward push will exert a leverage that will lift the nail straight up. When the nail has been raised a little, release the grip, take a lower hold on the nail, and repeat until the nail has been en-

tirely withdrawn. (It is good to place a thin piece of metal under the jaws to prevent injury to the wood surface.) Once you have mastered this method of extracting a stubborn nail you will marvel at the ease with which it is done.

WOOD DOUGH OR PLASTIC

Wood dough is often called plastic wood. The name is incorrect, as that is a registered trade name of a popular brand of wood dough, just as Duratite is the registered trade name of another brand. In recent years, wood plastic has been used interchangeably with wood dough.

Wood dough dries quickly and may be sanded, planed, drilled, or carved. It will hold nails or screws and can be used to fill cracks, such holes as nail or knot holes, and even for building up broken-off wooden parts. It is one of the cheapest and quickest materials for repairing. If properly applied it will make a strong and permanent repair, but it has one limitation: no matter how carefully it is smoothed, stained, and finished, it will seldom be entirely unnoticeable in a surface. The main reason for this is that, like stick shellac, it has no grain, in contrast to the wood in which it has been used.

Wood plastic is best used in inconspicuous places, or in those places where a part must be built up, then shaped or carved, stained, and finished. Use it also in places where the repair requires strength, the ability to withstand moderate shock without chipping, or where nails or screws must be employed.

Wood dough is composed of finely ground wood, mixed with a binder and softened with quickly evaporating materials. Most of it comes in "natural" color (something like light oak), to be later stained, if desired, but it is also available in colors to match various woods.

Wood plastic comes in tubes and cans of various sizes. Immediately after using any, close the container tightly, as the solvent evaporates very rapidly, causing the contents to harden. Additional solvent may often be purchased for softening wood dough that has thickened beyond practical use, but that which has dried too far can never again be softened for use. When a prepared thinner is not available, a high-grade lacquer thinner is recommended by many stores as a substitute.

How to Use Wood Dough or Plastic

While the instructions on the container should be followed to the letter, here are some tips that you should keep in mind:

1. See that the place where the wood dough is to be applied is thoroughly dry and free from dust and dirt. However, wood dough will stick to old paint if the surface has been roughened.

2. Apply it to the spot to be filled or added to, taking extra precautions to keep it from the surrounding surface. Pack it deeply into holes. Wet the tip of your finger and press it firmly in place. Allow to dry thoroughly.

3. Strip off the surplus with a sharp knife or chisel and, if on a finished surface, sand smooth with 7/0 or 8/0 abrasive paper, taking care to sand only where applied. Wood dough shrinks slightly in drying. If the place to be filled or added is large, use several applications, one over the other, but only after the previous one has dried thoroughly. Finally, build up the surface to a height slightly higher than the desired final level. This coat is to be cut and smoothed down.

4. When it is necessary to build up a part and there is sufficient depth, drive screws partly into the surface to be repaired, leaving the heads exposed but beneath the surface of the repair, when cut down to the proper level or finished by carving. The wood dough should be packed tightly around the screws. This gives added hidden strength to the repair when finally completed.

5. If when applying wood plastic it should get on the surface surrounding the repair, embedding deeply into the pores of the wood, it can be removed by sanding. But it is better to use lacquer thinner (not to be used on a lacquer finish). The material should not be harmful to other finishes.

If wood plastic must be stained, it would be wise to place a coat of wood dough on a piece of scrap wood. Allow it to dry, smooth and sand, and then apply a coat of stain. After the stain has dried, compare the color with that of the place in the piece where the repair is to be effected. Stain usually lightens somewhat in drying and, if too dark, can't be removed. (A single coat of about one-quarter white shellac and three-quarters denatured alcohol, applied carefully to the smoothed surface of the wood dough repair, will greatly lessen the absorption of stain.)

WOOD PUTTY

Many handymen prefer wood putty, also known as rock hard putty, to wood plastic. Each has its advantages, and both have equal importance in a shop. Wood putty, which can be purchased at paint and hardware stores, is a ready-mixed powder to which water is added when used. Its advantages over wood plastic are that the best types harden more quickly and with less shrinkage, result in a smooth finish, are preferable for use under non-transparent finishes, and can be colored with dry powder color to match wood surfaces.

The disadvantages are that wood putty does dry to a flat surface and, even though stained, does not look like wood. Consequently, it is a poor material to use on a surface that will be conspicuous, such as in building up a broken-off part. That can be done better with wood plastic. Furthermore, neither wood putty nor wood plastic should be used for filling small holes in wood surfaces, where they will be conspicuous. Stick shellac is the perfect material for such work.

How to Use Wood Putty

Here are some pointers to remember when using wood putty:

1. Put as much as you believe you will use immediately in a waxed-paper cup or small tin can, add only a very small amount of cold water at a time, and stir to a heavy dough. Once the putty starts to set, it can't be retempered, that is, resoftened, by adding more water.

2. Dampen slightly the hole or crack to be filled and the immediate surrounding surface, apply the dough, and pack it down with a dampened finger to slightly above the desired level, to allow for possible shrinkage. Take care to keep it off the surrounding surface.

3. Wipe the surrounding surface with a dampened cloth over a finger and allow to dry. Then shave off any surplus with a knife.

4. If the wood putty is to be stained with a dry powder color, add the color to the dry putty powder, but make the mixture

2-6. Here's a good trick to anchor securely thick patches made of water putty or wood dough. Drive one or two screws into the damaged area, making sure their heads are below the surrounding surface, but not all the way down against the damaged area. Now when you apply putty or dough it can encapsulate the screw heads for a good grip.

slightly darker than the wood to be matched, as it lightens in drying. If necessary to stain a patched spot or crack after the wood putty has dried, paint it first with white shellac thinned with denatured alcohol (about 6 to 1) in order to prevent the stain from soaking in and darkening too much. Test the color before applying it to the repair.

Vinyl patching material is used by some woodworkers, and it is very easy to use. However, it is rather difficult to spot-stain, since there is very little penetration. This material is applied as directed on its container.

STICK SHELLAC

Stick shellac is used for filling cracks, small holes, dents, or gouges in either solid or veneered wood surfaces. It is more often used in hardwood furniture, such as maple and mahogany, where, since such pieces require a fine finish, every small hole or depression should be filled smoothly. It is used extensively by professionals in restoring fine antiques and for repairing high-grade and highly finished new furniture that may have received surface damage in shipment or from handling.

The end of a shellac stick is softened with heat and applied with a flexible spatula where needed. This is called burning it in. When such a repair is properly finished, it is unnoticeable in surfaces having no grain, but stick shellac should not be used in surfaces with a distinct grain, except for small areas, since the repair

would show clearly. This shellac is produced in a great variety of colors and shades, from light buff through brown and into deep red, to match different woods and finishes. Some manufacturers produce these colored sticks in two types: transparent and opaque.

Stick shellac is sometimes difficult to find. It can usually be purchased in the larger paint stores. If not, an inquiry to a cabinetmaker or one of the better woodworking shops will disclose their source of supply. Mail order houses such as Constantine's and Craftsman (see page 4) also sell stick shellac. A set of about ten shades will be found sufficient for most work. However, if it is easily available, it would be a good plan to purchase various shades as needed. One stick should last a long time. It would be good, too, to own a color chart. Many manufacturers furnish them, and they are for sale by their dealers.

How to Use Stick Shellac

Stick shellac is fairly easy to use, especially if you remember the following tips:

1. A place to be repaired with stick shellac should be cleaned thoroughly of dirt and old finish. Scratching or pricking holes in the bottom of the repair area will give better holding power.

2. Select a stick shellac of the correct color and shade to match the finish of the wood to which it is to be applied.

3. Melt the end of the stick with an electric soldering iron, holding the stick against the iron and directly over the place to be repaired, and permit the molten shellac to fall upon that spot. Exces-

2-7. Cracks and scratches are easy to fill with stick shellac, which comes in a variety of colors to match most woods. To use, melt the stick over a clean flame or with a soldering iron and drip it onto the damaged area. Spread evenly with a thin knife warmed over the flame. Let cool, then scrape level with the surrounding area, using a razor blade or cabinet scraper.

sive heat will burn the shellac, destroy the color, and create bubbles. By the way, the point of a medium-sized screwdriver or the large blade of a pocketknife may be used to heat and melt the stick shellac, if you do not have a soldering iron. Heat will destroy the temper of the metal, so the tool should be an old one.

4. Before the shellac hardens, flatten it out in the depression with a dampened finger or with the blade of a small spatula. The depression should be filled slightly higher than the surface. If necessary, melt and add more shellac. Finally, heat the blade of the spatula over an alcohol spirit lamp and smooth the surface. Allow it to stand until thoroughly hard. Incidentally, a tool for smoothing the shellac can be made from an old round-ended table knife, by heating and bending its blade at a 45-degree angle about an inch from the end. Also remember that a spirit lamp that burns alcohol or canned heat (a jelly substance bought in cans) must be used for heating tools. An inexpensive one can be purchased or made from the base of a small oil can, with wadded string in the top for a wick. Since gas or wood flames leave a deposit of carbon (soot) on the metal, they shouldn't be used, as this will discolor the shellac.

5. Cut the raised shellac down flush with the wood surface with a sharp knife or razor blade, or, better still, with a sharp chisel, laid flat on the surface with the beveled edge of the blade up.

6. Finish the surface of the shellac with either a worn piece of wet or dry finishing abrasive paper, with pumice stone, or with rottenstone and oil.

7. If you wish to repair with stick shellac a surface that is to be stained later, the stain should be applied and allowed to dry thoroughly before the repair is made. Stains change color slightly as they dry, and it would be impossible to select the proper shellac color for the repair until the resin has dried.

8. The use of opaque stick shellac for deep cracks or depressions, and the transparent type for those that are shallow, results in a more professional job.

TO REPAIR A BROKEN CORNER OR EDGE Stick lacquer or stick shellac may be used to re-

2-8. Repairing a broken corner or edge with stick lacquer or stick shellac

pair a broken corner or edge on veneer or solid wood. With tongue depressors and masking tape, build a form in which to mold stick lacquer or shellac. Fill the form with lacquer or shellac. When hard, cut the form away gently with a razor blade and remove carefully. Apply the finish coat. Don't use this technique if edge damage is extensive, since the shellac is brittle and vulnerable to chipping.

REPAIRING CRACKS DUE TO SHRINKAGE

When two boards that are placed edge to edge in furniture shrink cross-grain, there will be a crack between them. This condition is often found in the tops of tables, dressers, cabinets, etc. The directions given for the repair of these cracks when they run the full length of the boards are intended to apply to such cases. They may also be used for cracks occurring in other parts and types of furniture. The procedure is as follows:

On Tops That Can't Be Removed

Remove from the crack any accumulation of dirt, old glue, or paint. Usually this may be accomplished with a thin knife blade, although it sometimes is easier to scrape out with the teeth of a worn hacksaw blade. Either must be handled with care.

Fill the crack with stick shellac of the right shade of color. In the case of a wide crack, this filling will be a slow and tedious job, but it is the only true method to use on high-grade furniture. If the work is done properly, the crack will not be visible, except that it will show no grain.

Wood dough may be used for the repair, but it is almost impossible to stain it to the proper color and not have it conspicuous, no matter how carefully it is smoothed, stained, and finished.

On Tops That Can Be Removed

Remove the boards and clear dirt, old paint, or glue from the edges. Roughen or scratch the cleaned edges to give the new glue a "tooth" to hold onto. Place the boards together again and test for close contact. If necessary, plane the edges at high spots. If the boards were held in place with screws, fill the screw holes with wood dough, packed in firmly, since the boards when replaced won't assume their exact original position. Apply waterproof glue to the edges of the boards and place them together on a level surface, over waxed paper, with their ends evenly in line. Draw them firmly together with two bar clamps or a wedge clamp. Wipe off squeezed-out surplus glue with a damp cloth. Don't release the pressure for 24 hours or handle roughly for 48 hours.

Replace the boards in their former position and refasten by the same means as originally used. Where convenient, use small angle irons and mending plates for additional strength and holding power. Strength may also often be added to the ends of boards by toenailing them in a manner that cannot be seen.

REMOVING DENTS AND BRUISES

Dents and depressions in furniture surfaces may usually be removed in softwoods, and most hardwoods, by the use of water or water and heat. (However, this method will seldom work satisfactorily with hard maple, which must be sanded to remove dents.) Various procedures are as follows:

For Softwoods—without Heat

In this method water only is used. Apply the water to the depression with a fingertip until the water level is above the surrounding surface. Allow the water to absorb into the wood, adding more until the surface of the depression has lifted higher than that around it. The wood will shrink back a little as it dries. To hasten water absorption, prick a few minute holes in the surface of the depression with a very fine needle. Such holes will close up and be invisible.

For Hardwoods—with Heat

Fill the depression with water as described for softwoods. Then heat the tip of a spike (a worthless screwdriver or blade of an old pocketknife is also good), and place it in the water until it steams, taking care not to burn the wood with the heated tool. Repeat until the wood fibers are raised to or above the surrounding surface.

Using a Marble or Thimble—with Heat

This is a good technique for a depression *near* a glued joint. First, fill the depression with water as described for softwoods. Then place a clean ink blotter carefully over the water. Press the blotter into the depression with a child's marble or the rounded end of a sewing thimble. Hold a moderately heated iron against the top of the marble or thimble, causing the water to steam and the wood fibers to swell. It is important to remember that water will soften the old-type animal glue, causing joints to loosen or give way.

Using a Woolen Cloth—with Heat

This method is fine for large or obstinate depressions *away* from glued joints. Lay a damp cloth on the depression and place over it a moderately heated iron.

2-9. Removing dents and bruises with a wool cloth and electric iron

The warm moisture will cause the wood to swell and raise back to the normal level.

When any of these techniques is applied to a wood surface without a finish, smooth it later with fine abrasive papers of grades from 120 to 320. Of course, water applied to a nonwaterproofed final finish will turn it white. For methods of reviving the color and finish, see "Removing White Spots or Rings," page 77.

WOODEN DOWELS

Dowels are cylindrical pieces of hardwood (usually birch) from which are cut short sections, called dowel pins, that are used in fastening furniture. When glued into holes directly opposite each other, they hold two members of the furniture piece together. Dowel pins give a hidden strength in flush joints, since they pass through the joint into matching holes and are invisible from the outside. For example, in the construction of tables, the top is usually made of several boards, doweled and glued together, edge to edge, to appear as a single board. The upper frames and stretchers are usually doweled into the legs. The arms of chairs, if butted against the back, and seat members are doweled. The spare leaves of extension dining tables are doweled to make them match and fit together, but here these pins are glued into the holes on one board only.

Dowels may be purchased from hardware stores and lumber yards. They ordinarily come in 3-foot lengths and are from ⅛ to 1 inch in diameter. The type of doweling having a spirally grooved surface is the best. These specially made pins are sold in short lengths by mail order houses. Their grooves allow excess glue to escape.

When making doweled joints, plan your work in advance. There are two factors to consider:

1. The thickness and length of dowel pins should be in direct proportion to the strain to which the joint is to be subjected. Thick, wide, heavy boards exert more strain on the joint and require heavier dowel pins. Dowel pins are seldom used more than 4 inches long and, where possible, not less than 2 inches. (One-half the length goes into each board.) The length is often limited by the thickness of one or both boards.

2. When it is possible to use two or more dowel pins at a joint, it will be better and stronger than if only one were used. Two small pins are stronger than one large one, and two pins provide a more widely distributed holding power. Keep in mind that a joint may often be reinforced from the underside or inside surface with angle irons or mending plates.

Marking for Dowel Holes

Marking for dowel holes may seem difficult to the beginner. The holes must be bored directly opposite each other, on an exact mark, so that when the dowel pins are placed in the holes the surfaces of the boards thus doweled come together properly, as had been planned. Marking for the holes is a relatively simple matter, but the procedures must be carefully followed. The two methods, according to where the dowels are to be used, are as follows:

EDGE JOINTS Used when two boards of *equal thickness* are to be doweled together, edge to edge. *Example:* Tabletops.

1. With a pencil, mark the sides of the boards that form the undersurface, unless it is obvious from the finish on one of the surfaces.

2. Clamp the boards together with the ends *flush* and the edge surfaces to be marked for the holes *upward* and *level* with each other. Have the undersurfaces of the boards outward, as the finish side might be damaged by the clamps or vise, if used.

3. Measure from the ends of the boards the spots you wish to mark for dowel holes. Hold a try square firmly against the side of one board, at those spots, and draw lines across the edge surface of both boards with a knife blade or the point of an ice pick or awl. A pencil line will be too coarse.

4. With a rule (a steel-type rule is best), locate the exact middle of each board edge. Measure from the *outside* surface on each board. Make a small hole on the line at those points, with the point of an ice pick or awl. Enlarge the hole slightly with a center punch. These holes indicate the exact center of the hole you are to bore for the dowel pins.

When there are more than two boards to be doweled together, as in a tabletop, the center boards will have to be marked and bored on both sides, to match the holes in the adjacent boards. Therefore, the boards should be marked (1, 2, 3, etc.)

1.

2.

3.

4.

2-10. How to use dowels in furniture work:
1. Mark the exact position of each hole to be drilled with scriber and square. This enables you to center the dowel in the piece of lumber. 2. Use a doweling jig, where possible, to obtain a perfectly aligned hole. Different-size tubes are used to match the drill size. 3. Hold the *piece to be drilled rigidly; use an auger or drill through the jig and the resultant hole will match with the companion piece, to take the dowel. 4. Place the dowel pins in the drilled holes to align two narrow boards when making a wide one out of them. The pins mark the center of the holes.*

5.

6.

7.   8.

5. Mark the center of the hole accurately and let the drill press do the rest of the job. If the board is held properly, the hole will be perfectly vertical. 6. Guide the work into the drill, using a built-up woodblock jig whenever you convert your lathe into a drill press. The woodblock jig assures positioning.

7. Make miter joints strong by using two dowels at each corner. Use the blind method, as shown in photo 4; the dowels fit the inside of the miter. 8. The open-doweling method requires a hole drilled completely through one piece into the next, the glued dowel then being driven into both holes. (Continued on next page)

9.   10.

(Figure 2-10 continued)
9. *Eliminate drilling through wood surface by using the blind-dowel method, which protects the surface of the wood and assures a good finish.*

10. *Force the dowel and glue into the drilled hole. Some dowels have grooves to hold glue for tight joining. Wipe off excess glue after the dowels are in.*

on the underside, to designate the order in which boards and edges go together. The adjoining boards must be treated as pairs.

There are small, inexpensive dowel jigs (available at hardware and specialty tool stores) that simplify the job of doweling by automatically centering holes and guiding the drill. If you do much repair work, they are easily worth their price.

BUTT JOINTS These are furniture joints in which the end of a board or other member butts against the side of another. In most cases the dimensions of these boards or members differ at the joint, a smaller one butting against a larger. Here, the exact place where the smaller member butts against the larger must be deter-

mined and both members marked for dowel holes, directly opposite each other. For instance, in table construction, the ends of the upper side members of the frame (thin boards) butt against the sides of the legs (wider, thicker, and usually square).

The procedure for marking butt joints is as follows:

1. From heavy paper, make a template that is the exact size and shape of the end of the smaller board by placing the end of the board on the paper and drawing around it with a sharp pencil. Cut the paper on this line and, if necessary, trim it so that it will be the exact size of the board end. Write "top" on one side of the template.

2. Measure and locate the spot on the template where you wish the center of the dowel holes to come. (Wherever possible, use more than one dowel pin.)

3. Place the template back on the end of the piece from which it was drawn with the "top" mark *outward,* and then prick through the dots into the wood.

4. Place the template in the proper position on the surface of the piece to be butted against, with the "top" mark *inward,* and prick through the holes in the template into the wood. The reason for this is that, should you have the mark for the hole or holes *off* the center line in the template and were it placed on the second surface with the "top" mark outward, the holes marked would be on the opposite side of the center line.

5. Enlarge the holes in both pieces with a center punch. These indicate the center of the holes to be bored for the dowel pins.

6. It must be remembered that the holes don't go all the way through the board or member butted into, and that the dowel pins are hidden in the joint. Therefore, it is impossible to locate the spot for the holes except on the faces into which they are to be bored. Follow the steps carefully.

The procedure for marking two boards of equal thickness and width that are to butt against each other is the same as that given above.

Drilling Holes for Dowels

It is assumed that you have already planned on the thickness and number of dowel pins to be used at each joint. Proceed as follows:

1. Use a drill or auger bit of the same diameter as that of the dowel pin selected. It is advisable to use twist drills for holes of small diameter. Use auger bits for larger holes.

2. Drill the holes, where marked, to a depth of about ¼ inch deeper than *one-half* the length of the dowel pin, if the hole is to be small in diameter. When the hole is of larger diameter (⅝ to 1 inch), the added depth should be about ½ inch. The extra depth is to allow space for excess glue in the bottom of the hole. (One-half the length of the dowel pin goes into each hole.) It is essential that the holes be drilled exactly perpendicular to the face of the board. A dowel pin will not slip freely into the holes in both members to be fastened if one hole is at an angle to the other. To aid in drilling a perpendicular hole in the face of a board, stand a try square upright on it, the steel-rule part up, next to the bit. If the hole is being drilled in the end of the board, tack small sticks of wood on two sides of the board, extending above it a few inches, to serve as a guide. By these means you can tell with considerable accuracy whether you are drilling in a truly perpendicular position.

Holes may be drilled to an even depth by the use of a bit depth gauge or, as it is more commonly called, a doweling jig. A gauge may also be made by wrapping a piece of masking tape around the bit at the depth desired.

Preparing Dowel Pins

It is important that dowel pins do not bind in the side of the holes, that their sides be grooved to create an avenue of escape for excess glue. Proper length is critical, too. Prepare them as follows:

1. If the dowel material is not of the kind that comes with a spiral groove, cut the groove yourself with a triangular file. This should be done on the dowel material before the pins are cut to length. The pins should not be a "sloppy" fit but should slide into the holes with use of the fingers alone. A proper fit permits air to escape and excess glue to be forced up the sides when the dowel is put into the hole. Since the holes were drilled with a diameter the same as that of the dowels, even the spirally grooved dowels may have to be eased a little, with abrasive paper or a file.

2. Saw the pins from the piece of doweling to a proper length to fit the hole depths. Take these depth measurements with a small piece of doweling or a nail. Make allowance for the extra depth in the hole to take care of excess glue. When a dowel pin is to be used in a hole that has been drilled from the outside of a surface, where later it will be seen, cut it a little longer. After the glue has set and dried, carefully trim it as close as possible and later sand it to the surface level.

3. Bevel the edges at the ends of the pins slightly, to permit easy entrance of the pin into the hole, and to allow the glue to pass up along the sides of the pin.

When there are a number of pins to be cut and installed, mark the holes and pins with a corresponding number, to tell you where each pin is to go. (In doing handwork, it is impossible to drill holes to the same length.)

Gluing Dowel Pins

Before gluing dowel pins in place, first test to see if the pins will go into both holes without binding. If they won't, the holes may not be directly opposite each other, or they may not have been drilled perpendicular. In either case, it is best to plug up the holes and redrill them, or start again and drill new holes, depending upon the circumstances and conditions found. Sometimes the hole may be slightly enlarged or the pin made a little smaller in diameter. When everything is in proper order, the pins and the contacting surfaces may be glued as follows:

1. Apply glue to the sides of the holes with a matchstick or nail. Apply glue to the contacting surfaces. Don't use too much glue, particularly in the holes. Use white or yellow glue unless you need waterproof glue. In that case, use an epoxy glue.

2. Insert the pins in the holes of one member and put the other member in place. Wipe off any glue squeezed out with a damp cloth. The two members should go together firmly with hand pressure only. If too much pressure is used (as when clamped) and the pieces are forced together, the result will be disastrous cracks, often caused by too much glue. The bottom of the hole fills and the glue is unable to force itself up along the sides of the pin.

3. Bind the parts firmly together with clamps or a tourniquet, being sure the parts are properly aligned. Keep in a warm room to dry.

Dowel Pin Repairs

A dowel pin that holds a furniture leg in place sometimes breaks, leaving one or both ends in the holes. Bore the dowel out of the hole with a brace and bit, or a hand drill with straight-shank drills slightly smaller than the diameter of the dowel. Never bore beyond the depth of the dowel because the hole may become too deep or the bit in some cases may go through to the other side. Usually you can tell when to stop because boring through the hardwood dowel is slower than boring through the softwood of the furniture. With a small chisel or penknife, chip and force out what remains of the dowel, but don't cut the hole any larger. Wash out the glue with vinegar. Then select a new dowel that fits the hole snugly. If the parts of the joint don't come close together, the dowel may be too long. Cut a piece off the end of the pin, round the cut with a sharp knife or sandpaper, then follow the directions for gluing.

REPAIRS WITH NAILS

One of the easiest ways to reinforce repairs is to use brads or finishing or casing nails. These three types of nails all have small heads that are easy to conceal by countersinking and covering with stick shellac.

However, these nails are quite thin and easy to bend if you are not careful when driving them; they may also split the wood. You can solve both problems by predrilling. The usual method is to use a twist drill slightly smaller than the diameter of the nail being used. But you can also drill the pilot hole with a nail of the same size you will use for the repair. Simply cut the head off the nail and insert it in a drill's chuck. Then drill the pilot hole using the chucked nail instead of a bit.

Surprisingly, this method gives good holding power, because the nail doesn't really cut away and remove wood from the hole. Rather it forms the hole largely by pushing the wood fibers aside. The resulting hole is therefore a little smaller than the nail you will drive into it, which means it will fit more snugly.

The only difficulty you may have in drilling a hole with a beheaded nail is when using very thin brads. Since they are made of soft steel, they must be properly centered in the chuck, and care taken against bending the brad while drilling.

Many joints—for example, spindles, slats, rungs, stretchers, arm posts, and legs—may often be given added strength by using this method of repair, after the parts have been glued and assembled and if the joint is near an edge.

Such repairs may be accomplished by drilling a hole in the side of the part with or into which the other part fits, at an angle and depth so that the hole passes through the center of the part that fits into or with the other part. A full-length, small-headed nail is then driven into the hole. Should the nail head be in an exposed position, it may be driven under the surface with a nail-set and the hole filled with stick shellac, of a color to match the surface, or with wood dough or wood putty, which may be stained.

Practically every joint shown may be strengthened with nails used in this way, if they can be driven in from an outside surface. Even splits near an edge of wood ⅛ inch thick may be repaired by this method. The procedure is as follows:

1. Choose a small-headed nail of the thickness and length deemed best for the work. Cut the head off close, center in the chuck of a hand drill with a short bite, and secure firmly.

2. Drill the hole without allowing the face of the chuck to touch the wood surface, thus marring it. When using thin nails, hold the drill steady and straight so there will be no undue strain on the nail. When drilling into the edge of a very thin board, be sure the hole is centered and parallel to the sides.

3. Using a tack hammer, drive a *whole* nail (of the same length and thickness as the one used for drilling) cautiously, until the head is flush with the wood surface.

Toenailing is a method of driving a nail at an angle, through one wooden member into another, to secure them tightly together.

Examples: A vertical upright being nailed into a horizontal member; two boards matched against one another in a flat position and toenailed together at the ends.

The work is done, as outlined previously, by drilling the hole for the small-headed nail at an angle, while the boards are held or clamped together. The nail is then driven in place. Should the repair be located where it may be seen, the nail is driven below the surface with a nail-set

and the hole filled. Use as large a nail as possible for the greatest strength.

FURNITURE JOINTS AND FASTENINGS

Many beginners, and perhaps some experienced amateur workers, have little knowledge of the various types of joints used in furniture construction. Among those most commonly used are butt, miter, dowel, mortise and tenon, dovetail, tongue and groove, and plain edge. Each type of joint may be cut by a variety of methods, especially the dovetail type, and each of these is called by a special name.

In restoration work, it is best that all wood joints be put together with glue. Where greater strength is required, it is advisable to give added support by mechanical means.

Following are listed the various types of joints, preceded by letters keying each joint to the appropriate illustration on page 44, with comments about them as to their uses and the kinds of mechanical support that may be used with some of them.

A. BUTT—END TO END Weakest of all joints. Should have mechanical support, unless otherwise held. If the boards are thick enough, doweling is best, as shown on pages 34–41. Can be supported with mending plates.

B. SCARF A simple method of repairing broken boards by cutting them at an angle and is strongest when cut at an acute angle.

C. SERRATE OR FINGER More complicated method of repairing broken boards. Usually cut by special machines and quite strong.

D. BUTT—END TO SIDE Very weak. Best reinforced with dowels, as in F. May be supported with a corner angle or flat corner iron.

E. MITER Weak. May be supported with screws, as in B, or hardware, as in D. Primarily used because it looks good and conceals end grain.

F. DOWEL Best reinforcement to use wherever possible. This drawing shows the corner of the upright piece cut away, for purpose of better illustration. This joint may be strengthened with mending plates.

G. MORTISE AND TENON A joint commonly found in high-grade furniture. This drawing also shows the corner of the upright piece cut away. The tenon (as illustrated) is an integral part of the horizontal piece (above the letter G), and is shaped to fit closely into the mortise, a rectangular hole, in the upright piece. A modification of this joint is cutting the mortise all the way through the upright piece, the tenon extending the full depth of the hole. The best mechanical means for additional support at the joint is with one or more dowels, to be installed crosswise through the tenon; mending plates may also be used.

H. DADO TONGUE AND RABBET There are many modifications of this type of joint. It may be reinforced with corner angles and flat corner irons.

I. SLIP OR LOCK CORNER A modification of the dovetail joint. (See J.) It is almost as strong as the dovetail and easier to make.

J. DOVETAIL This is a true dovetail, also called a cistern dovetail. There are various other types and modifications, required in complicated cabinet work. These joints are found mostly in well-made furniture and, if they are tight fitting and properly glued, should require no added support by mechanical means. When the joints are worn and support is needed, it may be supplied by building up each dovetail with small shims or with corner angles.

K. BLOCK The most common place a block is used is for securing tops to frames, as an added strength to screws that pass from the frame into the top. Not only should the blocks be glued in place but, for additional strength, holes should be drilled through them in two directions, which will permit screws to go through the blocks into both the frame and the top. Thus applied, they will give more strength and have more holding power than corner angles.

L. TONGUE AND GROOVE Not often used in furniture construction. Quite strong if well fitted. (See also illustration N.) The joint may be strengthened with mending plates.

2-11. Wood joints you should know

M. PLAIN EDGE The joint most commonly used in furniture construction (new and old) for tops, etc., made of several boards. When the boards are thick enough, the best mechanical strength (in addition to gluing) is with dowels. The boards may be held to the frame with blocks and corner angles, as directed in K, and the boards held together with mending plates.

N. TONGUE AND GROOVE VARIATION See L.

O. SPLINE A joint found mostly in finely constructed old furniture. The spline joint may be strengthened with mending plates.

METAL REINFORCERS

One or more types are recommended for use in various procedures throughout this chapter, including securing tops to frames, repairing loose joints or cracks, and holding formerly warped boards in place. Some examples follow:

Corner irons (also called angle irons) may be used to join a top more securely to a frame, as on the underside of a table. At least two should be used for each side.

Flat corner irons (also called L-plates) may be used on a flat undersurface near a corner, when a joint is mitered, with or without the joint being glued.

Mending plates (also called cleats) will reinforce, from the underside, two boards glued together. It is best to install plates a foot to two feet apart, according to the various circumstances encountered.

T-plates may often be used to advantage when a vertical member of furniture contacts a horizontal piece, such as reinforcing a leg to a frame member, or on a table.

TIGHTENING ROUND OR SQUARE FURNITURE JOINTS

More loose joints will be found in chairs and sofas than in any other type of furniture. Next come stands and tables. Most of these loose joints occur where one member joins another and the joint is either round or rectangular (here called square joints). Examples of such joints in chairs are the fitting of the back slat or splat into the back post and the fitting of the spindles into the back slat and seat. Examples in both chairs and tables are the fitting of the stretchers into the legs. Most of the square (or rectangular) joints are of the mortise and tenon type, while the round joint may be either a solid member, shaped round at the end, or a doweled joint that fits into a round hole in another member.

Joints become loose through hard usage and abuse, from lack of moisture in the place in which the furniture is kept, and from shrinkage in the wood. Joints must be tightened properly to effect a permanent repair. It is sometimes advisable to reinforce a tightened joint with added mechanical means, depending upon prevailing conditions and the type of joint. The simplest methods for tightening round and square furniture joints are as follows.

Tightening a Joint with a Wedge

A thin, hardwood wedge (maple is good) may be used to expand a round piece (rung, stretcher, spindle, chair leg, etc.) or a square or rectangular piece (tenon, slat, etc.) so it will fit more snugly against the sides of the hole into which it goes.

When reinforcing a blind mortise and tenon with a wedge, start the wedge into its slot, then fit the joint and drive it together. The wedge will hit against the bottom of the mortise and be forced into its slot. Back up the bottom of the mortise with a block of wood to prevent the wedge from possibly breaking out the bottom of the tenon.

This type of repair is easiest when the piece being wedged goes all the way through the piece into which it fits. Here's how the repair goes, using a leg fitting into a chair seat as an example.

Slip the leg into the chair seat as far as it should go, then mark it with a pencil. Remove the leg from its hole and saw a thin slot down through the center of the leg, stopping a bit short of the pencil mark. Next cut a thin wedge of hardwood, as wide as the end of the chair leg and about one-half inch longer than the depth of the slot. The thickness of the wedge is important. If it is too thin it won't spread the leg enough to make it fit its hole snugly. If it is too thick, it won't fit into its slot. To check, dry fit the leg in its hole and tap the wedge lightly into place. If it is too loose, make another slightly thicker. If it is so tight that you can't tap it into position, try a thinner wedge.

When the fit seems right, pull out the wedge and disassemble the joint. Coat the slot for the wedge, the hole, and the end of the leg with glue. Fit the joint together and drive the wedge into place. After the glue has set, trim off the excess wedge and sand smooth.

Wedge repairs are more difficult when the wedged piece does not extend all the way through. In that case you must be sure the wedge is the proper thickness and just a bit shorter than the depth of its slot. You cannot work by trial and error, because test fitting the joint may lock it.

After cutting the wedge, apply glue to slot, hole, and wedge. Start the wedge into its slot. Then slip the end of the leg into its hole and drive the joint together. Fitting the joint will also force the wedge into its slot. It's a good idea to back up your work opposite the end of the hole with a block of wood held in place with clamps. This can prevent the possibility that the wedge may press right through the end of the hole.

Tightening a Square Joint with a Shim

A very effective means of tightening square-sided joints, such as mortise and tenon, shims are best made of hardwood. They may be of even thickness or slightly tapered, but should be as wide as the hole. Apply glue to the hole and drive the shim into place.

Strengthening a Joint with a Screw

Should the joint be one in which the hole doesn't go all the way through the member into which another is placed, as stretchers or some mortise and tenon

2-12. Using wedges is a good way to tighten loose joints such as the mortise and tenon. Apply different techniques for the various types of mortise and tenon joints shown in these cutaways. Through tenon (above) is easier. Cut a slot in the end of the tenon and drive in a wedge thick enough to spread the tenon and lock it tight. Cut off the excess.

Blind tenon (above) is a bit trickier. A wedge must be cut the right length so that when the tenon is pressed into the mortise, the wedge is pressed into its slot. If the wedge is too short, it won't fit all the way into the groove in the tenon; if too long, it will prevent seating of the tenon.

joints, it may be strengthened by inserting a screw through the base of the hole into which the second part is placed, and into the end of that part. In such cases, a hole for the screw head should be drilled from the outside of the larger piece, and a smaller hole for the screw shank and thread should be continued through, so that, when the screw is inserted, its head will be beneath the wood surface. This can be plugged later with a small piece of dowel, glued in place, smoothed, and finished.

Plugging a Round Hole with a Dowel

When a rounded end of a furniture part has a loose fit in a round hole in another part, glue a piece of dowel of the same size as the hole into the hole and, when dry, drill a new hole for the part to be inserted.

Example: To fit a chair rung into a leg when there is a "sloppy" joint.

Tightening a Joint with Cloth

This method may be used on either a round or square joint. Cut some cloth strips narrower than the end of the part to be inserted into the hole. Put these cloth strips over the end of the piece in the form of a cross. Trim off the cloth on the sides from one-half to three-quarters the depth of the joint, since the cloth stretches when

2-13. Corner blocks glued and screwed in place are a good way to reinforce joints in weakened furniture. Here a block is being added to reinforce the skirt of a table, while the block for anchoring skirt to tabletop awaits screws.

going into the hole. Apply glue and put the joint together. Should the cloth protrude out of the joint, trim it off closely with a razor blade immediately after the joint is assembled, and wipe off any excess glue with a damp cloth.

SECURING FURNITURE TOPS TO FRAMES

Furniture tops must often be removed to make repairs and must usually be taken off when warps are to be removed from the boards. Obviously, the removed tops must be put back in such a way that they will be held securely in place. For example, when warps in boards have been corrected by application of moisture or steam, the tops must be secured to the frame immediately, or the warp may return.

The method of securing tops to frames is as follows:

1. Should a top consist of two or more boards, scrape any old glue from the board edges.

2. Fill any screw holes with wood dough. Pack in well with a matchstick and allow to dry thoroughly.

3. Turn the boards upside down and place them together, properly matched, over waxed paper on a flat surface. Glue the contacting edges and, if necessary, draw the boards together with a wedge clamp (see page 17). On small tops, this may sometimes be done better with bar clamps, with wood blocks under their jaws.

4. Turn the frame upside down and place it on the top. Locate its exact former position from the marks left at the edge of the frame.

5. Replace any screws that held the top to the frame and tighten securely (best done with a brace and screwdriver bit). The screws usually go through slanting holes in the frame.

6. Install glue blocks at the joint between the top and the frame, at each end of the frame side, and also along the sides. The blocks should be of hardwood (or semi-hard wood), glued in place and also held with screws, one screw going into the frame and the other into the top. Prior to installation, drill clearance holes through the blocks so that the screws will not bind in them, then countersink the holes. Use flat-headed screws, to take advantage of the pull against the head when the screw is tightened.

7. It is advantageous to use small corner irons at the corners, and, on small pieces where there is but little strain, corner irons may be substituted for the blocks. And if the boards have been warped, it would also be a good idea to install flat mending plates across the contacting edges of the boards of the top, about a foot apart.

REPAIRING DRAWERS

Furniture drawers get hard usage, and as a result they often become shaky and loosened in the joints more quickly than other parts of the piece. Usually, they must be taken apart completely in order to repair them. To accomplish this, use the following procedure:

1. Remove the drawer bottom. It slides into a groove from the back of the drawer and is usually held in place with a small nail driven through the bottom and into the end piece.

2. Care must be used in removing the sides if they are connected with each other by dovetail joints. To release the strain, pound on a small, flat board held against the side and next to the joint.

3. Clean any old glue thoroughly from the joints; apply heavy glue to both members and reassemble. A small brad driven into the joints will hold them in place. The drawer bottom acts as a square when reassembling, but be certain that the drawer will fit properly. Try it in the opening before the glue sets.

4. If the drawer drags along its sides, it may have to be planed or sanded. A slight drag may be relieved by rubbing on talcum powder, soap, or soapstone. If the drawer drags on its slides (bottom), the slides must be planed or sanded. If the drawer is too loose vertically, build the slide up by gluing thin strips of wood to it. Pieces of veneer are easiest to use. If one piece isn't thick enough, just add another layer. If a drawer does not slide easily, it may often be made to do so by applying furniture wax to the slides.

5. Many chests and drawers have wooden knobs or handles that have developed play from repeated use. Usually they are fastened from behind with blunt screws or bolts threaded into the wood itself. In many instances, the threads in the wood are stripped. This condition is easily remedied. Dip a piece of string into shellac and wind it around the threads of the screw or bolt, working the material into the grooves. This done, insert the bolt or screw, screw on the knobs or handles, and let the work dry out. A more difficult but more secure repair is to drill out the oversize hole and plug it with a dowel, glued in place. Then drill a new hole of the proper size through the plug.

MAKING AND INSTALLING
NEW CHAIR PARTS

Whenever it becomes necessary to replace a part of a chair that is difficult to make or install, have the work done in a professional shop, unless you are fully qualified to do this work and have the necessary equipment and tools. Such work includes the shaping of arms or carvings, or bows and combs for chair backs, and the turning of rungs, spindles, banisters, finials, etc.

The only instructions given here are for the type of work that should be within the ability of those with limited experience.

Round Chair Rungs

Rungs that are rather large in diameter may be made from an old rake or hoe han-dle. Those of smaller diameter are best made from a proper hardwood to match that used in the piece.

It is not usually recommended to taper replacement rungs for any length toward the ends. It is better to reduce the size of the new rung at the ends only to fit the hole, leaving a slight slope or shoulder on the rung at the edge of the hole. The joint must have a tight, or drive, fit. Therefore, the end beyond the taper should be round and straight. This may done with a sharp jackknife. Test for size by first whittling to the proper diameter at the end of the new rung. When it will fit tightly in the hole, twist the rung, thus marking it for continued reduction in size. Then glue and clamp it in place or use a tourniquet.

If an ornamental turned rung is missing, sometimes a similar one of the right length can be purchased at a secondhand shop.

Spindles for Chairs

When complicated turned chair spindles must be replaced, it is best to have them made. The type of round spindle with a bulb and taper toward both ends, such as those found on many Windsor chairs, is rather easily made with a drawknife and a spokeshave, or a short block plane. Shape the spindle roughly with the drawknife and, with the wood held in a vise, finish it with the spokeshave.

When the block plane is to be used for the finish, hold one end of the shaped spindle in one hand, place the other end against a very thin block nailed to a workbench, and force the spindle to bend, while using the plane with the other hand.

By bending the spindle outward, the bulge of a bend may be shaved off, and in this manner it may be shaped inward on both sides of a center bulb. Be sure to shape the ends of the spindle to fit closely in the holes in the top back rail and the chair seat. Test before installing.

A spindle of this type may be installed by bending it. A turned or thick spindle that will not bend may be installed by drilling the hole in the top back rail a little deeper. The spindle is first pushed up into the back rail and then let down into the hole in the seat. Apply glue to the holes before installation.

Odd-shaped Back Pieces

Many of these pieces that are not turned may be easily shaped with the same tools used for making spindles, by a worker handy with tools. Such parts include arrowhead slats and splats (sometimes also called slats). However, such pieces as a banister back slat, which is turned and then sawed in half lengthwise, should be made and installed by a professional.

Corner Blocks for Added Strength

Such chairs as occasional and dining room chairs, which have a padded cloth-covered seat, are subjected to much greater strain than chairs with solid wood seats. They must depend almost entirely upon the strength of the joint in the frame of the seat to hold them together. To give support to the seat frame, the padded seat should always be held in place in the frame with screws. Screws often do not

2-14. *Using dowel to repair the leg of an upholstered furniture piece*

give sufficient support, and the front legs become loose or the side members of the seat frame loosen at their juncture with the back posts. The same condition may often be found in the frames of over-stuffed chairs, sofas, and other types of furniture as well.

The best means of repairing and strengthening such loosened joints is with hardwood corner blocks (birch is good), glued in place and held with screws. The procedure is as follows:

2-15. When an entire part of a piece of furniture is damaged or missing, it is best to make a replacement. Here is a replacement arm for a rocking chair, cut to rough shape and being drilled for spindles.

1. Take out the padded seat by removing the screws (on the underside) that hold it to the frame. Working with overstuffed furniture is difficult, since the padding and sometimes the springs must be removed, so if you are not qualified to do this work, it is best left to a professional. Simple upholstery repairs are discussed in Chapter Eight.

2. Cut triangular-shaped blocks to fit into the four inside corners of the seat frame. They must fit into the corner, and the edge surfaces must contact the seat frame evenly. When possible, the blocks should be at least 1½ inches thick and the side edges over 3 inches long.

3. Drill clearance holes through the hypotenuse edge of the triangular block, at an angle, for the screws to go through into the seat frame, and countersink for the screw heads. The holes must be larger than the screw-shank diameter so they will not bind.

4. Apply glue and screw the blocks in place.

LENGTHENING LEGS

You may sometimes wish to lengthen the legs of antique furniture, when the lower ends have been rotted away due to a damp floor, or when legs have become shortened by years of hard usage. Also, the bottom of a leg may have been split or damaged beyond repair, or it may have

2-16. *When your straight chairs turn into rocking chairs, you can tighten up those loose joints quickly without taking them apart for regluing. Use a ¼-inch drill to sink holes at 45-degree angles ½ inch from the end of each rail into the posts, taking care not to penetrate too deeply. Cut ¼-inch dowels to fit the holes, shaping the ends with a pocketknife. Cover these with glue and drive them into the holes. The stretchers can be tightened the same way.*

broken off. A repair can be made by adding a piece to the bottom of the leg. Two methods of doing this follow.

1. If the bottom of the leg is straight (round or square), the easiest method is to dowel a new piece to the bottom, after the leg has been cut off squarely. The new piece should be a little thicker and longer than the original. When the glue has dried, the added section may be shaped by filling and sanding and then cut off to the proper length.

2. If the bottom of the leg is turned, a new turning should be made to match an existing one. This turning can be shaped at the top, with a straight shaft, to fit into a hole to be drilled in the leg bottom after it has been sawed off even. This eliminates the need for a dowel pin.

It is best to have the turning made a bit larger at the top than the leg into which it is to fit, so that, after it is installed and the glue is dry, it can be shaped down to size. This is a precautionary measure, for, should the hole in the bottom of the leg not be drilled in the exact center, and should the turning to be added be of exact size, the two pieces would not match.

The repair should be made with hardwood and, if possible, of the same kind of wood. After it is shaped it may be stained and finished.

CORRECTING UNBALANCED FURNITURE

Often a piece of furniture may wobble or rock because one or more of the legs is longer or shorter than the others. There are two rather simple procedures for correcting this condition.

Adding to the Legs

If the variance in the legs is slight, a felt chair tip (screwed in place) or metal chair guides (in the shape of a dome with claws, to be pounded in place) may be added to the bottom of the short leg or legs. The former may be available only in furniture stores, but the latter are commonly found in hardware stores.

Cutting Off the Legs

This method of correction is a little more difficult. The problem is not only to cut off the correct amount from the leg bottoms, but also to have the cut parallel to the floor, so that the cut end touches the floor evenly at all points. Proceed as follows:

1. To correct the balance, put a small block of wood of the proper thickness under the short leg. This must be done on a level surface.

2. Place another block of wood, of the same thickness as the first, on the level surface, against each of the longer legs. Move it around the circumference of each leg, in turn, marking the leg with a sharp pencil, so that there is a circular line on the leg at the exact level of the top of the block.

3. Saw off the leg (or legs) along this mark, on its lower side (leave the line), and if the marks and saw cuts are true, all legs will touch evenly at all points.

4. Bevel off the edges of the saw cuts slightly with a file, and put a small amount of stain on the bottoms of the newly cut leg bottoms. If you find that you still do not have a perfect balance, because of an error in drawing the line or in cutting, this may be corrected by filing the bottom of the leg a little.

If the furniture to be corrected has a flat top, it would be wise to place a spirit level on it before doing any of the work, to make certain the top is level. The line around the leg for the saw cut may sometimes be made better with a sharp chisel, provided the block used as a gauge is large and thick enough. (Place the back of the chisel on the block and move it around the leg.)

When it is desired to cut a considerable length off the legs and balance them, first mark each leg with a pencil (measured with a rule) at the desired point where the legs are to be cut off. Choose a block to be used as a gauge, and measure its thickness. Then saw off all the legs at a distance below the pencil marks of the thickness of the block, and at an angle you believe to be correct, so the leg bottoms will fit flat on the floor. Then proceed with the steps related before, marking the block as a gauge, sawing off the legs at the mark, correcting any error in balance, tapering the edges with a file, and staining.

USING OLD WOODS FOR REPLACEMENT

Whenever possible in restoring old furniture, use old wood for patching or for replacement of a part. A surface patch must match the rest of the piece in texture and color or it will be conspicuous.

New wood used for replacement is difficult to treat so it will resemble the old wood exactly. Even when stained and finished to agree in color and feeling with the old wood, there will nearly always be a difference in its appearance, due to the variation in grain and texture that age alone can give it.

Old wood will often take color merely from the finish applied to it. The natural oils in woods dry out with age and leave them more porous than new woods. The porous surface of old wood has a different texture from that of a new wood of the same species and grain. When a clear liquid finish (such as varnish or shellac) is applied to old wood, it results in a much darker color than on the new wood. (See "Wet Test for Color," page 120.)

A proper wood for a replacement part (particularly for a surface patch) may sometimes be gotten by using a piece from the furniture to be repaired. In well-made furniture, such a piece may often be found in the frame, or in such places as the parting rail between drawers, or other places normally out of sight. Before removing such a part, make certain it is of the same species and grain of wood.

It is a good plan to accumulate old woods and keep all scraps, if they're large enough. Old pine boards, maple bed sides or ends, tables (or just tops and leaves) of walnut, cherry, oak, mahogany, and other woods may often be picked up at reasonable prices from Salvation Army, Goodwill, and secondhand furniture stores, as well as from cabinet shops. It is worthwhile having a supply on hand, whether or not it is needed for immediate use. Keep the old wood in a place away from new wood, and guard it carefully.

PATCHING SURFACES

A small dent or hole in a wood surface can often be repaired with stick shellac of the correct shade and color, or with stained wood dough, so that the repair will not be noticeable. However, when the grain of the wood shows through the surface finish, neither of these materials is practical for a surface patch.

Such surface damage should be repaired by a wooden patch. In order to secure satisfactory results, the wood used for the patch must be correct as to species, texture, grain, and age and must take a finish that will blend it into the surrounding wood and thus be invisible. If such wood is not available, use a wood of similar grain that you can stain to match the color of the adjoining wood.

Any wood used for a patch must be thoroughly seasoned or the color will lighten greatly while seasoning, unless deeply stained. It should also be cleaned thoroughly to remove any former finish or accumulated dirt, and should then be smoothed with a fine abrasive paper.

Shallow Patches and Plug Patches

A shallow patch fits into a "grave," a hollowed-out space with vertical edges and a level bottom, cut to size and excavated with a chisel. This kind of patch is used to repair deep bruises, partly rotted surfaces, broken-away surfaces, etc. The depth and size of the grave depends upon how much of the injured surface must be cut away to get into sound wood and true it up to receive the patch.

A plug patch is used when it is necessary to cut a hole all the way through the board, to remove dry rot and injuries that extend through the wood.

The Shape of the Patch

The shape of the patch is very important. Its grain should match as nearly and as exactly as possible that of the surface into which it is to be placed. For this reason, the grain in a patch must run in the same direction as the grain in the surface. If it does, the side edges of a patch will scarcely be noticeable when they run with the surface grain. The ends, however, should be cut at an angle of 45 degrees with the surface grain. An end edge, if left at right angles to the surface grain, would be very evident.

Figure 2-17 depicts five shapes that will be adequate for most properly designed patches and shows how they should be placed in the surface to be repaired. You will note that, where the end edges of the patch cross the grain in the surface, they do so at an angle of 45 degrees (except for the diamond patch), and the side edges run with the grain in the long patches.

To make a template for the patch, follow a procedure such as this:

1. Measure, with a rule, the length (with the grain) and the width (across the grain) of the place to be patched. Be sure to include all of the damaged or rotted area so that the patch, when in place, will be entirely in sound wood.

2. Choose the type of patch you believe will be best suited for the size and shape of the hole and the circumstances of its position.

3. Make a cardboard template, following the measurements taken of the type of patch chosen. Draw to size, using a straightedge and a 45-degree angle (except for a diamond patch). Cut straight, clean edges with a sharp knife or razor blade.

4. Lay the template (lengthwise with

2-17. The five recommended shapes for patches (top to bottom): square, diamond, double arrow, reverse arrow, and parallelogram

the grain) on the surface and over the place to be patched. Mark closely around the edges of the template on the surface with the point of a sharp knife.

Digging the Grave for a Shallow Patch

The work sounds a bit tricky, but it's not too difficult if care is used.

1. Cut down with a sharp chisel, then, with a mallet, hit the chisel lightly into the surface along the lines marked from the template. Hold the chisel with the beveled cutting edge inward and perpendicular to the surface. Cut square corners.

2. The surface included within your

lines is to be cut down to the correct depth. Start about ½ inch back from the far end. Place the chisel blade at right angles to the grain of the wood and at an angle of about 45 degrees with the surface. Pound the chisel lightly with a mallet to raise chips. Move the chisel back about ¼ inch toward you and continue until you reach the near end. Holding your chisel bevel side down, chisel out these chips until you have reached the proper depth. Be sure the bottom is level and the depth uniform.

The depth of the grave is important. When a shallow patch is to be glued in place, its upper surface should be slightly higher than that of the surrounding area. This can later be sanded down to make both areas equal. A chisel with deep-beveled sides, as well as a deep bevel on the blade, is best for this work. The beveled sides aid in cutting clean corners, and the deep bevel in the blade makes it easier to cut chips and to smooth the bottom of the hole. The cutting edge of the chisel should be straight and very sharp. The work is more difficult with a chisel having square sides and only a shallow bevel on the blade, even when equally sharp.

Cutting a Hole for a Plug Patch

For this type of patch, a hole of the correct dimensions and with smooth, perpendicular sides is cut *through* the thickness of the board. Proceed as follows:

1. Bore holes (about ¾ inch in diameter) with a brace and a bit through the board and in each corner within the lines you drew around your template with a knife point. The holes should be close to the lines, but not touching, at the corners of your outline. (For a smaller patch use a correspondingly smaller bit.) A sharp auger bit is necessary to produce a clean hole. When possible, a piece of wood should be held firmly against the undersurface where the point is to come through. This will prevent the undersurface from being torn or splintered. If this is not possible, reduce your pressure on the brace as the bit comes through the undersurface.

2. With a keyhole saw or saber saw cut off the hole for the patch. Keep your saw cuts straight and a little inside the lines for the patch.

3. Remove the wood remaining to the lines with a wood file. The sides of the hole should be properly squared at the corners and at right angles to the surface.

Making a Patch

The following procedure applies as well to a shallow patch or plug patch:

1. Lay the template on the wood you are to use for the patch, being sure that the long dimension is lengthwise with the grain. Mark around the template with a *sharp* pencil.

2. Saw or cut the patch to approximate size, leaving the lines. Test the size by matching it with the hole into which it is to fit.

3. Finish the patch to nearly exact fit. This may be done on thin patches with a sharp knife, or with a file or small plane on thick patches. Follow by rubbing the edges with a piece of moderately fine abrasive paper placed over a flat block of

wood. The edges must be clean cut and square.

Make the patch after the hole has been prepared. You may experience difficulties in cutting and trimming the hole to the lines of the template or you may find further rot in the wood that could not be seen from the surface. In such cases, a new template must be made, since the patch cut from the original template will no longer fit.

The patch should fit the hole exactly. It can be made to do so with careful workmanship, a particularly important point when the patch is in a conspicuous place or when installed in furniture with a distinctive grain.

Gluing a Shallow Patch

Mix some clear epoxy glue. Apply this glue sparingly to the sides and bottom of both the grave and the patch, then press the patch in place.

Gluing a Plug Patch

The first two steps in the following procedures are for gluing a plug patch, while 3, 4, and 5 apply to both kinds of patches.

1. Mix some clear epoxy glue and apply it to the edges of the patch and the sides of the hole. Press the patch in place, leaving its surface slightly above that of the surrounding wood.

2. Hold the patch in place by inserting a small brad or pin in the cracks on two opposite sides so that it will not slip too far into the hole. Remove these fastenings when the glue has begun to harden.

3. Wipe off excess glue and allow the patch to dry for 24 hours.

4. If glue is permitted to remain in the cracks at the surface level, it will show through the finish. When the glue has thickened, but before it has hardened, scrape it out with a pin for a short distance down into the crack. This can be filled later with wood dough (which will take a stain) or with stick shellac of the proper color. This is important if the patch doesn't fit the hole exactly.

5. Sand the patch down to the level of the surrounding surface. Sand with the grain, using #320 abrasive paper. Take plenty of time, as a careless rush job will show up under a finish in the completed work. You cannot avoid rubbing the edges of the surrounding surface.

Staining Patches

• Stain is usually necessary to match the color of the patch surface with that of the old surface surrounding it. This will require a little experimenting. It should be done on a surplus piece of the wood used for the patch.

• A paste filler may be needed on the patch to secure the correct surface texture.

• If the patch was made of old wood, the proper color may often be obtained by using linseed oil without a stain. Often this may be determined by making a "wet test" (page 120).

• It is almost impossible to match the color of the patch exactly to that of the surface. If the match is not exact, it may be necessary to stain the entire surface.

• If the patch material has been taken

from a part of the furniture being repaired, it may match exactly in color by the application of the correct finish alone, provided the woods are of the same species. A sealer coat should be applied before and after a paste filler.

Finishing Patches

When the patch alone is to be given a final finish, it is best to use the same materials that were used for the original finish of the piece. The two finishes will then match more exactly. Usually when you have to patch furniture, you intend to refinish the entire piece. In such cases, you can use different materials for the new finish from those that were originally used, especially when you plan to stain the entire surface.

VENEER

Veneer is a very thin layer of wood, usually cut from the more expensive species of hardwood and chosen for its beauty of wood patterns or grain. The veneer may be glued to a thicker board base of another species (usually less expensive) that does not have the cherished patterns or grain. In many early American furniture pieces, pine was used for the base.

The wood patterns in veneer often match, as on table and dresser tops, or as on old Victorian drawer fronts, where two pieces have been cut out of the same grain pattern (often a crotch) and butted together in reverse position. The effect, as you may have seen, is one of beauty.

Veneered furniture is more apt to be damaged by hard usage, age, and dampness than solid wood. You may often find marks resulting from flowerpots or hot utensils having been placed on them. Any of these may break or mar the veneer or cause the glue to loosen, resulting in such defects as raised edges, cracks, blisters, or waves. Often sections of the veneer lift from the base.

The furniture you are to repair will, most likely, be veneered with mahogany, walnut, or rosewood, as these are the woods most commonly used for veneer. They are beautiful pieces when the veneer has been cut from the proper angles of the grain and from such selected sections of the tree trunk as limb crotches, stumps, or abnormal growths in the trunk.

Repairing Veneer

General information on this special type of repair and the methods used is as follows:

• Where there is a choice, use the method of repair that will permit you to glue the old veneer back in place without cracking it. Such cracks will leave lines in the surface that will show through the finish.

• If any lines do show, fill them with stick shellac of the proper color and shade.

• When it is necessary to replace a part of the veneer, use material of the same color, grain, and thickness as the old. If you do not have any on hand, take a small sample from the furniture to be repaired to a cabinetmaker. Use an old piece of veneer whenever possible.

• When a piece of veneer is cut to the size

2-18. Below: Veneers often come loose during overzealous stripping. Here a piece of mahogany veneer has lifted at the corner of a drawer front. To repair, lift the veneer gently with a thin blade and scrape or wash away old glue beneath it. Then apply fresh glue.

Below: With glue in place, clamp down the veneer tightly, using a scrap of wood to distribute the clamping pressure evenly. Be sure to place a piece of waxed paper or aluminum foil between the block and the repair to prevent the block from becoming glued in place.

of the patch, it is best that the edges be trimmed on a bevel slanting inward, so that it fits tightly when clamped. This makes a closer fit when sanded.

• Veneer darkens with age. Therefore, since new material will be lighter in color, it will have to be stained. This should be done before it is trimmed, as the stain may expand or warp the veneer. After the patch has been trimmed its edges must be stained, but, before staining, sand the edges lightly to get them smooth.

• New glue will not stick over dirt or old glue. Both should be removed with a knife blade that is sharp, thin, and pointed.

• Yellow or white glue is the best kind to use for this type of repair. Apply the glue thinly to the hole or patch, insert the patch, and cover the area with waxed paper. Clamp a flat block of wood over this or place a weight on it. Allow the glue to dry for 4 hours; then sand with #320 abrasive paper to level the patch to the adjoining surface.

• Small veneer repairs are not difficult. If the surface affected is large, it might be best to take the work to a cabinet shop, which has special equipment. You may be

2-19. *A veneer punch like the one shown here can be used to cut away a section of damaged veneer. Place it around the damaged area and give a few sharp raps with a hammer. Then chisel away waste.*

2-20. *A veneer punch like the one shown in Figure 2-19 can then cut a replacement patch out of a piece of new veneer. The patch will fit perfectly, and its irregular outline will make it difficult to spot.*

able to hold a newly glued piece of veneer in place on a small curved surface by using a sandbag, but a larger curved area will require a special mold. Also, an extensive flat surface may require a large press.

SMALL DEFECTS   A great variety of small defects is often found in a veneered surface. Among these are bruises, dents, and chips. Stick shellac should be used for the repair of such a defect whenever it is away from the edge of a surface; but, since this is quite brittle and may be broken off easily, it should not be used on corners or edges. Should the defect be at the edge, use wood dough. When hard, sand smooth, stain, and apply a finish.

Small, shallow depressions from bruises may often be repaired by the same method as that given later for plywood. This involves raising the surface with moisture. It may not be successful with very thin veneer, but it is worth trying. If it fails, use stick shellac.

LOOSE EDGES   There are two methods for this work, their selection depending on the conditions you find. They are as follows:

Method 1   If there is no dirt under the loosened veneer and there is life left in the old glue, this method should work. At least it is worth trying because of its simplicity. Proceed as follows:

1. Lift the veneer slightly with the blade of a small spatula, being careful not to break or injure the veneer. (The same spatula used for applying stick shellac will do.)

2. Work a little water or spray with an atomizer under the veneer.

3. Heat the spatula blade over a spirit lamp (wipe off any carbon deposits if you use some other method of heating) and run the spatula back and forth under the

1.

2.

2-21. Large-scale damage in veneer is best repaired by hand cutting a patch from new veneer. A good shape to use is a diamond. 1. Here the patch, already cut with a sharp utility knife, is being placed over the section of damaged veneer. The utility knife is cutting out the damaged veneer, using the patch as a template. Cut carefully, starting with light pressure on the knife. After going all the way around the patch once, make a second pass, applying more pressure. It's better to apply light pressure several times around than to attempt to cut all the way through the veneer in one try.

2. After cutting all the way through the damaged veneer, chisel it away, being careful not to damage the surrounding veneer. Clean all the old veneer and scrape away old glue.

3.

4.

3. Finally, glue the patch in the pocket you have cut for it. The old veneer had been applied with contact cement, so a similar cement is being used for the patch.

4. The finished patch blends well with surrounding veneer. Sanding and finishing will make it even more inconspicuous.

loosened veneer to heat the water and soften the glue.

4. Cover the veneer with waxed paper, a block of wood, and a clamp, or use a weight in place of the clamp.

Method 2 If there is any dirt under the veneer, proceed as follows:

1. Scrape out the dirt and old glue carefully.

2. Spread fresh glue on the end of the spatula blade. Lift up the loosened veneer slightly, insert the blade under the veneer, and press down the veneer. Withdraw the spatula, leaving a thin deposit of glue under the veneer.

3. Squeeze out the excess glue, wiping it off with a damp cloth, or the veneer may bulge. For this you can also use a roller similar to that used in photographic work, rolling it toward the edge. Clamp the veneer or hold it with a weight.

The tool used for this work should have no sharp corners on the blade, which might tear the veneer. The type of spatula recommended has a rounded end. If you do not own this type of spatula, a piece of heavy paper cut with rounded corners may be used for inserting the glue.

BLISTERS AND WAVES These are raised places on the surface of veneer (much like blisters on the skin, as from a burn) that are caused by an excess of moisture, either from the air or because a liquid has been spilled on the surface and allowed to remain until it has penetrated through the veneer to the glue beneath. This results in the glue softening and the veneer swelling. The proper method to use for repair

depends on the circumstances in each case.

Method 1 (unbroken surface) This method is simple. Whether it will work depends on the condition of the old glue and whether there is enough moisture in the wood below the veneer.

Place a moderately heated iron on the raised veneer surface gently enough so that it will not cause a crack. The iron should not be so hot that it will ruin the finish. The heat should draw out sufficient moisture from the base wood to soften the old glue and make it stick. Leave the iron in place for 24 hours, reheating the iron occasionally. (If this method fails, use Method 4.)

Method 2 (broken surface) When the raised veneer is broken and a piece is missing, it is usually best to cut out that section and repair with a patch, as follows:

If you have the broken piece or pieces and they still are in good shape, often a very satisfactory job can be done by flattening the edges that are intact with a moderately hot iron over a damp blotter or cloth. Next, glue in place the loose piece or pieces, being careful that the edge lines do not show. Clamp or hold with a weight for 4 hours (over waxed paper).

Method 3 (cracked surface) If there is no dirt under the surface, use this method. If it does not work because the old glue will no longer hold, use Method 5. Proceed as follows with Method 3:

1. Fill the air pocket with hot vinegar and keep the piece in a position that will prevent the vinegar from running out. Let it stand from 8 to 12 hours and then drain

off any vinegar that hasn't been absorbed. The vinegar is not to remove the glue but merely to soften it.

2. Dry the area with a moderately heated iron over dry blotting paper. The heat will shrink the veneer back to a flattened position and the blotting paper will absorb the moisture.

3. Lift the edge of the crack with a knife blade and, using an eyedropper, insert glue through the crack under both sides. Rub the surface, away from the crack, to spread the glue. Then rub it toward the crack and wipe off excess glue with a damp cloth. Clamp or hold with a weight for 4 hours (over waxed paper).

Method 4 (cracked surface) When there *is* dirt under the veneer and this dirt can be easily removed, use the following method:

1. Make a cut with a razor blade, directly *across* the crack, down to the flat surface on both sides. If necessary, cut the *crack* down to the surface through the center in both directions, thus leaving four attached flaps.

2. Scrape the old glue off the bottom surface and from the underside of the flaps. Scrape any glue from the edges of the cut or flaps to permit the edges to return to their original positions without interference. If necessary, dampen with a wet cloth to make the veneer pliable.

3. Insert glue under the veneer and press the flaps down in place. Wipe off any excess glue with a damp cloth and clamp or hold with a weight for 4 hours (over waxed paper).

Method 5 (cracked surface) When there *is* dirt under the veneer and it is dif-

ficult to remove, use the following method:

1. Make a cut along three edges of the raised veneer with a razor blade. Two of the cuts should be with the grain and the third across the grain. This makes a flap.

2. Raise the flap and scrape away the dirt and old glue from the bottom surface and the underside of the flap. Glue, clamp, or hold with a weight for 4 hours (over waxed paper).

MISSING VENEER If any of the veneer is missing it will have to be replaced with an inlay that should be of the same thickness and grain pattern as the surface into which it is to be placed. Proceed as follows:

1. Trim the place in the veneer to be repaired so that it will have straight and vertical edges. Two sides of this grave should run with the grain and the other two sides directly across the grain, or at an angle to it, depending on how conspicuous the patterns in the veneer are and how closely the inlay pattern should match the sound veneer. For this purpose use a straight-edge and razor blade.

2. Make a template from a piece of paper. To do so, lay the paper over the "grave" and rub a finger around the edges, producing lines on the paper. Cut on those lines to fit the hole.

3. Place the template over the veneer to be used as the inlay and mark along the edges with a sharp-pointed pencil. Trim the inlay with scissors to size and check it for correct fit into the "grave."

4. Glue and clamp or hold with weight for 4 hours (over waxed paper).

2-22. *Blisters in veneer can be reglued by injecting fresh glue with a hypodermic needle, then pressing flat with clamps or heavy weights. If you can't find a hypodermic needle, slit the blister with a razor blade and work glue in through the slit.*

2-23. *Blisters in veneers that were applied with old-fashioned hot hide glues can often be removed with heat. Place a sheet of foil over the blister and heat with an iron. This may soften the old glue and restore its grip. Remove the iron and immediately apply pressure until the glue cools.*

2-24. *Small checks at ends of tabletops, drawers, etc., can be repaired by filling them with thin slivers of veneer. Glue the veneer in place and let it dry. Then trim with a chisel and sand smooth.*

Veneer may be purchased from some lumber dealers who specialize in cabinetmaker's supplies, as well as from mail order houses that cater to craftsmen. Some of these mail order outlets also sell special veneer punches that will cut out damaged veneer and also cut a perfect patch automatically. They are expensive, but worth the money if you have a lot of patching to do.

If only a small piece is needed, or if it is impossible to locate a matching piece of veneer, you may be able to "borrow" a piece from the back of the furniture unit or from some inconspicuous corner where a missing piece would be much less noticeable. To do this, lift up a small piece of the veneer with a sharp chisel, then cut it out with the point of a sharp knife. With careful cutting and fitting, a surprisingly good job of patching can often be done— particularly if you make the patch irregular in shape rather than a square or rectangle.

Sometimes wood plastic of a matching color may be substituted for a missing piece of veneer.

REMOVING BOARD WARPS

In furniture, the most severe warps are often found in the hinged drop leaves of tables and hinged chest or stand tops, since they are not secured in a flat position from the underside. To a lesser extent, warps often occur in the tops of tables, dressers, chests, and stands. This warping is found most frequently in tops that are not fastened securely enough to the frames from the underside or when there is not a sufficient number of properly placed glue blocks or screws to hold the top securely in place.

One important cause of warping is the failure on the part of the cabinetmaker to apply the same finish to the bottom of a board as he did to the top, a point to be remembered when you are finishing furniture. This neglect allows a greater amount of moisture from the air to penetrate the wood from the undersurface than from the top, causing the board to warp.

A board may twist lengthwise with the grain, but it warps across the grain only. Furthermore, the board edges of furniture always tend to warp up toward the finished side. This is the concave (inward curved) side of the warp. The reverse side of the board is the convex (outward curved) side.

If the top or leaves of furniture are badly warped, you will want to correct this condition. A slight warp is permissible by the standards of the collector. In fact, such slight warpage often adds a note of charm to the piece.

If a wide, one-piece board used as a top for furniture is not too badly warped, it may often be clamped back and properly secured in place. However, this work should be done with great care, the clamps being tightened only a little at a time. A narrow or badly warped board should never be forced to flatten out. Disastrous cracks will result.

It is important to examine the frame, to see if it is sound and rigid. Any work to tighten a frame should be done before attempting to remove a warp. Next, examine the warped surfaces and select a method for removing the warp. This will be determined by conditions and circumstances, such as the degree of the warp, the thickness of the warped boards, and their location in the piece. Various methods are used for tops, table leaves, and other such parts, as related in the procedures to follow.

All the procedures call for careful planning of the work, and care and prompt action is required to obtain satisfactory results. When using methods employing moisture or steam, the materials for holding a board in place after the warp has been removed should be on hand before any work is started. There are four methods for removing board warps, as follows:

Removing Warp with Moisture

This is the simplest method of all. It rarely results in a permanent correction and it is impossible to tell in advance whether it will work or not. That depends on the ability of the wood pores to absorb moisture or the angle or grain when the board was cut from the log. Therefore, correcting a warp by this method should be followed immediately by securing the board flat by mechanical means, before the moisture dries out and the warp has a chance to return. This method is best for boards that may be secured in place, especially from the underside.

Examples: Furniture tops or table drop leaves held flat with cleats.

1. Fill any screw holes on the underside of the board with wood dough. Pack the wood dough deeply and allow it to dry thoroughly.

2. Lay the board on damp grass in the sunlight or over wet burlap before a heated stove, with the concave side up. It usually takes from one to several hours for the board to flatten out, the time depending on the degree of the heat applied, the thickness, width, or density of the wood, and whether or not there are open pores. It may be necessary to remove paint or finish to permit a board to absorb moisture. Usually the back of a board used in furniture has little or no finish, so that is the side to be placed downward to absorb moisture. It is important to recognize that wide tops and wide table drop leaves are usually made of more than one board, glued together, side by side. When warped, such pieces usually give way where glued and each board warps independently. Because waterproof glue was unknown when old pieces were made, any glue still holding at such joints may give way when moisture is applied.

3. If and when a board has flattened, secure it immediately, before it dries, to the place from which it came. If it was held with screws, replace them. It is advisable to give additional reinforcement by holding the board in place with corner irons and mending plates whenever it is possible to use them. When cleats are to be fixed to a board to hold it in a flattened position, the work should be done immediately after the warp has been removed. (See page 69 for more information on cleats.)

4. If it is necessary to secure a board temporarily in a flat position, do so by clamping rigid strips of wood on both sides near the ends and at the center. Otherwise, the warp may return.

There are many modifications of the above method, mostly complicated and to be avoided. A brief example would be when several boards are involved, as in removable table leaves. They are stacked with wet sawdust between and around them for days, removed, restacked with cleats between them, gradually flattened with clamps across the boards about a foot apart, and allowed to dry. The clamps are made of heavy wood, wider than the boards, with long bolts through holes near both ends. The bolts are tightened in rotation, little by little, so that the pressure won't crack the boards.

Removing Warps with Steam

Warps that are stubborn and cannot be removed by the first method will usually submit to this one. With it there is a far better chance that the warp correction will be permanent than if the warp is removed by Method 1, as the penetration goes all the way through the board.

1. Remove all paint and surface finish to permit penetration of moisture. (Various methods are given in Chapter Four.)

2. Have the board steam treated in a steam box. Such boxes are not too common, but you should be able to learn where such work is done by inquiry at a cabinet shop or lumber yard.

3. Follow Steps 1, 3, and 4 under Method 1.

If the warped board is extremely dried out or of the type that has open pores, it is sometimes advisable to apply a single even coat of half pure white shellac and half denatured alcohol, so that the moisture will not be absorbed too rapidly. However, inquire at the shop to do the steaming before applying it.

Removing Warps with Grooves

This method, which may be new to some workers, is a very satisfactory way to remove warps. It is done with a power saw. Since the grooves are cut on the reverse side of the boards only, it leaves the face undamaged, a point in its favor. But this method can be used only on parts of furniture that can be removed to be sawed, such as a tabletop, and should never be used on a part where the grooves

may later be seen, such as table drop leaves. Remember, too, that the grooves will show if the ends of the board are visible.

1. On the reverse side of a flat wood surface, the side that swells outward, saw slots (grooves) lengthwise where the warp occurs about 3 inches apart and to a depth of about three-quarters the thickness of the board, with a power saw. The grooves should run lengthwise with the grain of the wood for the full length of the board, but should stop just short of the ends, so they won't be visible on the end surfaces.

2. Replace the board (or top) and secure to the frame by the means previously used (usually screws). Reinforce with corner irons and glue blocks.

In cases of extreme warpage or with thick boards, it is best to straighten the warp from the grooved board (or top) before attempting to secure it to the frame, to avoid cracks. This may usually be done by Method 1 or by laying the board over wet burlap before a heated stove with the grooved side down. This method is similar to that used by carpenters in building construction, when a flat molding is placed around a curved wall surface by sawing cross-grain slots close together on the reverse side of the molding.

Removing Warps by Sawing Boards in Strips

This method of removing a warp must be done in a shop equipped with the large power tools required for boards wide enough to warp. The work cannot be attempted on boards too thin to plane level, as is necessary in the final operation. Usually boards should be in excess of one inch in thickness for this method to be used, but it may be used on boards of lesser thickness, if the warp is not too great. This method is best for such items as table leaves that are hinged to hang down and the reverse side of which can be seen, as the operation results in a smooth finish on both sides.

For your information, the work is done as follows: The board is cut lengthwise with a ripsaw into strips about 3 to 4 inches wide. The cut edges are smoothed on a joiner, alternate strips turned *upside down* and glued together under pressure. When dried, the board is put through a planer and then sanded on both sides. This eliminates the alternating convex and concave curves that were on both surfaces, due to every other board having been turned over. This procedure for removing a warp destroys all evidence of age and wear, and the board is thinner. The new surface, when finished, will seldom match the rest of the furniture in color or tone, which is why many workers object to this method. When it is possible to use cleats on the reverse side of the board, that method of straightening a warp is preferred by many.

CLEATS ON HINGED TABLE LEAVES

The best method for keeping a hinged table leaf flat, after a warp has been removed by moisture or steam, is to install cleats. The method is relatively simple and is acceptable to most collectors. The work should be done immediately after the warp has been removed and before the leaf has had a chance to dry out. The cleats should have been prepared previously; the glue, screws, and clamps should be at hand.

Cleats are installed on the underside and across the grain of the leaf. They should be set in from the ends of the leaf, in a position from which they will not interfere with the frame or legs when the leaf is hanging in a vertical position. Usually, two cleats only are used, one near each end of the leaf. However, if it is possible to install a third cleat near the center of the leaf and still not have it interfere with the frame-arm or brace (which swings out from the frame to hold the leaf in a horizontal position), the additional support furnished by this third cleat is desirable.

The procedure employed is as follows:

1. The cleats should be of hardwood (oak is good) to be effective. On medium-width table leaves the cleats should be ¾ inch thick and from 1 to 1½ inches wide. Their length should be to within an inch of the width of the leaf. When a cleat is installed, its narrow edge is placed against the board.

2. To make cleats, saw them lengthwise from a board of proper thickness for the *narrow* edge and of a determined width dimension. When a cleat is made in this manner and installed on its edge, it gives the greatest resistance to bend.

3. Use flat-headed steel screws of the proper length to go through the cleats and take a good hold in the table leaf. (Since

brass screws are made of soft metal, they are apt to break off if the leaf is hardwood.) Drill holes through the narrow width of the cleats, not more than 6 inches apart and large enough to give free clearance for the shank of the screw through the cleat, and countersink with a rose drill so that the screw head will be flush with the surface. Round off or taper the upper ends of the cleats so they will have a neat appearance, then sand off the upper edges.

4. Take an accurate measurement of all four corners from the edge of the leaf to the leg or frame. If the table isn't too large, it would be best to turn it upside down over cloth or paper while doing the measuring. Draw lines from these measurements, representing both side edges of the cleats. Leave enough clearance so the cleats will not interfere with the leg or frame when the leaf is in a hanging position. The lines must be parallel to the board ends. Recheck your measurements and marks. It is most important that they be correct.

5. Remove the finish from the surface where the cleats are to be installed to assure the glue holding. Apply yellow or epoxy glue to the contact side of the cleats. Secure the cleats to the leaves with screws, driven in tight with a screw bit and brace, being careful to place the cleats in the exact position between the drawn lines. Wipe off the excess glue with a damp cloth.

6. Apply clamps over the cleats to hold them firmly to the leaves. Place in a warm room and permit the glue to dry. Should the cleats be installed immediately after the warp is removed, the leaves will contain moisture.

7. Stain the cleats to match the underside of the leaves.

8. After the leaves are thoroughly dry, seal the underside of the leaves with a coat of varnish or shellac. This helps prevent absorption of moisture from the air, which was the cause of the warp.

Cleats are often applied by this method to the undersides of the hinged tops of chests, stands, etc., after a warp has been removed. In these cases, when space will permit, they are most frequently installed under the extreme ends of the top.

Another method of keeping a board flat, after a warp has been removed, is with hardwood dowels. Holes are drilled from side to side through the board edge, and dowels are inserted and glued. The drilling requires accurate workmanship and is best done with a power tool. The boards must not be too wide or too thin. This method is rarely used, but it is good to know about it.

FURNITURE CASTERS

Casters used for furniture are usually the stem-and-socket type. The stem is the round shaft on the top of the caster. Near the top of this shaft is a slight groove. The socket, called the ferrule, is the hollow tube made with a beveled top and a plate, with upturned jagged teeth, at its base.

To install casters, proceed as follows:

1. Measure the outside diameter of the socket tube. This is usually ⅜ inch for smaller casters and ½ inch for larger ones.

2. Drill holes in the center of the bottom of the furniture legs, about ½ inch deeper than the length of the socket tube, to allow the stem to protrude through the tube. If the furniture legs are small in diameter, wrap friction tape around their bases to give added strength to the wood while drilling. If this isn't done, the legs may split, especially if the bit is not sharp or the wood is very dry. The bit should be the same size as the diameter of the socket tube.

3. Pound the socket gently into the holes until the jagged teeth engage firmly in the wood of the leg bottom.

4. Insert the stem in the socket and hit it sharply with the palm of the hand. This forces the stem through the beveled top of the socket, where it is held by the groove. Finally, remove any friction tape.

Here are three methods of tightening loose caster sockets:

1. Shred steel wool, twist it, and work it into a string. Wrap it tightly around the socket, cover it with epoxy glue, insert it in the socket hole, and drive it into place.

2. Wrap the socket with tough paper or cloth, glue, and insert, or wrap it with friction tape or rubber bands and insert.

3. Fill the hole into which the caster fits with wood dough that has been thinned by additional solvent. Assemble the caster with the stem in the socket and drive it to its full depth in the hole before the wood dough has a chance to harden. Twist the stem around several times and work it up and down a bit to make a space at the end of the stem so it won't bind when the wood dough hardens.

three

Reviving
Old Finishes

Many novice furniture restorers will laboriously strip and refinish an old piece of furniture when the job is not really necessary. They waste time, energy, and money and at the same time rob the piece of some of its authentic charm. A piece of old furniture is never quite the same once it has been completely redone. So avoid overrestoration.

If the piece isn't disfigured, for instance, leave some indications of age—the marks of the cabinetmaker, some signs of wear. The proof that a piece is an antique, and its commercial value as well, often rest on these marks.

Many old pieces of furniture *need only to be cleaned.* If the original finish is smooth, adhering well, and isn't chipped, do not remove it. Removing the original finish of a valuable piece, if it is in good condition, would destroy much of its value and character. So, don't assume that an old finish must be completely removed and a new one applied. The condemna-

tion of the old finish often results from jumping to conclusions too quickly after a casual inspection; such condemnation results more often from inexperience and not knowing that the existing finish can be revived.

Old finishes often become dull and drab in appearance merely from an accumulation of dirt and grime from long usage. Both shellac and varnish finishes will take on a milky effect from dampness, while varnish will check or alligator when the atmosphere is too dry. Under normal conditions, this could have been avoided if the furniture had had the proper care. (See Chapter Nine.)

The finish on furniture is subject to scratches and marks from carelessness or accident. It may become stained by acid or ink, or it may have white spots or rings left by hot dishes, water, or alcohol. Many of these blemishes can be removed while leaving the finish intact.

Methods and materials to be used for

3-1. It is nearly always possible to identify the wood in a piece of furniture by inspecting its underside, where bare wood is usually exposed. Often, too, the manufacturer stamps the species name here. Some of the things to consider are: Is it plywood, veneered, soft- or hardwood, open-grained or close-grained? What is the age of the wood (antique or modern) and design (inlay, carved, etc.)? Now form a mental picture of the finished product—type of finish desired, upholstery, grain, color, and general appearance. Let this serve as your guide and the refinishing chore will seem much easier.

reviving the entire finish, or for spot work, are described in this chapter. The effort to revive an old finish is well worth trying. Should it fail, little time and material will have been wasted. The old finish may then be removed and a new one applied.

TEST BEFORE CONDEMNING AN OLD FINISH

It is always best to test these simple methods of restoring an old finish by trying them on a small area. If the results are not satisfactory, the old finish can then be removed and a new one put on without any harm having been done. Some old furniture, such as the Hitchcock chair and the Boston rocker, were constructed of wood that was intended to be painted, and these should be restored by painting, although those still carrying their original paint can often be revived.

Generally speaking, checking and white on an old finish are signs of bad adhesion. A simple test of brittleness and adhesion is scratching an old finish with the edge of a coin. Make the test in an inconspicuous place, because the scratches will probably whiten. (The test scratches may be removed as described later in this chapter.) If you can't scrape through to the wood with relative ease, you probably can get away with rejuvenation instead of removal.

You will sometimes find the varnish on furniture made of such hardwood as mahogany, maple, or walnut in bad condition due to age or abuse. Such a finish may have been marred, dented, or scratched. If its condition isn't too bad, it can usually be satisfactorily revived. But when it is very badly checked or alligatored there is no alternative but to remove the old finish and replace it with a new one, suitable to the type of furniture and its use.

It is often difficult for the amateur to determine what kind of an old clear finish was used on a piece of furniture. It may be shellac, varnish, or lacquer, with no definite characteristic to indicate the finish that was used.

A test to show whether the material was shellac can be made by applying denatured alcohol with a rag to a small area (free from wax) to see whether the finish will soften or rub off, since shellac is always thinned with alcohol.

To distinguish between varnish and lacquer, treat a small area (free from wax) in the same manner, but with lacquer thinner. Lacquer will soften or rub off with this material, which will not be harmful to varnish. Very often a heavy lacquer finish may be distinguished from one of varnish by the mere fact that lacquer is almost crystal hard as compared to varnish.

CLEANING MAY RESTORE FURNITURE

If the finish is smooth, use a furniture cleanser-conditioner to:

1. Clean wood and restore the natural grain and color.

2. Disguise scratches and retard checking.

3. Remove cloudiness and dullness caused by smoke, grease, and dust.

4. "Winterize" furniture to withstand the dryness and heat of rooms in fall and winter.

There are a number of products made for reviving old finishes. These are often sold in grocery, hardware, and paint stores, but it may be best to inquire at a furniture store for special types of products. Most of the commercial products are for general cleaning of dulled surfaces. When this work is completed, as directed on the container, the piece should be finished with a good furniture polish or wax. Some products will do a much better job than others in the complete elimination of foggy, cloudy, milky, or faded conditions, while others will usually remove white spots, rings, or other blemishes.

No harm will be done to a finish that is basically in good condition by the use of a good commercial product made for the purpose, provided it is used correctly. It should be tried on a small area to see how it works. The balance of this chapter gives treatments for various ailments on finished surfaces, and in some cases special products are recommended.

REVIVING A CLEAR FINISH

The condition of an old clear finish may often be such that it can be revived satisfactorily with a single coat of the same kind of finishing material that was originally used.

Wax should be removed before attempting to revive a surface. This may be done with a cloth dampened with turpentine or a product especially made for the purpose.

Wet a rag with the solvent and carefully scrub the surface of the finish, covering every square inch. Then rub dry with a clean cloth and repeat. It is vitally important to do a thorough job of cleaning. Some furniture waxes and polishes contain silicones, which do a great job of protecting the finish but will repel most finishes applied over them. The fresh coat of finish will "crawl," leaving tiny craterlike bare spots called "fisheyes." There are additives you can buy at paint stores or from such outlets as Constantine's (see page 4) that when mixed with a finish will keep it from crawling. Still, it is best to remove the silicones rather than to rely on additives.

After the wax is removed, the piece should be washed with a solution in the proportions of 2 heaping tablespoons of sal soda to 1 gallon of hot water to remove traces of grease, etc. Rinse with clear water, wipe with clean, dry cloths, and allow to dry thoroughly. On veneered pieces, use the solution sparingly, washing, rinsing, and drying each surface independently and quickly, so as not to loosen the veneer.

When the piece is dry, sand it lightly with #320 sandpaper (to give the new material a "tooth"), apply the finish material, and allow it to dry. Then complete the finish to the smoothness desired (as directed in Chapter Six) for the type of finishing material used.

Another very good cleaner-conditioner can be made by mixing three-quarters boiled linseed oil (buy commercially prepared—don't attempt to boil linseed oil at home) and one-quarter gum turpentine in a glass container with a tight-fitting lid. Shake well before using. You can store the mixture indefinitely in a tightly closed container.

To apply this cleanser-conditioner, it must be heated. To do so, pour a layer of the oily mixture onto the surface of a pan of hot water. Apply the solution to a small area at a time. Keep excess moisture away from joints, to prevent the glue from softening. Rub the surface with the mixture, using a toothbrush on carvings and grooves. Dip a 3/0 steel-wool pad into the solution and rub lightly with the grain to remove dirt, if needed. Dip a clean cloth in clear, warm water, wring, and wipe the surface. Wring dry for shellac surfaces. Wipe the surface with a dry cloth. Discard the mixture when cold. Do *not* reheat—it is flammable and it will become gummy.

After cleaning, use furniture polish or wax, if desired.

WASHING SOILED FURNITURE

There are three basic methods of washing soiled furniture, as follows:

Method 1 is commonly used for light cleaning. Wash the piece thoroughly with a soft, clean rag and warm water to which a small amount of pure white soap has been added. Wipe dry with clean cloths.

Method 2 is used for badly soiled pieces and is especially suitable for varnish finishes. Wash the piece with a mixture of 1 quart of hot water, 3 tablespoons of boiled linseed oil, and 1 tablespoon of turpentine. (Turpentine aids in cutting dirt; oil lubricates, feeds, and polishes.) Use an old double boiler to keep the mixture hot, since it is flammable. Rub the wood with a soft cloth that has been wet with the solution, then polish with a soft, dry cloth. Repeat if necessary.

Method 3 is especially useful for removing stubborn dirt and stains and may be necessary only for spot cleanups. Use a cloth dampened with a product such as Weldwood Cleaner and Thinner. This contains some powerful solvents that will remove many types of dirt, yet it is safe for most finishes. Before using it on a piece, however, test it on an inconspicuous area to make sure it won't harm the finish. While this type of cleaner is very strong, it probably is safer for veneered work than the first two methods.

Great care must be taken when washing veneered surfaces with water to prevent moisture from getting into the glue and loosening the veneer. When the veneer is not broken or cracked, wash only a small area at a time and quickly wipe it dry. Should the veneer be in poor condition, the surface is best cleaned with a commercial product made for the purpose. Remember that water also damages shellac, so do exercise care when employing a cleanser-conditioner containing water.

REVIVING WAXED SURFACES

A scratched or spotted waxed surface may often be revived by rubbing it with a little turpentine on a soft cloth and then rewaxing it.

REVIVING FOGGY, CLOUDY, MILKY, OR FADED FINISHES

It is difficult to state just what materials and methods to use to revive extensively overcast or faded finishes. It may at times require a bit of experimenting. Any wax on the surface should be removed. Sometimes this itself will remove an overcast, especially when turpentine is used as the cleaner.

1. *Shellac finishes* may often be revived with a mixture of 2 parts paraffin oil and 1 part white shellac. Apply and rub with a cloth for mild cases, but with a pad of 3/0 steel wool, for severe cases, rub with the grain. Wipe dry with a clean cloth.

2. *Varnish finishes* can generally be revived with a mixture of half raw linseed oil and half turpentine. Apply as in Method 1.

3. *A foggy appearance* should be treated with a mixture of 1 quart of clear water to which has been added 1 to 2 tablespoons of vinegar. Dampen a clean cloth and rub with the grain.

4. *A milky effect* on varnished surfaces, particularly in damp climates, is probably due to an inferior grade of varnish. A good rub with a mixture of half raw linseed oil and half turpentine will sometimes improve or entirely remove the defect. Use a closely woven cloth of hard texture. If the piece is not improved, it will need to be refinished.

5. *Commercial furniture refinishers* are made for the purpose of reviving old finishes. Apply as directed by the manufacturer. These products—available at paint and hardware stores—are strong solvents. Essentially what they do is melt the old finish and blend it together. If overapplied, they can remove the old finish down to the wood.

When applying any of these materials to carvings and other raised or depressed surfaces, use a small hand brush dipped in the mixture. Then dry with a cloth. Use a pointed stick under the cloth for depressions.

In all cases, after cleaning use furniture polish or wax, if desired.

REMOVING WHITE SPOTS OR RINGS

Most white spots or rings on a furniture finish may be removed. The method employed depends more upon the depth of the damage than upon using a particular method for various types of finishes. However, finishes that are very thin must be treated by a less severe method than that used on those which are thick.

It is best to attempt to remove the white spot first by simple methods, using mild abrasives. If not successful, it will then be necessary to use more drastic means. The following methods run from the mildest to those requiring special materials or coarser abrasives.

1. Dust cigarette or cigar ashes over the spot or ring; dip a cloth into a lightweight oil—sewing machine oil, lemon oil, baby oil, olive oil, or raw linseed oil. Then rub lightly *with* the grain of the wood. Apply lightly to the entire surface to prevent spotting; wipe the surface with a soft cloth.

2. Dip your finger into lightweight oil, then common table salt, and rub the spot with the mixture. If the white spot is old or very deep, much rubbing may be needed.

3. Dip a cloth in clear water, wring it, then hold it up to the mouth of a bottle of household ammonia to moisten. Whisk the damp cloth over the spot lightly and quickly. Rub with a dry cloth. This method is especially good for a varnished surface.

4. Rub with rottenstone and some lightweight oil on a cloth as described in Method 1.

5. Rub with a thick paste made of grade 3/F pumice powder and lightweight oil, using a cloth as described in Method 1. This method is especially good for a varnished surface.

6. Use a commercial product for removing white spots from furniture, following the manufacturer's directions.

If the white on a surface is successfully removed, follow with an application of furniture polish, after a slight interval, to permit the cleaning materials to evaporate or harden. If the white cannot be removed, it will be necessary to refinish the surface or the entire piece.

REMOVING SCRATCHES

On woods with a *natural finish*, use a furniture cleanser-conditioner (see page 74) to clean and blend the color of the scratched area with the natural finish. To disguise minor scratches, use broken pieces of the meat of nuts, such as pecan, English or black walnut, Brazil nut, or butternut. Rub diagonally along the scratch until it darkens.

On woods with an *oil finish*, use a 3/0 steel-wool pad dipped in lightweight mineral oil, *boiled* linseed oil, or baby oil. Rub carefully with the wood grain. Wipe the entire surface with a cloth slightly moistened with oil, then with a dry cloth. In badly scarred instances use boiled linseed oil.

On woods with a *shellac finish*, use a shellac thinner or denatured alcohol solvent to soften the shellac around the scratch.

On woods with a *varnish finish*, use gum turpentine to soften the varnish and cover a small scratch. You may also employ a commercial scratch remover; use as the label directs.

On *stained* woods with a *natural finish*, use a stain to blend with the old stain, of the color and type originally used on the piece, if possible. For example, on wood stained yellowish-brown, use a base of walnut stain and a small amount of yellowish maple over the base. Dry, and apply the type of finish used originally.

To color a scratch, apply colors in oil (such as burnt umber), thinned with turpentine, or varnish stain, ready mixed in wood colors. If too concentrated, add the stain to a clear varnish of the same brand; or use a commercial scratch remover. Set the container in a pan of hot water before applying.

To apply a stain or solvent to a scratch, proceed as follows: With your finger or a small pointed brush, apply the stain or solvent diagonally along the scratch, feathering it out toward the edges. When dry, rub the surface with a lintless cloth. It may be necessary to repeat the process after 24 hours. When dry, rub varnish or shellac finishes with pumice and oil, lacquered surfaces with rottenstone and oil.

Deep scratches may be filled with a stick lacquer or shellac of a color shade that matches the finish most closely. (See pages 30–32.)

When scratches have been removed, revive the finish with furniture polish or wax.

REMOVING PAPER ADHERING TO A SURFACE

To remove paper that has adhered to a wood surface, pour enough *warm* lightweight oil on the surface to saturate the paper. Let it stand. Rub lightly with a 3/0 steel-wool pad. Apply more warm oil; rub again. Wipe the surface with the oil, then with a dry cloth.

REPAIRING GOUGES, HOLES, AND BURNS

When wood finishes are gouged or burned, repairs may be made on the existing finish. Or, during refinishing, burns, holes, and gouges may be filled after several coats of the new finish have been applied and are dry.

To remove discoloration or char, scrape the charred spot or darkened edges of the holes with a knife blade or a 3/0 steel-wool pad wrapped around an orange stick or pencil. Brush out the scrapings with an old toothbrush. To bleach the area, sponge it with denatured alcohol. Repeat the process, if necessary. If further bleaching is required, try a dilute solution of oxalic acid (paint store item).

If the damaged area is *shallow*, fill it

with several coats of colored sealer or varnish, if stained. Or use a clear sealer or varnish.

If the hole is deep and *no larger than a thumbnail,* fill it with stick lacquer or shellac. (See pages 30–32.)

If the hole goes clear through, use wood putty or wood dough underneath. (See pages 27–30.) Fill the top with stick lacquer or shellac.

REMOVING INK OR DARK SPOTS

Ink spots are difficult to remove. Ink penetrates deeply into wood, especially when the surface is not finished, as is often the case with old desks. The stain may usually be minimized and sometimes removed by the application of pure household ammonia, or a saturated solution of oxalic acid. It is often necessary to use repeated applications. (See pages 101 and 102.)

When an ink stain is only on the surface of a finish, it may usually be removed with a mixture of pumice stone and light oil made into a paste. Rub with the grain of the wood, using a soft cloth. Clean off with turpentine on a clean cloth.

When ink spots are on top of a finish and do not completely bleach out with treatment, they may often be completely removed by scraping the finish. However, this is useless to attempt for stains on bare wood.

Dark spots may often be bleached out with ammonia or the oxalic acid solution, as outlined above. If not, they may have to be scraped.

CORRECTING CHECKED AND ALLIGATORED FINISHES

Many different terms are applied to those finishes that have dried out, leaving shallow or deep grooves that look like the skin of a snake or alligator. Those with very fine lines are here termed *checked* while those with deep lines are called *alligatored.*

It has been considered a hopeless task to correct an alligatored finish satisfactorily. However, it is advisable to take the time to try, using a furniture refinisher. If it is unsuccessful, no harm will be done. It may aid in the removal of the old finish, preparatory to applying a new one. With checked finishes the fine lines or grooves can usually be corrected so well with a furniture refinisher that they will scarcely be noticeable.

Directions for using furniture refinishers vary from brand to brand. The usual procedure is to rub the material onto the finish with steel wool. Solvents in the refinisher soften the old finish, and rubbing with steel wool packs softened finish into the cracks. You can keep adding more refinisher and rubbing with clean steel wool until the finish either smooths out to your satisfaction or is removed down to bare wood.

REPAIRING A SPOT WORN THROUGH THE FINISH

This work is the bane of refinishers. There is nothing difficult in the procedure, except that it takes time and much care in selecting or mixing a stain that will ultimately match the surrounding color. Applying a finish over the stain and rubbing down is the simplest part of the work.

The following method is for the use of standard products:

1. Prepare the spot and feather the edges by rubbing lightly and carefully with #400 wet or dry finishing paper. Use water as a lubricant on the paper for a varnish finish and baby oil for a shellac finish. Clean off and allow to dry completely.

2. Apply a thin wash coat to the spot, using the same material that was used for the original finish. This is to keep the stain from penetrating into the wood pores, so that it may be removed if not the proper shade. (See "Preliminary Wash Coats," page 121.)

3. The spot is then stained. It is wise to check for the exact shade of color before the stain is used by applying it (if possible) to an unexposed part of the piece. When satisfied with the color, thin the stain considerably and apply coat after coat until you have obtained an exact match, allowing each coat to dry thoroughly. Each coat of stain adds color. Sand lightly with used 7/0 or 8/0 finishing paper between coats.

4. Apply enough coats of the same kind of finishing material as was used for the original finish to produce a smooth and high gloss. Allow each coat to dry completely. Sand lightly between coats with worn, fine paper, as used for the stain.

5. The last coat of finishing material on the spot must then be rubbed down to match the surrounding finish in texture.

For an ordinary *semigloss* finish, use 2/0 or 3/0 steel wool, rubbing carefully with the grain. For a smoother grade of this finish, use #400 wet or dry finishing paper. Follow the directions in Step 1, above.

For a *polished rubbed* finish, smooth the spot with grade 3/F pumice powder and a rubbing pad, using water on varnish and light rubbing oil on shellac.

6. Complete the finish by waxing or using furniture polish over the entire piece.

It is advisable to use an oil stain for this work, as it may be more readily removed than any other type of stain material should the color not match properly. (See "Oil Stains," page 126.)

RESTORING BRASS HARDWARE

Brass hardware—handles, keyhole plates, handle plates, escutcheons, hinges—is favored for its durability and appearance. If the original brass hardware remains, it adds to the value of an old piece, so restore it if possible.

To polish solid or pressed brass, apply a commercial brass cleaner or household ammonia. Or remove the brass hardware gently, if you can, and soak in household ammonia briefly. Then rub with 3/0 steel wool, and clean in warm, soapy water. Rinse and dry. Rub hard-to-remove spots with hot vinegar and salt or lemon rind and salt.

To polish antique-finish brass, use pure lemon oil (not lemon oil polish).

To polish brass finishes, apply a commercial brass cleaner or a thin paste of rottenstone and commercially boiled linseed oil. Wipe off paste with a cloth moistened in boiled linseed oil. Polish with a dry cloth. Allow it to dry on the brass before polishing. Wash, rinse, and dry.

When the brass finish on hardware has peeled, you cannot restore it. You may paint the hardware off-black to cover discoloration, if you wish.

REVIVING PLASTIC SURFACES

While laminated plastic cannot be classified as old or antique material, it's used a great deal in furniture making.

Laminated plastic surfaces can become dull and shabby in spots from excessive wear or when abused by the use of harsh abrasives. To bring back the new look, clean occasionally with a low-luster cream polish or a silicone-based wash—the wax will protect against wear, making daily maintenance easier because spilled things will not stick. On badly worn areas, a single-step auto cleaner-polish will provide great improvement. Pour a little on a thick pad or clean, soft cloth and rub on the worn area, using long, even strokes and rubbing with the "grain"—that is, the length of the pattern. Do not use a circular motion, as this might cause swirl marks. Rub until an even gloss develops, then wipe with a clean cloth. Apply a cream polish or a silicone-based wax.

Do not try to remove spots from laminated plastic surfaces with abrasive cleaners, which damage the surface of the plastic. A treatment with an automotive cleaner, as just described, will remove most spots and will not scratch the plastic.

If a laminated plastic surface should become loose from its base, scrape away the old adhesive as best you can. Make certain both surfaces are dry. Then, with a spatula, spread a waterproof countertop adhesive (but not contact cement) in the crack, according to the manufacturer's instructions. Then clamp or weight the plastic in place. If the plastic is under tension at a nearby point—for example, if a faucet escutcheon is bearing on it—release the tension before clamping the laminated plastic in place.

CLEANING MARBLE

Small scratches on marble surfaces can usually be eliminated by rubbing them with a very fine abrasive paper, such as #600. Then wet the surface with water, sprinkle on a little rottenstone, dampen a cloth, and rub briskly until a shine appears.

While large scratches and pit marks can be removed by rubbing evenly with abrasive materials of successively finer grit sizes and polished as above, the job is rather difficult and is best done by a professional marble dealer.

Stains can be removed from marble surfaces. After soaking the stains in very hot water, you can start the cleaning with a stiff brush and one of the more powerful detergents. If you apply pressure during the scrubbing and then rinse with clear water, most of the stains will disappear. If any are left, you can make use of cleansers with a lye or other *alkaline* base (plain lye soap, for instance, or cleansers with a lye content), since marble is basically limestone and won't be damaged by this type. Avoid acid cleansers of all kinds, as they destroy marble. Be sure to rinse well, for marble is quite porous and dirty water can sink in deeply and stain it.

Oily stains made by butter, salad dressing, cream, etc., should be removed before waxing. Place a white blotter soaked in lighter fluid over the spot and let dry. Repeat several times if necessary. If the stain is still visible, make a paste of talcum powder and lighter fluid. Spread it over the spot. As the fluid evaporates, it is drawn up into the powder, pulling the stain with it. If this does not remove all the stain, bleach with an application of hydrogen peroxide to which a drop or two of ammonia has been added.

To remove marks that have been etched into the polished surface by alcohol or acids in fruit juices, sand gently with the finest sandpaper. Then rub with rottenstone on a damp, soft cloth. Tobacco stains may be bleached out with an application of hydrogen peroxide.

To clean marble safely and apply protection at the same time, use a cream polish or a silicone-based spray wax. These waxes are especially recommended for white, rose, and beige marbles. For additional protection on black and porous travertines, follow cleaning with a light coat of paste wax and polish thoroughly while the wax is moist.

If a marble item should break, wash the edges if dirty and let them dry thoroughly. Then apply an epoxy glue to one edge, press together, and clamp securely. Allow at least 24 hours before removing the pressure.

CLEANING LEATHER

Leather on tables, chairs, and other furnishings may be renewed and maintained by washing with saddle or castile soap and water. Avoid using furniture polishes, oils, and varnishes on leather. These often contain solvents that will make leather sticky.

To clean leather on furniture, use lukewarm water with mild soap flakes (such as Ivory) and a teaspoonful of vinegar. Dip a clean, soft cloth into the water and rub it over the leather. Then, to wash off any suds, go over it with the cloth wrung out in clear, lukewarm water. When it is thoroughly dry, polish the leather with a lamb's-wool shoe brush or a dry, soft cloth onto which you have squeezed a dab of neutral leather dressing from a tube. This cream also comes in liquid form in a bottle and may be obtained at any notion counter or shoe repair shop. Never use polish on leather; it will weaken the surface.

four

Removing the Old Finish

When it is obvious that the old finish must be removed or when you have determined, from the test described in Chapter Three, that its removal is necessary, the question then arises as to the proper procedure to follow to ensure the best results and cause the least amount of damage to the wood surface.

There are three techniques you can use for removing an old finish.

1. *Using paint and varnish remover* In liquid, paste, or semipaste form, these are combinations of several chemicals that soften the old finish so it can be lifted off with gentle scraping or washed off with water.

2. *Mechanical removal* This means that the job can be done by hand scraping and hand or power sanding.

3. *Heat* This method accomplishes removal by using a portable blowtorch or an electric heating tool to burn off the old finish.

Of the three, the best and least harmful method of removing an old finish is with the use of a commercial paint and varnish remover. Incidentally, there is no difference between a paint remover and a varnish remover, and the industry usually refers to the material simply as paint remover.

Both the mechanical and heat methods of finish removal are not recommended for the home handyman. The original wood surface may be destroyed by scraping with sharp tools or glass, by planing, or even by cutting too deeply with abrasives. Also, a beginner may risk gouging the surface when using a scraper or sanding machine for the first time. The mellowness and texture (patina) in the old wood are built up by age, years of use, and repeated rubbings. Once removed, patina cannot be restored.

With the heat method of removing a finish there is a danger not only of fire, but

4-1. *Three techniques for removing an old finish:* upper left, *paint and varnish remover;* upper right, *mechanical removal;* lower right, *heat removal.*

also of scorching the wood. In addition, the heat technique is often slower than either one of the other methods, so it is foolish to take the extra risks involved.

You should not use lye to remove wood finishes, because it burns and pulps the wood. It is difficult to remove and to counteract its action, so the new finish often remains sticky and does not dry. It may even come off in a short time.

EQUIPMENT YOU WILL NEED

No job should ever be started without proper tools. The same rule applies for stripping old finishes. Rigid paint scrapers are not advisable, as their sharp edges have a way of gouging the wood, in spite of the greatest care. For removing finishes that have been softened by a good paint remover, you'll find a broad, round-cornered putty knife useful for shoveling away thick layers of old paint. In most cases 2/0 steel-wool pads will remove the sludge. The basic equipment is:

a good paint and varnish remover
denatured alcohol solvent
gum turpentine (if the remover contains wax)
a putty knife
a wide wall spatula
an old or cheap bristle paintbrush (about 2½ inches wide)
orange or lollipop sticks
burlap ravelings or twine
an old toothbrush
burlap squares
2/0 steel-wool pads
clean old cloths
newspapers
covered containers for remover and alcohol
covered metal container for used rags and papers
waterless hand cleaner

Old clothes or a washable coverall are recommended.

Paint removers, cleaning solvents, and finishing materials in general must be handled with care and certain precautions must be followed. For instance, the FLAMMABLE or KEEP AWAY FROM FLAME warnings on containers mean that the products give off flammable vapors *at room temperatures*. When you open the container, flammable vapors come out of the opening. And as these vapors mix with the air, they will burn or explode if a spark or flame ignites them. As soon as you spread one of these substances on a surface, the vapors circulate much faster. The striking of a match, the operation of a light switch, or even the flame in a gas pilot light can ignite such fumes. In addition, paint-remover fumes are dangerous to persons with heart and pulmonary disorders.

To prevent any problems, take the following precautions when using finishing materials or cleaning solvents:

1. Read the manufacturers' labels and heed their warnings.

2. Work outdoors if possible. If not, provide good cross ventilation to carry vapors away quickly, to prevent toxic effects from breathing fumes, and to reduce the danger of fire.

3. Don't smoke in the area where you use flammables.

4. Do not let containers of flammable liquids stand uncovered. Replace caps immediately after pouring finishing liquids.

5. Place rags or papers used in finishing in metal-covered cans after use, or destroy them at once. Don't leave them crumpled in open containers. Under certain conditions they are subject to spontaneous combustion and can start fires in your home.

GENERAL RULES FOR REMOVING OLD FINISH

When removing an old finish or paint from wooden furniture surfaces, it would be wise to abide by the following rules:

1. Do nothing that will harm the patina or the original surface, unless it is in such bad condition that drastic methods are called for or unless the piece is to be painted.

2. If you plan to replace the old finish with a new clear type, all old finish must

be removed so that the new will hold properly.

3. When removing old paint, it is not only permissible but acceptable to most collectors that the marks of wear through the years, as well as traces of color from the old paint, be allowed to remain, so that they will show through the new finish. Traces of old paint add interest to the piece by their variations of color, and are evidence of age. However, old paint should not be left on in thick patches or blotches.

4. Usually stubborn paint can be removed down to a satisfactory level, but it is often impossible to remove it all, particularly from cherry, mahogany, and walnut.

5. Before attempting to remove an old finish or paint, it is a good plan to scrape off a small area, in an inconspicuous spot, to determine the condition of the finish and the number of coats that have been used, and to inspect the undercoat. If this undercoat is found to be of the refractory type, the necessary materials for its removal should be at hand before the paint and varnish remover, if used, has had a chance to dry.

6. For the final cleaning, after using a remover, use a cabinet scraper or knife blade on joints, corners, and angles on flat surfaces. Use steel wool to clean out carvings, turnings, moldings, cracks, and crevices. Some workers make scrapers of hardwood, with a beveled edge and handle, instead of using a metal scraper, as wood is safer and cannot injure the surface. Orange sticks, wooden meat skewers, and sharpened hardwood dowels

make good tools for use in small places. The points of such tools should be covered with a piece of cloth. Doweling, of various diameters, that has been cut on the end at an angle of 45 degrees, makes a fine tool for removing softened finishes from grooves or moldings.

7. If the old finish is shellac, you don't need a paint and varnish remover. It can be taken off with denatured alcohol solvent and 2/0 medium steel wool. To test for a shellac finish, see page 74.

8. After using any kind of material as a remover, the piece must be allowed sufficient time to dry thoroughly. This usually takes 24 hours or longer. If shellac is to be used as a sealer or for the finish, and the wood is not completely dry or traces of remover have not been properly cleaned from the surface, the finish may turn white or discolor. Moreover, many materials (other than shellac) used for a final finish may not dry hard over some of the old finishes, if any has been left on a surface.

9. Remove all hardware, table leaves, and doors from the piece before applying the paint remover. You can save yourself some work by keeping remover off any surface that doesn't need to be stripped. Mask off a cane seat and glass, for instance. Prevent accidental spills by plugging screw holes for pulls, hinges, etc.

10. Clean the hardware carefully. Pour some paint remover in an old glass bowl and dip hinges, pulls, and other hardware in it. Varnish and paint will come off the metal fairly quickly. Wipe away residue with a cloth, then spray the hardware with clear lacquer to keep it bright.

SELECTING YOUR
PAINT REMOVER

Commercial removers are solvents rather than corrosives. They act more slowly on older paints than on new, but they are the only materials that can be used with safety. They attack the vehicles only, such as linseed oils used in paint, or the resins in shellac, varnish, and lacquer. They won't injure a surface by burning it or leaving marks and won't be harmful to glue or raise the grain of the wood. As they contain no water, they may be used on veneered surfaces without causing the veneer to loosen. When properly applied and then washed off, solvent-type paint removers leave the surface clean.

These removers are available in a thick, waterlike consistency and in semipaste and paste forms. They are sold under many trade names and are made from various formulas. Some contain paraffin or wax. They may be purchased in containers—from one pint to a gallon—at most hardware and paint stores. Solvent-type paint removers are, of course, more expensive than other materials that might be used (such as lye), but, because of the excellent results from their use, they are highly recommended. Always read the full directions on the container.

Some professional workers prefer the thin liquid form of remover, claiming it is best for speeding up the work. But for the average home handyman, a thicker liquid (more like syrup) is preferred. It will "stay put" better when applied, remain wet longer, and is less wasteful.

The key active ingredient in good paint removers is methylene chloride; the best removers contain around 90 percent methylene chloride. Unfortunately, most labels do not list proportions of ingredients, so there's no way of telling how much methylene chloride a particular remover contains. *Family Handyman* has tested several removers and found Zar and Rock Miracle to be very effective and fast working. Close behind were Saf-te Strip, Zip-Strip Semi-paste, and Wonder Paste.

In choosing a remover, stay away from those containing paraffin or wax. These materials used to be fairly common in paint remover formulas but are being used less today, as the wax often remains behind on the surface of the wood after the finish has been stripped, interfering with the proper drying of subsequent finishes.

"Rinse-away"-type removers are not usually recommended for fine furniture wood, since they have a tendency to burn or stain them, and since the water used with them may damage the bare wood. In addition, they are expensive to use.

HOW TO REMOVE OLD FINISHES

Dislodging layers of old paint or varnish isn't difficult, but patience, time, and perseverance are required. Here are the basic directions for using paint remover:

1. Place the piece to be worked on over layers of old newspapers (on a table if the piece is small), in a good strong light, and if possible, with the top surface in a hori-

1.   2.

3.   4.

4-2. Removal of paint: 1. Apply paint remover to the table top with a brush. 2. Scrape the softened paint off with a scraper. 3. Apply water-rinsing paint remover with toweling. 4. If the remover used includes a waxy retarder, follow the scraping operation with a rinse of paint thinner—alcohol, solvent, or turpentine.

zontal position. If you work outdoors, stay out of direct sunlight, as it will cause evaporation of solvents before they have had a chance to work. On the other hand, avoid working in temperatures below 68 degrees F—cold slows down the action of removers.

2. Shake the remover thoroughly, pour

a small amount into a can or jar, and apply thickly with a full brush in one direction. Do not rebrush.

3. Let the remover stand, without touching, for a period of from 10 to 20 minutes, or until the paint or finish "lifts." This is indicated by a crinkling of the surface. Do not let the remover dry. If it begins to dry, apply an additional coat and wait for it to act.

4. When the surface covering has lifted, remove it with a dull putty knife. The corners of the knife should have been rounded off to prevent gouging. To remove the accumulation of remover and finish, wipe the knife on a piece of old newspaper from time to time.

5. Wipe off as much of the remaining finish as possible, using burlap squares (best) or crumpled paper.

6. Scrub the surface with a small brush dipped in denatured alcohol.

7. Wipe off with several clean cloths.

8. Rub the surface with steel wool, dipped in denatured alcohol.

9. Wipe with cloths dipped in alcohol. This not only cleans the traces of remover from the surface but neutralizes its further action. Follow by wiping with clean rags dipped in turpentine or paint thinner. Then wipe with dry rags. This will remove any remaining wax or silicone polish that may have been used on the finish in the past.

10. Allow the piece to dry thoroughly (at least 24 hours).

Turned and Carved Surfaces

Removing the old finish from grooves and carving requires a little more patience and work. Here is how it should be done:

1. Apply the remover, as previously instructed.

4-3. Liquid and semipaste paint removers may be poured onto flat surfaces, then spread with the edge of a piece of fairly stiff cardboard. This provides even distribution.

2. When the finish "lifts," wipe off as much as possible with a burlap square.

3. Scrub crevices and grooves first with a toothbrush dipped in remover, then with a larger brush dipped in denatured alcohol.

4. Clean turnings as well as possible by holding a pad of steel wool (dipped in alcohol) in the hand and using a twisting motion. Follow with the use of threads from burlap or steel wool, twisted into narrow strips, for the final cleaning of turnings. Clean crevices in carving with an instrument such as an orange stick or a meat skewer, with a piece of cloth over its end.

5. Allow at least 24 hours for complete drying.

Additional Tips on Finish Removal

Here are thirteen "lucky" tips on finish removal:

1. Circumstances may be found where some of the steps given here may be shortened or even omitted. Some experts add another step (after Step 5). They brush the surface lightly with remover before the final cleanup.

2. If any of the old finish is still visible in spots, this must be removed by repeating the procedure or the new finish may not dry in these places.

3. If any streaks of color are left on the surface, dip a clean cloth in alcohol, wring it out, and wipe the surface with long, light strokes.

4. If the piece must be repainted, the new paint will adhere better if the surface is sanded smooth. The only reason for re-

moving the old paint is to have an even surface upon which to apply the new.

5. After the upper coats of paint have been removed and it is discovered that the undercoat is of the refractory type, the surface should be kept moistened by applying one or more coats of the remover.

6. If there are several coats of paint and these are found to be difficult to remove, several layers of the remover should be used, one on top of the other. Cover with layers of wet burlap or cloth and allow to stand for several hours or even overnight. If this covering is kept wet, the old paint can usually be removed with a putty knife. The action of the remover on old paints is very much the same as that involved in removing several layers of wallpaper. They both sometimes come off layer by layer.

7. The drawers and doors should be removed from the piece before using a remover.

8. Whenever possible, apply removers to flat surfaces in a horizontal position. This may be accomplished by turning the piece. Put small pieces and parts on a table or workbench, over old newspapers.

9. A large piece sometimes cannot be turned over or moved to a horizontal position, so the remover will have to be applied to a vertical surface. In such cases, tilt the top of the piece toward the surface to be worked upon by placing blocks under the opposite surface. In this way the remover will not run onto unfinished horizontal surfaces.

Example: When using a remover on the front surface of a dresser or a cabinet from which drawers or doors have been removed.

1.

2.

3.

4.

4-4. Removing varnish from a fine furniture piece:

1. Apply varnish remover with a brush, spreading in one direction as evenly as possible. The removal liquid permeates the finish while a retardant covers the surface to slow evaporation. The old finish is softened and gradually raised from the wood in blisters. The area covered on the first application should be small; increase gradually until the maximum surface area can be covered and removed before the remover and varnish begin to harden again.

2. When the chemical has done its work, the varnish is removed. For flat surfaces, or where there are scratches or burns, a metal scraper does the job very well. The depth of the cut is determined by the angle of the scraper and the pressure applied. Two-handed pressure at an almost perpendicular position will cut through to the wood, while one-handed light pressure at about a 30-degree angle will merely skim off the top varnish coat, leaving the others there.

3. Crevices in carvings require special treatment. An additional application of removing liquid is brushed into the crevices; a sharpened orange stick and a fiber brush dipped in alcohol, wielded with care and patience, will eventually rout out the most stubborn deposits.

4. Follow the varnish-removing process with an immediate application of alcohol. A rag should be thoroughly soaked until the alcohol runs on the wood when applied. All varnish removers carry a retardant vehicle in the fluid; this is often wax, which must be removed or the finish that you apply will not dry correctly.

4-5. A can opener makes a good tool for scraping softened finish from grooves. Be sure the opener is not too sharp or it may dig into the wood. Dull it slightly with a file if necessary.

10. Any remover that has gotten onto bare wood should be wiped off with a cloth dampened with denatured alcohol. Otherwise it will leave a stain on the wood.

11. Get rid of dirty burlap pieces, cloths, and paper on which you have wiped the putty knife or placed the removed finish.

12. Spread out cloths clean enough to be used again, so that alcohol will evaporate.

13. A paintbrush used with removers becomes unfit for other uses. Clean with denatured alcohol and then wash with hot soapy water for further use with removers. Use bristle, not synthetic, brushes.

REMOVING REFRACTORY PAINTS

You may find another disturbing factor in the removal of paint from antique furniture. This arises when the only coat of paint, or perhaps the undercoat of many layers, is a refractory (obstinate) type, which has penetrated deeply into the wood pores. Before the days when linseed oil was used as a vehicle in making paints, many paints were made by mixing a pigment with skim milk or buttermilk. These pigments may have been soot (lampblack) from kerosene lamps or colors from the earth, such as sienna (brown) or iron oxide (red). Refractory paints were used generally on pine, because of a desire to cover knots or other imperfections in the wood. They produced an effect that made cheap woods appear more beautiful. It is said that finely grained and finished furniture was often covered with this paint to make it appear less valuable in the eyes of the tax appraiser. However, we cannot understand why so many fine woods were thus painted.

This stubborn paint may often be successfully removed by the following method:

1. Apply a heavy coat of the remover and allow it to stand a while in an attempt to further soften the old paint.

2. While the remover is still wet, scrub

4-6. Varnish removal with steel wool. When there are only surface scratches, it is best to remove the varnish with a pad of fine steel wool. The steel wool can be used dry or wet with commercial alcohol or alcohol-based antifreeze. This complete process may have to be repeated. If the manufacturer wanted to hide light grain streaks or knots, he used a deep-colored filler and varnish stain. It took two applications of remover to bring up the grain on this chair.

the surface with pads of grade 1 steel wool. Turn each pad to a new surface when the old one is filled with paint and remove all paint possible, repeating Steps 1 and 2 as long as any paint can be removed.

3. Scrub the surface with a fresh pad of steel wool dipped in denatured alcohol and wipe with a rag.

4. With a knife, carefully remove any paint remaining in joints and corners.

5. Allow to dry for 24 hours and smooth by sanding, followed by steel wool.

If paint remover won't remove a refractory paint, you can try some other means of removal. It is a good plan to start with the least harmful and then try the others later.

The first suggestion is to use denatured alcohol. Next try sal soda or trisodium phosphate, and lye as the last resort. Refractory paints may be red, black, green, or brown. If you find in advance that the undercoat is black, it is best to remove all coats by scraping, as a liquid remover will drive black deeper into the wood grain. This will leave a gray color that even bleaches will seldom lighten.

Denatured Alcohol

This method is the easiest because so little equipment is required and is less messy than any of the others. Try it first; it may do the trick.

Moisten the surface with denatured alcohol and use 2/0 steel wool or 6/0 abrasive paper, rubbing with the grain of the wood. Wipe off occasionally with a clean cloth, moisten the surface again, and continue rubbing. Finally, wipe off with a clean cloth dampened in alcohol. If the paint is well into the wood grain and there is more of it left than you feel is desirable, try the procedure for using shellac (page 96).

Sal Soda or Trisodium Phosphate

A solution of sal soda should be used while the surface is still wet after an attempt to remove the paint with a commercial paint and varnish remover. Trisodium phosphate (a powerful alkali often used in water softening) may be substituted for the sal soda. Neither will harm the wood, but they should not be used on a veneered surface, since the water will soften the glue holding the veneer. You can get sal soda at your grocer's, in pound packages. Trisodium phosphate, in the form of small crystals, will be found in most paint and building supply stores.

Here is the equipment you need:

two medium-sized galvanized or
    enamel pails
a cotton dish mop with a long handle
a large scrubbing brush (8 or 10 inches
    with handle, if possible)
hot water, both for making the solution
    and for washing it off
a supply of sal soda or trisodium phos-
    phate (2 pounds is usually enough for
    a piece of moderate size)

Glasses or goggles should be worn while doing the work. Use rubber gloves and old clothes with long sleeves. (Either solution will burn the skin.) The work should be done on a cement floor with a drain, or outside in the shade. Here's how to use sal soda or trisodium phosphate to remove a refractory type of paint:

1. Dissolve 1 pound of either sal soda or trisodium phosphate in a pail containing 5 quarts of hot water. Have the other pail filled with hot water only.

2. Apply the solution sparingly to one surface, using a dish mop. This surface should be in a horizontal position, if possible.

3. Let stand less than 1 minute and then scrub vigorously with the scrubbing brush for a few seconds.

4. Dip the scrubbing brush in clear hot water and wash the surface.

5. Continue applications of solution and the scrubbing until you have removed enough of the paint or until you are convinced that some other method must be used.

6. Use clean cold water to flush off the surface, and then, if you are satisfied with the result, turn the piece so that one of the other surfaces will be horizontal and repeat the procedure.

7. Use a hose to flush all surfaces *while scrubbing thoroughly*, particularly in cracks and grooves.

8. Keep the piece in the shade. Direct sunlight will cause the wood to warp. Let it dry thoroughly. This will usually take several days.

Either of these solutions, in hot or cold water, is excellent for cleaning a piece following the use of paint and varnish remover, particularly where the remover has dried and left a considerable amount of paint color on the surface. Scrub with clear water and dry, as above. Do not, however, use these solutions to clean fine work or veneered pieces. They will raise grain and loosen veneers.

Lye

Lye is a dangerous substance for anyone to handle. It is a powerful caustic and has a chemical reaction that causes even the most stubborn paints (refractory type) to powder instead of lifting (as do paint and varnish removers). Lye should never be used to remove other finishes.

Lye is inexpensive. Its action is quick and thorough. But knowledge of its properties and great care in its use are necessary. It will burn certain woods, turning them black, and must, therefore, be washed and scrubbed off completely and thoroughly, particularly from any cracks and crevices. Unless the *utmost* care is taken in removing all residue, it will raise the wood grain and spoil any later finish you may apply.

A strong solution will destroy clothing, burn the skin, and injure the eyes. It is least harmful to hickory, maple, and pine but should never be used on open-grained woods such as butternut, chestnut, oak, or walnut. It will ruin cherry or mahogany and should not be used on veneers, because of the water in which it is mixed. These warnings should *not* prevent you from using lye when it is necessary.

In your first attempt at using lye, select a piece of furniture of little value, either intrinsic or sentimental. If you will use it only on the woods suggested and make sure that you have washed off every trace, you should be successful. Don't attempt to use lye unless you have the proper equipment and are willing to spend the time it requires.

Here's the equipment you'll need for lye work:

  two cans of lye (13-ounce size)
  a supply of white vinegar
  a 10-quart galvanized or enameled pail
    (never use an aluminum one)
  running water with hose attachment

You should have a long-handled cotton dish mop, brush, glasses or goggles, gloves, and old clothes. The work should be done on a well-drained cement floor or outdoors in the shade. The directions for lye use are as follows:

1. Fill the pail half full with *cold* water. Pour in the lye from the two cans. Dissolve by stirring with the mop and then fill the pail with more cold water. The water should never be poured onto the lye, since this will cause it to foam up out of the pail. Have water running slowly through the hose.

2. Using the long-handled cotton dish mop, apply sparingly to a horizontal surface.

3. Let it stand for about 30 seconds and then scrub vigorously with the brush.

4. Wash off with the hose and continue scrubbing.

5. Repeat until enough of the powdered paint has been removed from all the surfaces, turning the piece so that you always work on a horizontal one.

6. Scrub well with water from hose and a brush, working deeply into cracks and crevices, until all the slippery film of the solution has been removed.

7. To neutralize the caustic action of the lye, wash with vinegar on a clean cloth.

8. Place the piece in the shade and allow it to dry thoroughly for 24 hours or longer. Direct sunlight may warp the wood.

This solution is very strong. The secret in removing the paint without burning the wood lies in not letting the solution remain on the surface long enough to injure it. The more often and more quickly you apply the solution and wash it off, the less danger there is to the wood. It is nearly impossible to apply the solution to one horizontal surface and not have it get on an adjoining vertical one. Therefore, these other surfaces should be scrubbed off at the same time, as in Step 3 in the lye procedure.

Should there be spots of paint that are stubborn, let them remain, rather than continue the use of the solution, for fear of injury to the wood. These may usually be removed easily with a cabinet scraper after the wood is thoroughly dry.

REMOVING DEEPLY BURIED PAINTS

A deeply buried paint may often be removed entirely or partially by a simple procedure. This paint is usually that which is left after you have removed the previous coats with remover or by light scraping. Because of its simplicity, this procedure is worth trying.

1. Apply a liberal coat of shellac with a brush and let it dry for at least 24 hours.

2. Use the remover as previously directed. All or part of the buried paint may come off with the shellac.

Removing Paint Hardened by Heat and Containing Dirt

Heat from the sun or a hot stove will often soften a finish, and when it has cooled and hardened again, dirt and dust

will be found embedded in it. A commercial remover will often fail to remove it, particularly in those cases where another coat of paint has been added over the dirt.

This paint can often be removed by applying a mixture made of equal parts of linseed oil and turpentine. This is rubbed into the surface, allowed to stand, and then cleaned off with fine steel wool dipped in turpentine. If necessary, this process is followed by a light scraping.

Removing Old Varnish with a Scraper

Very old varnish will, at times, be found to be so flaky that it can be removed easily with a cabinet scraper or the sharp blade of a large knife without injury to the wood surface or destruction of the patina. This should be attempted only by those familiar with the use of such tools. Clumsy use of a scraper can damage the wood.

REMOVING FINISH FROM STENCILED CHAIRS

You may, at some time, wish to remove old varnish from a Windsor or Hitchcock chair or a Boston rocker, without injury to the paint or the stencil design with which they are so often decorated. The stencil may have been covered with paint that you want to remove, leaving the stencil intact.

The removal of old varnish is simpler than the removal of paint. However, both require careful and delicate handling. Either may often be removed in part by light scraping and the balance by the following method.

If you suspect that a stencil has been painted over, first experiment at the spot where you might expect a stencil to be. There is usually one on the front side of the top back. Use a scraper with care to remove only the hard outer coat of paint so that the materials for removing (see below) can penetrate the undercoats more easily.

The decoration of furniture, by painted or stenciled designs, is a specialty and hence beyond the scope of this book. Some such pieces can be restored if the condition of the outer surface is not too bad. They must then be refinished by a fresh coat of shellac and wax or with varnish and a rubdown (see Chapter Six).

Following are the methods to use in removing an outer coat of varnish or paint.

Removing Varnish

Try to soften the varnish by applying denatured alcohol on wads of cotton to small areas. If successful, wipe off the varnish. If this does not work, try a mixture of equal parts of benzine and alcohol. Finally, try a mixture of equal parts of pure turpentine and alcohol. These solutions are given in the order of their strength.

If none of these will soften the varnish, clean off a small area and apply a light coat of a commercial remover. When the varnish starts to lift, stop the action by washing off the remover with alcohol on a wad of cotton and start again. Repeating this process may bring results. The great

difficulty is in knowing when to stop, in order to save the stencil.

Removing Paint

Use fine 3/0 steel wool dipped in alcohol and a sharp knife blade, or delicately use a scraper, as in the procedure for removing refractory-type paints (page 92).

A good alternative to stripping furniture yourself is to have the work done at a professional stripping shop. A good pro can do the job for little more than the money you would have to spend for paint remover, and he will save you hours of tedious work.

But if you are going to entrust a valuable piece to a professional stripper, first make sure he knows his business. Go to his shop and check it out. Examine pieces that he has stripped that are waiting for pickup by customers. Ask yourself how much more work they will need before they can be refinished. Is all the old finish off? Is the wood smooth, or is it pulpy, rough, or fuzzy? Have veneers lifted or blistered? Are joints loose and wobbling? If you like the looks of pieces the pro has stripped, by all means give him a try. If not, find another shop.

Most commercial strippers use the same paint removers you would. Chemicals may be put in a tank into which your piece is dunked and allowed to soak, or they may be hosed over your piece. Hosing is generally the safer procedure since it gives the stripper better control over where the remover goes. Dipping can allow the chemical to soak into joints and may attack some old synthetic glues.

Some pros also use tanks of lye. If so, they should use them only for stripping such things as shutters and iron furniture.

Lye soaks are too strong for any kind of furniture. Never allow any of your furniture to be stripped in a lye bath.

4-7. *If the wood revealed by removal of an old finish is in good condition, it may require only a light steel wooling to prepare it for refinishing.*

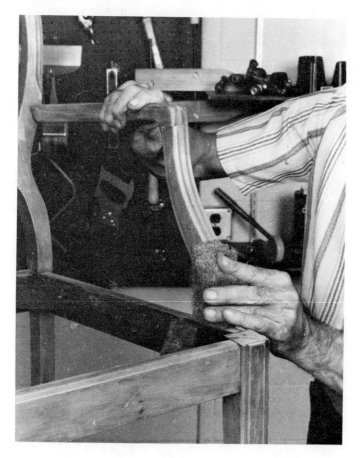

five

Preparing for a New Finish

This is the turning point in the work. Thus far you have been given general instructions for repairs and the removal of old finish. Now you are ready to prepare the surface for a new finish. This requires careful workmanship and full knowledge of the necessary procedures and methods, as the quality of the final finish depends directly on this preparation.

Before starting the work, make a thorough inspection of the piece, especially after you have removed any old, heavy paint. You may find dents, holes, cracks, and other damage that were not previously visible in the surface and that will require repairs. This must be done before preparing for the new finish.

Some of the procedures in this chapter are seldom used, but all are described to give you a full knowledge of them. Included are bleaching, sanding, scraping, staining, sealing, and filling. The number and choice of those to be used for a single job are determined by the type and condition of the wood, after a former finish has been removed. Each procedure is accompanied by information as to when and why it is used. Some are necessary, according to conditions, and some are a matter of choice.

BLEACHING

Bleaching was once used largely to achieve the "blond" look in vogue during the 1950s. Today it is used mostly to remove undesirable stains.

After the old finish has been removed from a surface, any darkened or discolored spots that may remain can be lightened or entirely removed by the proper use of a bleach. Although you may feel justified in wishing to remove all traces of old stain and marks of discoloration from antique furniture, these, in most cases, add to the charm of the finished piece and may be left when they do not show too plainly through the new finish. Some collectors prefer that a certain amount of this evidence of age and usage be left. However, when working on pine or maple, it is best to remove discoloration and freshen up the surface.

Types of Bleaches

There are four common bleaches used by home handymen to lighten wood and help remove undesirable stains. They are:

PREPARED BLEACH The simplest method of getting a good bleach is to buy a prepared bleach, which usually comes in the form of two solutions that may be applied successively or mixed together, according to the directions on the label. Such bleaches are sold at some paint stores and through such mail order outlets as Constantine's (see page 4).

HOUSEHOLD PRODUCTS Sometimes a laundry bleach in which sodium hypochlorite is the bleaching agent (Clorox, for example) is effective for such woods as maple, walnut, and gum. Household ammonia is a good bleaching agent on all but dark woods. It is, however, best for spot work only.

OXALIC ACID This bleach works only when a mild bleach is needed. Under this condition, it can be used quite success-fully for such open-grained woods as oak, chestnut, and ash. Some professional strippers use it routinely to remove the slight discolorations created during the stripping process.

HYDROGEN PEROXIDE Probably the most satisfactory but most expensive bleaches are those based on a strong solution of hydrogen peroxide (30 or 35 percent). This concentrated commercial-grade bleach should not be confused with the 3 percent solution used as an antiseptic.

Using Prepared Bleach

Commercially prepared wood bleaches, as previously stated, are two-solution preparations that must be intermixed or applied in successive steps. All contain strong chemicals, so it is important that rubber gloves be worn to protect the hands. An apron or old clothing should also be worn, since these bleaches will attack most fabrics—and follow label directions carefully! These powerful bleaches are best for overall work. They are difficult to control when spot bleaching.

The bleach can be applied with a brush or a sponge and should be allowed to dry on the surface until the desired effect is reached. The instructions will tell whether neutralization or rinsing is required. After bleaching and rinsing have been completed, the piece of furniture should be allowed to stand until thoroughly dry. Then sand lightly with very fine sandpaper to remove the raised grain. However, be careful not to sand more deeply than the bleach has penetrated.

1.

2.

3.

5-1. How to bleach: 1. Apply bleach according to the directions for the particular brand. Be sure to wear gloves to protect your hands.
2. When the bleach has remained on the surface for the required time, usually 5 to 15 minutes, apply neutralizer as directed. 3. Allow the wood surface to dry for at least 24 hours. A light sanding with a block will be necessary, for bleaching raises the grain.

Using Household Products

Most household products are better for spot work than they are for large areas. Here's how to use laundry bleach and ammonia as bleaching agents:

1. Apply the product full strength over the spot or surface of the wood.

2. Wash the product off with clear water after it has been on the surface about 15 minutes. Check to see if the desired color has been attained. If not, repeat the treatment.

3. When the right color has been achieved, rinse the entire surface with water.

4. Let the furniture stand to dry for at least 48 hours.

Using Oxalic Acid

Oxalic acid isn't expensive. It can be purchased at a drugstore in either crystal or powder form. It is also sold by some paint stores. The following is the procedure for using oxalic acid to bleach wood:

1. Prepare a solution of oxalic acid by dissolving 1 ounce of the powder or 2 ounces of the crystals in 1 pint of very hot water. Some woods, maple in particular, respond more readily to a solution of 1 ounce of oxalic acid crystals and 1 ounce of tartaric acid powder (available at drugstores) in 1 pint of very hot water.

2. Using a large brush, apply the solution (hot) to the entire surface, from which the finish has been removed, or to a spot with a small brush. In the case of a spot, work the solution carefully to the edges with the brush. It is recommended that you bleach an entire surface rather than remove a spot only. However, you may be very successful in spot bleaching when the outline of the spot is clearly defined. If your efforts to remove a spot are unsuccessful, no harm is done, since the entire surface can then be bleached.

3. Let the solution remain for 10 to 20 minutes and then wipe it off with a damp cloth. If the discoloration has not been bleached sufficiently, repeat until you obtain the color you are after.

4. When the proper result has been secured, wash off the solution with 1 part ammonia in 10 parts of water. This will neutralize the bleach and stop its further action. Then wash with clear water and allow the piece to dry for at least 24 hours.

Removing Discoloration

You may find that the surface of a piece, particularly pine or maple, has a gray or faded appearance. It may be freshened and brought back to a more satisfactory color by the following procedure. (This is recommended for a surface that has just been cleaned with a paint and varnish remover and before it has again dried.)

1. Scrub with laundry detergent in water that is just under the boiling point. Wash off with hot water and wipe with a cloth.

2. While the surface is still wet, apply a hot solution of oxalic acid. Let this stay on for about 10 minutes and then wash it off and neutralize its action with ammonia or vinegar. Let it dry thoroughly.

This treatment will raise the grain of the wood, but it usually removes the fine particles of colored pigment. The grain will settle down again when dry and can be sanded later. The surface won't have the appearance of new wood, but, if circumstances are favorable and the work has been done properly, it should have an even mellowness.

Removing Grease Stains

Frequently, oil and grease penetrate the wood of tabletops, cheese or meat boards, and salad bowls. It is necessary to remove as much grease as possible from the surface so that the new finish will adhere.

A grease stain from animal fat may usually be removed by an application of commercial cleaners, used for removing spots from clothing. In a well-ventilated area or outdoors, scrub the surface with a dry-cleaning solvent. Scrub first with a brush, then with 3/0 steel wool. Allow to dry thoroughly. Repeat two or three times, allowing about a day for drying between treatments.

Another method of removing this type

of grease stain is to make a paste of whiting (sold at paint stores) and a dry-cleaning solvent. Apply to the greasy surface. Leave the paste on the wood 24 hours, then brush off. Repeat the paste treatment, if necessary.

If the grease spot is of vegetable origin, it will usually respond to the use of acetone. This may be purchased at a paint store. The remover should be applied to the spot with a small artist's brush, then worked around with the brush and removed with a piece of absorbent tissue paper. The operation should be repeated until the spot has been removed.

If the surface feels sticky after the old finish has been removed, it's an indication that some of the old finish remains. The solution is to apply another coat of remover to the entire section.

If the surface appears smoky after removing the old finish, wash the section again with denatured alcohol.

SANDING AND SMOOTHING

Any surface on which a new finish is to be applied requires smoothing, an operation that brings a surface to a fine, silky condition without destroying the patina and the evidence of age and usage. Many pieces are free from any finish or paint and need no repairs. However, these must go through the smoothing operation as well.

The smoothing of a wood surface, free from a finish, is done with abrasive papers (commonly called sandpapers) by first working with relatively coarse papers, followed by those of finer grit. Steel wool is often used for final smoothing, and at times it is necessary to use a scraper to smooth a surface that is to be followed with fine abrasive papers and steel wool.

The degree of smoothness a piece requires depends greatly on the type of the article and the wood of which it is made, as well as the type of final finish that is to be used. For example, a crude piece of pine furniture does not call for as smooth a surface as a well-designed piece made of hardwoods, nor would the final finish be smoothed to the same degree.

Abrasive Papers and Emery Cloth

It is important that you understand the various kinds and types of materials used as backing for abrasives, since only the correct type should be used in any specific step in your work. They must be of the proper grade or weight to accomplish the purpose effectively and speedily, yet without damaging the piece on which you are working. Such understanding can best be gained by here describing the various abrasive sheets, their backing, and the type and grades of grit used on them, in accordance with their distinguishing numbers. Instructions are also given in the use and proper handling of the various types and grades.

Flint paper is coated with a type of quartz, off-white in color, that occurs as a natural mineral deposit in the ground. Flint paper has little use in furniture restoration. Its cutting edges are dull and do not cut well, crumbling in use and then rolling around under the paper as you sand, creating small gouges in the work. The glue used to fasten the grit to the paper is cheap, and the paper backing is brittle. About the only use for this type of sandpaper is removal of gummy finishes that will clog any paper in seconds. In this case, the cheapest paper is the best.

Aluminum oxide paper is made with a synthetic abrasive, created in an electric furnace. It is the most common abrasive paper sold today, and the most useful all-around paper available. The brown abra-

sive is sharp and wears well. Garnet is better for fine sanding, and silicon carbide for smoothing finishes, but otherwise aluminum oxide is the workhorse paper of today, both for hand and power sanding.

Garnet paper is made with a reddish-brown natural mineral that wears well. When it breaks down with use it creates more sharp cutting edges, so that even as it wears it continues to cut well rather than scratching. Most professionals consider it the best paper for final sanding in

5-2. *Sandpaper for wood finishing. Sandpaper is made of these four minerals: silicon carbide, aluminum oxide, garnet, and flint.*

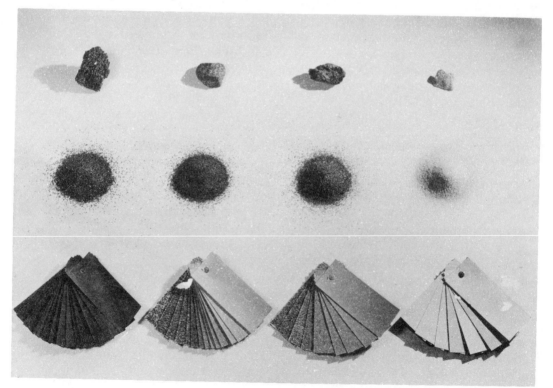

the finer grades, especially when it is made on the lightweight A backing.

Silicon carbide paper is made with a black man-made abrasive. It is generally manufactured with waterproof backing and glue. Its main use is for smoothing an existing finish and for sanding between coats of varnish and enamel. The most useful grits to buy are 320, 400, and 600; these are the fine grits you need for sanding finishes.

Emery cloth is also black like silicon carbide, but it doesn't cut as well. Emery cloth really has no good application in furniture work. Some workers use it for smoothing turnings on the lathe because its cloth backing holds up well, but you can do the same job better with aluminum oxide or garnet paper reinforced with tape.

BACKING Backing is the material to which the various types of abrasives are glued. This may be paper, cloth, fiber, or a combination. The paper and cloth types come in a standard size of 9 inches by 11 inches, and we shall deal only with these.

Paper backing is tough and of a special quality. It comes in various thicknesses, called weights, as follows:

A-weight is a soft, pliable grade of paper used where flexibility is required, as in final sanding just before you apply the finish. Try to buy garnet paper with this backing. Otherwise, you needn't concern yourself with backing weights.

C- and D-weight papers are thicker and are used for the more demanding hand-

sanding jobs. Most of the paper you buy will have this weight backing.

E-weight, the heaviest of the backing papers, used primarily for machine sanding.

Cloth backing comes in two grades, as follows:

Lightweight material is marked *J* and is used for a backing on emery cloth for handwork and on some finishing and polishing cloths.

Heavyweight material is marked X and is used with power tools.

Some manufacturers distinguish the weight of the backing by producing it in different colors.

CLASSIFICATIONS OF ABRASIVE PAPERS AND CLOTHS The reverse side of most abrasive papers and cloths is printed to show the grade of density or type of abrasive and often the weight or quality of the backing.

Finishing paper is the name applied to those papers designated as *A* or lightweight and which have a fine or extra-fine grit.

Cabinet papers are the papers known as C- or D- (medium) weight and have grit of medium fineness.

Closed-grain papers contain thickly applied abrasive grains and are the papers most generally used.

Open-coat papers are papers whose abrasive covers only 50 to 70 percent of the backing surface, leaving a certain amount of space between the grains. This increases the pliability of the paper, allows faster cutting with less pressure, and is used on the softer woods, which tend to clog the surface of the paper more rapidly.

Wet or dry papers are papers whose backing is waterproofed; they are made with only the finest grades of abrasives. In restoration work, they are used for the final rubdown with water, gasoline, or oil. They are sold under various trade names. Most of them designate whether they are for wet or dry use or are merely marked *waterproof.*

GRIT NUMBERS AND GRADES   The grit size (and thus coarseness or fineness) of sandpaper is designated by two different systems. One is called the grit number, the other the grade. The table at the right shows how these two systems compare and indicates which grits are best for which jobs. Some papers—especially the cheaper brands—are labeled without numbers or grades. They are called such things as fine, medium, coarse, and so on. These categories are vague and almost meaningless. If a paper does not have a grit number or grade stamped on the back, don't buy it.

MARKINGS   The form of marking on the back of the sheets may vary greatly among different manufacturers. Sometimes either the grit or the grade only is given and sometimes both. Also, information may or may not be furnished as to the weight of the paper or the kind of grit used, but it will usually be given as to whether it is the wet-or-dry type by denoting that it is waterproof, either by using that word or a coined one.

Example of marking: "3/0–120 A"

WORD DESCRIPTION	GRIT	GRADE	USE
Superfine	600	—	Polishing and finishing
	500	—	
	◆400	10/0	
	360	9/0	
	320	—	
Extra-fine	280	8/0	
	240	7/0	
Very fine	220	6/0	
Fine	180	5/0	Finishing
	150	4/0	
	120	3/0	
	100	2/0	
Medium	80	0 or 1/0	Cabinet
	60	1/2	
	50	1	
Coarse	40	1 1/2	Rough sanding
	36	2	
	30	2 1/2	
Very coarse	24	3	Coarse sanding
	20	3 1/2	

means the grade is medium fine, that it has 120 grit, and the weight (thickness) of the paper is A (thinnest).

You may have to guess at the kind of abrasive material used, but you should know it from the color. This paper may or may not be marked *finishing paper.*

SANDPAPER SELECTION CHART

USE	GRIT	GRADE	BACKING	WORD DESCRIPTION
Rough sanding and shaping	80	1/0	D	Medium
Preparatory sanding on softwoods	100 or 120	2/0 or 3/0	A	Fine
Preparatory sanding on hardwoods	120	3/0	C	Fine
Finish sanding on softwoods	220	6/0	A	Very fine
Finish sanding on hardwoods	220 to 280	6/0 to 8/0	A	Very fine Extra-fine
Polishing on all woods	280 or 400	8/0 or 10/0	J or X	Extra-fine Superfine

BUYING ABRASIVE SHEETS Standard sheets may be purchased from paint and hardware stores and are sold more cheaply in quantity than in single sheets. Most dealers will permit you to mix grades or types when buying, and, if you are doing much work, it is best to have a supply on hand, since many grades are needed and they do wear out quickly. Sometimes A- weight garnet paper is hard to find. If you can't find it in your area, you can buy it by mail order from Constantine's or Woodcraft Supply (see page 4).

The flint papers are by far the cheapest, but the other papers last so much longer, and do the work so much better and more quickly, that they are the least expensive in the long run. The reason is that the latter stand up under service and have better cutting edges. (When fed onto the paper or cloth, the grit is electrocontrolled, compelling the particles to stand on end with point upward, affording better cutting edges and corners.)

TYPES AND GRADES Abrasive papers are used for: 1. rough sanding and shaping; 2. preparatory sanding and smoothing; 3. finish sanding; and 4. polishing.

Number 1 paper might be used on very soft and rough wood as the first medium in smoothing, followed by grades of 1/2 and 1/0, but it is far better to make a rule never to start with a coarser grade than 1/0, to be followed by those of less coarse (2/0, 3/0, etc.), especially on hardwoods. It is always a good plan to take more time in smoothing with the finer grades of papers than to take chances of damage with the coarser ones.

For finishing, after smoothing, it is best to forget the intermediate grades beyond

3/0 and jump immediately to a grade from 6/0 to 8/0, for, with new paper, it is fine enough for most woods.

For polishing, use 8/0 or finer waterproof (wet or dry) papers, or cloths with water or proper oil as a lubricant, and finish up with pumice and rottenstone (should a finish call for them).

CLEANING AND USING OLD ABRASIVE PAPER Good abrasive paper is fairly expensive, but many home handymen are prone to discard it long before it has become unfit for further service. Papers clog up with powdered wood, but this may be removed with a small, stiff hand brush. Should the material be difficult to remove, as is the case when it is gummy, and if you know the type of that material, dip the brush in the proper solvent before scrubbing. When clean, allow the paper to dry.

Examples: For varnish, use turpentine; for shellac, use alcohol; for lacquer, use a lacquer thinner.

By such methods, the useful life of abrasive papers may often be doubled.

Used or dulled abrasive papers are of great value and are recommended for many stages of work. It is good to have a special place in which to store them.

TEARING AND FOLDING ABRASIVE PAPERS Great economy can be had from tearing or folding papers. A paper is torn best across the short (9-inch) dimension to form strips about 3½ inches wide. It can be torn by securing an old hacksaw blade (with screws) to the side edge of a board prepared for the purpose, with the teeth of the blade slightly above the flat surface, or it may be torn over an edge of a carpenter's steel square. The surface of the board can be marked with a scale to measure the width of the tear.

A full-sized sheet of thin paper may be folded in squares by first folding it in half on the 11-inch dimension, folding it again to one-quarter size, then again to one-eighth size. The folds should be creased firmly. The edges of the folds are useful for smoothing in angles or cleaning out cracks.

SANDING BLOCKS The best size for a sanding block is 3 inches wide by 5 inches long and 1 to 1¼ inches thick. It may be of felt, cork, or rubber. One made of hardwood (maple is good) is preferred because of its weight, and the long sides may be coved or shaped for easy gripping. The face of any hard block should be covered with rubber, cork, or heavy felt.

A block of this size may be used best with a sheet of abrasive paper cut crosswise into 5½-inch by 9-inch pieces. The paper is then folded to one-half that size (4½ inches by 5½ inches) and placed over the rubber face of the block, with the long dimension of the folded paper over the long way of the block. This leaves it slightly longer than the block, at both ends. The paper is turned up over the sides and gripped with the fingers. When worn it may be shifted to present new edge surfaces, then turned upside down, thus using practically all of the abrasive paper surface. Never tack paper to a sanding block.

There are many types of hand-sanding blocks that may be purchased. Some are

5-3. *Sanding blocks are indispensable in wood finishing.*

good and some poor, but most require special sizes of abrasive paper and do not utilize the full surface. A blackboard eraser, like the ones used in schools, may be purchased at most five-and-tens and makes an excellent sanding block. It is padded and of approximately the right size.

Rules for Sanding

The sanding of a wood surface is the least difficult of all procedures in restoration work, yet it is one of the most important parts of refinishing and must always be done thoroughly and with great care, whether accomplished by hand or with a power tool. If not done correctly, the surface will be a mass of scratches. A good sanding job is essential to a good finish.

When sanding, remember these three rules:

1. Always sand with the grain of the wood—never across the grain.

5-4. *Sanding sticks are good for fine work in tight spots. You can make your own by gluing sandpaper to thin strips of wood. Aerosol rubber cement is a fast way to do the job.*

5-5. Always sand off sharp edges and corners before finishing. Sharp edges don't finish well, chip easily, and can cause injuries. Use 120-grit paper wrapped around a block.

2. Use straight strokes with an even pressure, avoiding a twisting or circular motion.

3. First use a paper of as coarse a grade (grit) as the wood will stand without scratching, then finer ones until the surface is as smooth as the wood will become. The results will vary with the kind of wood.

Sanding Tips

Here are some very important points about sanding:

1. Planing and scraping are not substi-tutes for sanding. When such tools are used, sanding should follow.

2. Moistening will often permit better sanding on old and relatively smooth wood surfaces. Wring out a wet cloth and rub the surface. When dry, the fine ends of the fibers (termed wood whiskers) will be raised. Sand with a very fine or extra-fine grade of paper (6/0 to 8/0).

3. To raise the fibers of new woods (and veneer) before sanding, moisten the sur-face with a glue water (1 ounce of liquid glue, such as LePage's, to 1 pint of hot water). Dry and finish as in Rule 2 of the rules for sanding. Be careful of wetting ve-neers too much.

4. The general rule is to start and finish with finer grades of papers on hardwoods than on softwoods. Also, on softwoods it is better to use the "open-coat" papers, es-pecially when using the coarser grades, since these woods respond to sanding more readily than do hardwoods and clog up the paper.

5. Clean papers often by brushing and you will prolong their life and cutting power.

6. Sanding blocks or folded paper may be used to advantage on large surfaces.

7. The removal of paint or varnish must always be followed by sanding to get rid of any wax that may have been in the re-mover; otherwise a finish may not harden.

8. Inwardly curved surfaces may be sanded by wrapping the paper around wood dowels of various sizes, according to the curve. Soaking the paper with turpen-tine will make it more flexible.

9. Turned surfaces are best smoothed with paper of a fine grade (grit) torn into

narrow (½- to 1-inch) strips and worked back and forth in the grooves, holding the strip by its ends. Reinforce the paper by applying fiberglass strapping tape to the backing. Great care must be exercised in smoothing the bulge of turnings and long cylindrical surfaces (like chairs or table legs), or harm may be done. It is best that this work be accomplished with steel wool, especially on very old antique furniture, since these parts may have been turned by hand-powered lathes, resulting in slight ridges on the long surfaces that should not be obliterated. This will happen if they are sanded.

10. Sanding the edges and ends of the tops of tables, cabinets, etc., should be done with only the finest grades of abrasive papers, regardless of whether the part is of hardwood or softwood. Unless otherwise designed, the edges must be true and the corners square. Improper treatment of board ends may spoil an otherwise beautiful finish. They should be brought to an almost glazed surface by sanding with no coarser than an 8/0 sharp paper and finished with a worn paper of that grade or finer. When working on square ends, place the paper over a sanding block to make sure such surfaces are kept flat. Should the edges or corners be too sharp when this work is completed, relieve them slightly with light strokes of the sharp paper first, followed by polishing with the worn paper.

11. After sanding, and after using steel wool, all dust must be carefully removed by wiping with a tack rag. This is a cloth that is treated to attract and hold dust. It is usually available at paint dealers who handle wood finishes, or one can be made out of any piece of dry, lint-free cotton cloth. To make one, sprinkle the cloth with varnish that has been diluted with about 25 percent turpentine. Fold tightly, then wring the cloth out till almost dry.

12. Crude pine furniture will be greatly improved in its finished appearance if the top corners of the used surface, as well as the corners of nicks, and dents, are rounded down by sanding and smoothing to make them look as though such rounding had come from usage. The same is true of other parts or places on surfaces of crude furniture, if such work is not overdone. For example, a natural crack that runs only a short distance from a surface edge into a top will often look better if it is not filled but widened slightly along its edges and rounded on the upper corners of its outlet, by sanding and smoothing, just as though it has been worn into that condition. Also, many pieces of crude, yet attractive, early American furniture were fastened together with nails that either rusted or were used in such a manner as to leave holes around their heads. Others can be found that have narrow cracks between small partitions or parts. The appearance of such pieces will be greatly improved if these holes and cracks are carefully filled with wood plastic or putty and then sanded, to expose the top of the nail head and to remove the surplus wood dough from the surfaces around the cracks. The remaining dried wood dough should then be stained (with the use of a small artist's brush) to match the piece. This procedure ties the surface together and greatly improves the appearance of

the piece; in fact, you will be surprised at the improvement in eye appeal.

Power Sanding

Sanding can be done by hand or with a wide variety of power tools. Of the various power sanders, the so-called finishing sander is the most useful for the home handyman doing finishing and refinishing of wood furniture.

There are three varieties of finishing sanders: orbital, straight line, and dual action. Orbital action means the abrasive is moving in a flat, tight oval rather than straight back and forth. Each orbit, typically, is less than ¼ inch wide, so it's barely sanding against the grain; but you are doing just that, and enough to make cutting faster. This still produces a fine

A dual-action (orbital or straight-line) sander. Photo: Black & Decker

A belt sander with dust catcher. Photo: Sears

A disk sander/polisher. Photo: Black & Decker

5-6. Three basic types of power sanders are orbital, belt, and disk. The orbital type is good for fine finish work, and the belt sander can quickly smooth large flat surfaces. Avoid the disk sander for refinishing work as it leaves swirl marks and is difficult to control.

finish, while at the same time expanding the tool's capability for some rougher jobs. Many perfectionists, however, will not use orbital sanders. They think the circular action creates swirl marks with coarse papers and even with fine papers may cause muddy results when the wood is stained.

Straight-line sanders, with the abrasive moving back and forth, can be restricted totally to sanding with the grain and are for extra-fine finishing. There are enough jobs of that kind in the average house to let it earn its keep. The straight-liner doesn't remove much material, or do it quickly, but it does it with ultimate smoothness. And it does not cut corners, but gets up into them. It can almost completely eliminate the need for hand sand-

ing. At 9,000 strokes a minute, each 3/16 inch long, how can you compete?

The dual-action sander combines both orbital and straight-line actions, giving you the best of both worlds. You can start out with orbital action for heavier stock removal, then switch to straight-line action for finish and flush sanding. A dual-action sander doesn't cost quite twice as much as a straight-line and orbital sander combined, but it approaches it.

Both orbital and straight-line sanders work slowly—not much faster than you can sand by hand. If you have a lot of heavy sanding to do, a belt sander is a better tool. Stay away from the disk sanders. They can't be controlled well enough for furniture work.

Aside from differences in action, finish-

5-7. *The circular sanding motion that this disk sander makes is not recommended for furniture refinishing because it sands across the* *grain, leaving marks that are hard to remove.* Photo: Sears ing sanders differ in the size, shape, and kind of pad they have. The bigger the pad area, the more work a sander is likely to do. The standard size of sheet abrasives is 9 inches by 11 inches. Some sanders use half a sheet, others use a third of a sheet, still others a fourth, a fifth, or less.

A small pad is at its best in tight situations and on irregular surfaces. On broad, flat surfaces, the big pad goes to town. So an in-between size is a compromise that satisfies most handymen most of the time. But it may not satisfy you, and you're the one who's going to be using it.

The pad on which the paper goes may be either felt or neoprene (synthetic rubber) sponge. The felt may have a little more firmness and bite, especially good for flat surfaces. The neoprene may adapt to uneven contours slightly better and can be used for either wet or dry sanding. For some sanders, you can get either or both kinds and use them interchangeably. Some pads extend beyond the sides of the sander, which, it is claimed, makes them better for handling corners. The way the paper attaches to the pad may be of some significance to you, too. They all add up to the same thing, but some aspects may be more appealing than others.

Some sanders feel twice as heavy as others, either because of a difference in balance or because of an actual difference in weight. Weight is important. Pressure, which will slow the speed of the sander and cause its paper to clog, should not be

5-8. Felt sanding pads (right) are better for flat surfaces, neoprene for contours.

5-9. Without a dust catcher attached, this straight line/orbital sander can work more closely into corners. Photo: Sears

applied on a sander. The weight of the sander alone, plus the natural weight of your hand, is all the pressure required in normal operation. A heavier sander usually has a more powerful motor and will be more of a workhorse.

Sanders kick up a lot of dust. Often, a sander must be used in a living area, and occasionally you may find it necessary to sand with freshly painted surfaces nearby. You will always find it less pleasant in an atmosphere that is dust laden. To overcome these problems, you can use a dust collector. Many sanders have vacuum attachments available as an extra. Some have their own vacuum bag. Others have a hose that you can attach to almost any tank-type vacuum cleaner.

This will not exactly be "dustless" sanding, but most of the dust does get picked up. Removing dust as you sand enables you to sand faster—some say 25 percent faster. With no layer of dust to obscure your work, it's much easier to see what you're doing and how much more remains to be done. With a vacuum attachment it is necessary to place an enclosing skirt around the sander's pad. This skirt can be somewhat of a nuisance when you're trying to sand close to vertical surfaces and when you want to change paper. But you'll settle for these disadvantages to gain the greater benefit of getting rid of most of the dust.

The tank-type arrangement may offer a stronger vacuum than the integral back

5-10. Sanders with independent vacuum systems do dustless jobs.

Some sanders can be attached to any standard vacuum dust-collection system.

pickup. But the bag is handier to use. Just remember to empty it when it becomes about a quarter full and its efficiency will stay relatively high.

Selection of the right kind of paper is an important part of success. Don't use ordinary flint sandpaper. It's cheap to buy, but it wears out so fast it's more expensive to use. It's not made for the high-speed operation of power sanding.

The paper most commonly used for finishing sanders is aluminum oxide. Garnet paper is also used. Silicon carbide paper is used mostly for very fine finishing of lacquered and varnished surfaces.

For best results on a typical sanding job, use only open-coat paper with a grit no coarser than 1/2–60. (Some manufacturers say 1 1/2–40.) An open-coat paper works faster than a closed coat, doesn't clog, and produces just as smooth a finish. Possible exceptions are high-speed vibrating sanders. They can take closed-coat paper satisfactorily because their rapid action shakes dust loose remarkably well.

For many sanders you can buy abrasive sheets, in packages of ten to twenty-five, of the exact dimensions you need for your sander. The usual run of grit, from very coarse to extra-fine, is 40, 50, 60, 80, 100, 120, 150, and 220.

One accessory you can get for a sander is a felt rubbing pad. This pad, usually about ¼ inch thick, is used with finishing compounds on furniture. It can be used with loose abrasives, finer than any that come on paper. Another good accessory is a lamb's-wool polishing pad for "hand-finish" polishing of furniture and paneling.

When you start sanding, and when you finish, flick the switch only when the sander is not in contact with the work. If you start up or shut down while the sanding surface is in contact, you may make marks you'll be sorry about. If you have your choice of orbital or straight-line motion, use the orbital for such jobs as removing an existing finish, cutting wood down to size, or preliminary rough sanding. Use the straight-line for fine finishing, always in the same direction as the grain of the wood.

Begin with a grit coarse enough to accomplish the dirty work, then move on to a finer grit and a still finer grit until you're satisfied with the smoothness of the results. For a fine finish with a minimum amount of sanding, start with the finest grit that will remove the surface defects. On many projects you may want to round corners and edges slightly; they will look better, wear better, and hold finish better. When proceeding from coarse to fine paper, don't skip more than two grits at a time—ideally, no more than one. A good and perfectly legitimate progression might be from 60 to 80 to 120. For between-coat sanding of enamel and varnish, you won't want anything coarser than 220. Keep the sander moving. If you stop in one place for long you will make a rut. With a straight-line sander, if you go across the grain you'll tear the wood fibers. With an orbital sander, grain direction isn't quite so critical.

Sanding Sealers

A sanding sealer permits you to sand

wood smoother than would be possible any other way. It is possible to purchase a sanding sealer ready mixed, or you can make one by diluting 4-pound cut shellac with 3 or 4 parts of denatured alcohol. The latter is brushed on smoothly, allowed to dry, and then sanded.

When using the ready-mixed sanding sealer, stir it well before using, but do not shake. Thinning, which can be done with mineral spirits, is not required except for spray application, or when sealer is used as a wash coat or filler coat. Apply sanding sealer liberally in an even coat. When thoroughly dry, after two or three hours, sand lightly with very fine sandpaper. Two or three coats of sanding sealer are necessary when it is to be used as a complete finishing system; only one coat should be applied when used as a sealer under varnish. Remove all sanding dust before recoating or applying varnish.

Before using sanding sealers, it's good to keep in mind that they do have an effect on the penetration of stains and other finishing materials. If this could be a problem, run some tests on identical wood to determine the effect of the sealer on the materials that follow it, or forget about using a sealer. (See pages 130–31.)

USE OF STEEL WOOL

Steel wool is made of finely shredded steel and is a most important and economical material for use in many stages of restoration. Many finishers ignore steel wool and depend entirely on abrasive paper for smoothing, thereby losing the benefit of this most valuable material. It must be remembered that a poorly smoothed surface is likely to be a poorly finished one.

There are only six grades of steel wool that should be used for woodwork. They are as follows:

#3—the coarsest grade, rarely used in furniture work

#2—should be used on rough lumber only

#1—the coarsest grade that should be used on furniture

#1/0—the most commonly used of all grades

#2/0—used for rough smoothing

#3/0—the finest grade, used for final smoothing

Steel wool is commonly carried in paint and hardware stores. It usually comes in packages of sixteen individual pads, and it's best to have a package of each furniture type (#1 to #3/0) on hand. Steel wool may be purchased in small packages of mixed grades, but it's not too economical to buy it that way. It also comes in a large one-piece roll; if there is a choice, avoid this type, since it is hard to tear and roll into pads, which is the best way of using it.

Steel wool uses in refinishing are as follows:

1. After paint and varnish removers, as an aid in mopping up or cleaning off the messy residue left after most of the remover has been removed with a putty knife or burlap. Use grade #1 for this

work. It will not scratch when the surface is wet and it may be used to advantage when dipped in alcohol.

2. After sanding or scraping a surface, use the finer grades for greater smoothness. Start with grade #0 and finish with the finer grades in turn. Steel wool is best on hardwoods and is particularly good for smoothing turnings and carvings. On long turned surfaces (like table or chair legs), it will work rapidly and will not disturb marks or ridges left from the old, slow-turning lathes. Steel wool will put a smoother finish on end-grain surfaces after they have been sanded.

3. When stains are to be applied to a surface, it is better not to smooth the surface too much, to allow the stain to penetrate, but a light rubbing with fine steel wool will smooth the surface after the stain has been applied.

As steel wool is used it disintegrates into minute particles, many of which go into the air. It shouldn't be used outdoors because of the danger of its blowing into the eyes, and gloves should be worn to keep it from working into the skin. All traces of steel wool should be removed from your work after rubbing or they may stain the wood. The pads of steel wool fill with wood dust during use, and their life and cutting power may be prolonged if the dust is knocked out by striking the pad against something. New sharp surfaces may be brought to the top by turning the pads inside out, but it's not a good plan to add a new pad to an old one, for steel wool mats as it is used, especially in the finer grades.

CABINET SCRAPERS

A cabinet scraper is a difficult tool to use properly. Its sharp, hook-shaped edge removes a very thin shaving from the wood surface, and unless this edge is sharp and smooth, it won't do the work properly but will leave marks that will later show through the final finish. Watching an expert use a scraper is indeed a pleasure; in fact, it would be wise for an amateur to take lessons from such a person, both in the handling and the sharpening of the scraper. In the art of cabinetmaking, both operations are among the most difficult to perform correctly.

Scrapers are used in cabinet shops for final smoothing of surfaces after they have been planed. They are particularly well adapted for smoothing cross-grained boards, which are difficult to dress with a plane. Some experienced workers like to use the scraper for removing paint or varnish, but one should be sufficiently adept in its use or great damage may result.

One cause of damage lies in a scraper's not being properly sharpened (causing scratches), another in gouging the wood with the edge or corners of the scraper. There is less risk in using a scraper on hardwoods than on soft, since softwoods are more likely to rip and fuzz. Extensive sanding is then necessary to restore them to their proper condition. A scraper should not be used on old woods (such as pine) that have a beautiful patina, since some of this cherished surface is bound to be lost in the process.

Many experts warn against using a scraper on mahogany, walnut, or cherry,

5-11. *Cabinet scrapers like these are good for smoothing wood before finishing. They cut faster than sandpaper and are not as likely to chip the wood as a plane. Different shapes allow you to scrape a variety of surface contours, but it takes considerable skill to use them properly.*

since scratches on the surface of these woods will show through a clear finish. It is often difficult to remove color from maple without resorting to the scraper. However, the best rule to follow is never to use a scraper except as a last resort.

A scraper is a very handy and satisfactory tool for many small jobs and as a supplement to other tools, as in removing spots of paint left by a paint remover. It is also useful for removing paint from angles and crevices or as the only means for removing flaky paint from the legs of chairs, etc.

There are two kinds of scrapers recommended for use, as follows:

Hook Scraper

This scraper consists of a shaped wooden block into which is inserted a narrow, curved steel blade, placed crosswise in a metal groove at one end of the block. The handle end usually has a compartment for storing spare blades. Several manufacturers produce this type of scraper, which is available at hardware stores and tool supply houses. It comes with extra blades, and additional ones may be purchased as needed. In the hands of an inexperienced person, this tool can be a dangerous one, since the blade corners are sharp and apt to gouge a surface if not properly handled. The edge of the blade is beveled and will retain its sharpness for a longer time if burnished.

Blade Scraper

These blades are fabricated from flat pieces of hardened tool steel about $\frac{1}{16}$ inch in thickness. The type of blade most commonly used is rectangular in shape (in sizes up to 3 inches by 6 inches), while others are available in different shapes or may be ground to any shape required. The edges are squared, then hook turned and burnished.

It is worthwhile to practice using a scraper (of any type) on pieces of scrap wood before undertaking work on furniture. The following general rules are, for the most part, applicable to the use of both hook and blade scrapers.

1. Because of its construction, a hook scraper is drawn only toward the worker

and should be used with one hand. The tool should be tilted at the most advantageous angle, with just enough pressure applied to *shave* the surface properly.

2. Most of the work with a blade scraper is done on a plane surface, by pushing the tool away from the worker. The scraper is held with the fingers of both hands on the far side of the blade and with the thumbs on the near side. When working on a surface at a corner or adjoining a molding, etc., it is easier to pull the blade toward you. The blade can then be held in one hand. The angle at which the blade should be held is approximately 45 degrees, with the top slanting in the direction of the push or pull.

3. On plane surfaces (with either type of scraper), make the strokes as long as possible, exerting an even pressure. Lift the tool on the return stroke or you will dull the edge.

4. Scraping with the grain is best; avoid scraping across the grain or on an end grain. Scrape away from surface ends rather than toward them. When the scraper is held at a slight angle to the direction of the push or pull, the result is known as a "skewed cut." This type of cut is smoother and the blade stays sharp longer, but great care must be exercised to prevent a corner of the blade from gouging or scratching the surface.

5. If it is difficult to secure a smooth surface with a scraper, a light sponging of the surface with water before scraping will help.

6. The use of hand scrapers requires caution, since the blades are not held at a fixed angle or position, as are the blades in a plane or other types of tool scrapers. Consequently, on some kinds of woods, hand scrapers tend to follow the contour of the surface, cutting more deeply into soft areas and riding over hard ones.

7. When a scraper no longer lifts thin, curved shavings and shows a tendency to fuzz the surface, the blade needs to be resharpened. These same conditions may arise when the scraper isn't properly handled or the cutting edge has not been correctly sharpened or hooked (turned) by burnishing.

WET TEST FOR COLOR

Make a wet test to see whether a change in the bare wood will take place if a clear finish is applied. This test can be made on wood that has had no finish, or on a surface that is free from previous finish or paint and is sanded and smooth. The test will show the approximate color the wood will take when a clear finish is put on.

Merely wet a fingertip with clean water or saliva and touch the surface. The drier and more porous the wood, the greater will be the change in color. The most pronounced difference in color from this test will be found in softwoods like pine, while the change will hardly be noticeable in green or unseasoned woods.

Woods with open pores, whether they are softwoods or hardwoods, darken more after an application of a clear finish than do those with closed pores. Neither type of wood will absorb to a great degree until the sap has dried out.

PRELIMINARY WASH COATS

Some experienced wood finishers advise that a wash coat be used on a wood surface before a stain is applied. A wash coat is a mixture of 1 part white shellac to 6 or 8 parts denatured alcohol.

It stands to reason that no wash coat should be applied if it is going to lessen the penetrating ability of a stain, for without penetration a stain will not last. A wash coat may be beneficially used under certain conditions and circumstances, whether softwoods or hardwoods or those with large pores (called coarse grained or coarse textured) or with small pores (called close grained or fine textured).

The deciding factor is the condition of the wood. Some woods dry out greatly, depending on the amount of natural oils or gums they contain. Some old pine dries to the point where it powders when sanded. It sounds reasonable, and it is my contention, that when woods are considerably dried out, a wash coat is beneficial before the application of a stain. However, this must be judged by the worker according to the condition of the wood and the type of stain to be used.

When making a decision, it must be borne in mind that a wash coat of the type recommended has but a very small proportion of shellac and will be absorbed quickly and deeply into well-dried-out wood. It should never be used on woods that are not well seasoned. The purpose of the application is to seal the pores partially and to retard the absorption of a stain, but not to prevent its absorption into the pores to such an extent that it will remain upon the surface only. The rate or speed of absorption of a properly sanded and thoroughly dry, clean wood surface may be judged with much accuracy by making a wet test.

It is recommended that no wash coat be applied when water stains or spirit stains (reduced with water) are to be used, and it is not needed under a varnish stain or a penetrating sealer, for these materials both seal and finish. A wash coat is often beneficial when oil stains are used.

All brushwork with very thin materials should be done with as few strokes as possible. Three strokes only should be used— one stroke each way to lay the material on the surface and one stroke to tip it off (to remove or spread excess material). For this work a full-tipped brush (2 inches wide is good) is best, but don't overload it. Proceed quickly until the surface is covered.

STAINING WOODS

Stains are applied to bring out the full beauty of the grain or to emphasize the color of woods. They are also used to harmonize the color of a patch with the surrounding surface, or to match wood pieces of varying colors to bring them to a uniform color.

Stain will add color to wood that has no natural beauty of color in itself or if the color has faded. There is a definite need for stains in refinishing, but it is good to pause for consideration and not jump to conclusions before using it.

Woods with no color that are often stained or painted are:

basswood   poplar
gumwood   white pine

Light-colored woods that may be finished in their natural color or stained include:

ash   korina
beech   maple
birch   oak
chestnut   Philippine mahogany
elm   primavera

Stain is not usually used on veneers or woods with natural beauty and rich color, such as:

butternut   myrtle
cherry   rosewood
mahogany   teak
maple   walnut

These woods should be finished to bring out those characteristics and should not be stained. Any type of clear finish will darken a wood somewhat and magnify the beauty of the grain and the wood patterns.

It must be remembered that a stain is *not* a finish and that a finishing coat must be applied over it, except in the cases of varnish stains, penetrating wood-sealer finishes, and lacquer-containing stain.

It takes patience and experience to learn the art of staining, but the following general information should be of assistance.

1. A surface to be stained should not be too smooth, but should be dry and free of dust or other foreign matter before a stain is applied. When you can rub a nylon stocking over the surface without its catching, it is smooth enough for staining. Number 120 or 220 paper is fine enough for prestain sanding.

2. When the wood is extremely dried out, the surface should be treated with a wash coat as a preliminary coat before the application of some stains.

3. A stain should be tested for color, shade, or tone of color to match by applying it to an unexposed surface of a piece, or to a wood of the same kind, and allowing it to dry.

4. Stains of a similar type may be intermixed for shades of color and thinned for a lighter tone.

5. One coat of stain may be applied over another for a darker color. If a piece is of several colored woods, stain to the darkest shade.

6. A stain should be brushed or wiped on quickly in an even coat and without overlaps. It is best applied on a horizontal surface, as it may be smoothed out more evenly there. If it becomes necessary to apply it to a vertical surface, wipe out sags and runs evenly.

7. After a stain has been applied, all surplus should be wiped off with a lintless cloth. The longer the unabsorbed stain remains on the surface, the darker will be the final effect. Times vary as to when the excess stain should be wiped off, according to the type and thickness of the stain and the condition and kind of wood.

8. Care must be exercised in wiping the edges and corners of the piece to avoid removing too much stain.

9. It often requires two coats of stain to get a uniform color. There should be at least 24 hours between coats.

10. End-grain surfaces, which are porous, will absorb too much stain, often resulting in too dark a color. To overcome this, the surface should be well smoothed and, if necessary, treated with extra wash coats.

11. When insert patches are to be stained, it is usually necessary to stain the entire surface into which they are to be placed.

12. When applying a stain (or paint) to an article like a chair, it is always best to do all the inside of the underpart first, then the outside of the underpart, and, finally, the upper part of the piece.

13. All stains should be applied in a work area free from excessive heat or drafts.

14. Allow stain to dry for at least 24 hours, unless otherwise instructed. If a stain is not thoroughly dry, it will weep (blend) with the sealing coat to follow and won't dry.

15. A stained surface should not be smoothed with an abrasive until after a sealer coat has been applied and dried.

16. Colors don't appear true in artificial light, especially fluorescent light. Therefore, apply stain during the daytime in strong natural light.

17. Stain colors of the same type can be intermixed—oil stain with another color of oil stain, one water stain with another.

5-12. Before staining a piece of furniture, make color tests on a scrap of a similar type of wood. Apply a coat of varnish over the samples to see how they will look when finished, then pick the one you like best.

Commercial Stain Colors

Color charts, which are furnished by the manufacturers of the various types of stains, are supplied without cost to customers in those retail stores (paint, hardware, and builders' supply) where wood stains are available. These charts show the various colors, and each manufacturer has his own version of the shade of a color. These shades vary greatly and are often called by a coined name, rather than by the name of the wood they represent.

Those most commonly found are oak, maple, mahogany, and walnut. The various colors may be called by those names only, a coined name, or a name that is generally accepted as a shade of one of the colors. The colors and shades are as follows:

> *Oak*—light oak (yellowish); dark oak (brownish-yellow); golden oak (slightly reddish dark oak)
> *Maple*—maple (brownish-yellow); honey (reddish-brown); Vermont (brownish-red)
> *Mahogany*—mahogany (reddish-brown); dark mahogany (brownish-red)
> *Walnut*—variation of brown to blackish-brown

The colors on the charts may vary somewhat from the color found in the can, so when making a purchase it is good to have the can opened and the color tested by placing a small quantity on a piece of paper, into which it is quickly absorbed and on which it soon dries, because the wet color varies from the dried. All stains should be mixed in the daylight.

Water Stain

Water stain is considered by most professional workers the best for all-purpose use. It is by far the most universally used stain for mass production in furniture factories. For use in a home shop, it has both advantages and disadvantages.

The principal advantage is that it may be readily mixed by dissolving aniline dye powders in hot water, producing a concentrated solution that may be stored in glass bottles indefinitely and diluted to tints as needed. Also, with proper materials, colors may be made and intermixed that harmonize with true wood colors of various shades and tones, that don't fade or bleed, and that may be applied to a prepared wood surface without a preliminary sealer coat.

The disadvantage in the use of water stain, for an amateur, is that many workers do not care to take time or trouble to mix and store water stains when they are able to purchase oil and other types of penetrating stains in small containers, ready mixed and in colors to match various woods. Too, these stains do not raise the grain, while a water stain will. Another disadvantage in the use of water stains is that many paint stores do not carry the powders in stock, but you can buy them (for less money than any other type of stain) from Constantine's. A final disadvantage: water stains often do not penetrate well on wood being refinished. Remnants of the old finish interfere.

MIXING WATER STAIN Heat water to just below the boiling point in a vessel other than aluminum. Pour the aniline powder into the water slowly while stirring. Allow to cool, and store in a glass bottle. If the water is "hard" (containing lime) or not pure, use distilled water. The mixture should be in proportions of 4 ounces of powder to 1 gallon of water. Dilute this solution with pure water to the density of color or tint desired.

APPLYING WATER STAIN To apply water stain, the procedure is as follows:

1. Wipe the wood lightly with a damp sponge to raise the grain. Let dry, then sand *lightly* with #220 garnet paper. Now

you can apply water stain and the grain will not be raised again.

2. Apply stain with a brush, using long, straight strokes. Free the brush from stain on the edge of the container or by shaking it, then go over the surface, picking up surplus stain. Continue doing so, using long strokes, until the surface is even in color. Remove all excess stain from cracks and crevices with a small scrub brush.

3. When brushing is completed, wipe the surface with a cloth, using light, full-length strokes, picking up stain remaining on the surface, making the surface uniform in color and without streaks.

4. The end surfaces should be thoroughly wetted with water before stain is applied to an adjacent surface. Don't let such end surfaces become dry. Stain the end surfaces while wet and wipe off immediately, repeating if necessary. This method will keep the end surface from absorbing too much stain and becoming too dark.

When spots will not absorb the stain to match the surrounding area, rub them with 3/0 steel wool to open the pores while the surface is wet with stain.

NON-GRAIN-RAISING (NGR) STAINS Because water-soluble colors will raise grain, finishing manufacturers have developed stains in which powders are dissolved in a solvent other than water. Stains of this kind are known by various descriptive trade terms such as non-grain-raising, fast-to-light, and non-sand. They are, of course, more expensive than water stains because of the solvent used, but they offer one of the best types of stain for new work. Their rapid drying makes brushing difficult, but smooth coats are easily applied by spraying. Strictly nonbleeding, they can be used under any type of finish coat. They dry for recoating in from 10 minutes to 3 hours, depending on the manufacturer's recommendation. Ready-mixed colors are numerous, but if you wish you may obtain concentrated primary colors and mix tints to suit your individual taste. It is possible to mix the stain powder and the solvent, but the cost is about the same as for the ready-mixed product.

NGR stains are best applied by spraying. Because of their quick-drying nature (some of them are ready for recoating in 10 minutes), brushing is difficult. Also, because of the wetness of a brush coat, the stain tends to raise the grain of the wood, although it is strictly non-grain-raising when sprayed. These stains can be slowed down a bit with the addition of about 10 percent Carbitol or Cellosolve.

Use a large brush and apply the stain in a very wet coat. Always break up the job into convenient areas; do the legs, rails, and top of a table in separate operations. If it is impossible to do a lap-free job, dilute the stain to half strength with an equal amount of solvent. Apply two coats of this weak stain. Another way is to wash the work quickly with the stain solvent and then apply full-strength stain immediately.

When you spray NGR stains, apply a moderate coat, not too wet. Cover all inside edges first; do the top last. Use a small spray pattern, but fan it out by holding the gun a fair distance from the work. Always have a good light on the work, so that the color density can be properly evaluated. By spraying heavier on light wood and less on dark wood, it is easy to obtain a uniform color on mixed or off-color wood.

Oil Stains

Oil stains are best for the beginner and amateur worker to use. These stains not only are rich in tone and produce lasting colors but are generally available, inexpensive, and easily applied and stored. They do not raise the grain, causing wood feathers, nor do they conceal the natural wood grain or wood patterns; those of similar type may be mixed together for shades of color.

Oil stains are made of coloring matter with linseed oil as a vehicle, japan drier to hasten the drying of the oil, and turpentine used as a thinner, which carries the mixture into the pores of the wood and later evaporates. There are two distinct types of oil stains, as follows:

PIGMENT OIL STAINS   This stain is often referred to merely as an oil stain or a wood-finishing stain, without mention on the containers of the fact that it is a pigment type. The coloring matter is the same as that used in so-called colors in oil. The pigment settles to the bottom of the can and must be stirred before using.

Pigment oil stains are best on such close-grained woods as basswood, birch, cherry, gumwood, maple, pine, and poplar. If the stain is properly applied and wiped off, the small and closely spaced pores of these woods will not become clogged with the finely ground color pigment.

This clogging is the main drawback of this type of stain. If the stain is not properly wiped off, the opaque pigment can easily obscure the wood beneath it, creating a muddy look. Certain pigmented stains—Minwax, for example—also contain a certain amount of dissolved coloring agent in addition to the opaque pigments. For application on coarse-grained woods it is best not to stir the stain. This leaves the pigments in the bottom of the can and lets you stain with the relatively transparent coloring agents dissolved in the oil base.

PENETRATING OIL STAINS   This type of stain is usually referred to on the containers either as a penetrating material or described by a trade name, indicating that it is of that kind. Since the coloring matter is in liquid form, these stains are transparent. They are best for use on coarse-grained woods such as ash, beech, chestnut, elm, hickory, mahogany, oak, rosewood, satinwood, sycamore, and walnut. Since these woods have large pores and coarse texture, they will often clog up too much with a pigment stain, which would be detrimental to the finished appearance.

Penetrating oil stains should be used by preference on woods that are not well seasoned or old enough to have had their natural oils dried out, and on surfaces that are quite smooth, as they will penetrate better than stains of the pigment type. Some workers prefer them to other types of stains and use them exclusively, when available.

The greatest drawback to this type of stain is that when it is used on an extremely porous surface it penetrates deeply and is very difficult to remove, should the occasion arise. If prior tests are made for color, tone, or shade, there should be no need for their later removal.

Another problem with penetrating oil stain is finding it, as it is not usually carried by paint stores. To get it you will probably have to order it from a professional finishing house, such as Behlen's, where the minimum order is $25. For that reason, few amateurs use this type of stain.

INTERMIXING OIL STAIN COLORS Practically all the variation of colors you will need for staining furniture woods may be made by intermixing stains of three basic colors—maple (brownish-yellow), mahogany (reddish-brown), and walnut (true brown).

If the maple contains too much brown, it will be necessary to add light oak to the list, and should the walnut contain too much black, you'll need raw umber or burnt umber. To lighten the other colors, add gum turpentine to oil stains.

A small amount of oil stain goes a long way, especially when thinned with turpentine for lighter color tone. Buy only quality stains of the three colors and intermix for various shades of color. If necessary, you may add to these colors, as described earlier. To dull color that is too bright, add a small amount of deep Thalo green (blue-green) color in oil to an oil stain. To mask refractory or other stains, add a small amount of blue-green color, as when you dull color. CAUTION: Use a very little green to dull the red stain and to produce a reddish-brown wood tone.

Never buy cheap grades of stains. They are off-color, particularly the mahogany stain, which may be much too red. The walnut stain also may not be the true color of the wood it is to represent.

APPLYING OIL STAINS To apply oil stain, proceed as follows:

1. Test stain color on the underside of the piece to be sure it's appropriate.

2. Brush or wipe on an even and moderately thin coat of stain without overlaps, after having thoroughly stirred the stain, especially if it is the pigment type.

3. Allow to remain on wood long enough to penetrate and give the desired

COLOR GUIDE FOR MIXING STAINS

TO STAIN WOODS	START WITH BASE OF	ADD TO BASE
Brown (reddish)	Walnut stain	Reddish-brown mahogany stain
(yellowish)	Walnut stain	Brownish-yellow maple stain
Yellow (brownish)	Maple stain	Walnut stain

effect. Wipe off surplus with a lintless cloth before it sets. The stain should be allowed to dry 24 hours. Smooth lightly with 3/0 steel wool to remove roughness.

Spirit Stains

Stain powders soluble in alcohol make penetrating spirit stains, but they are also available in ready-mixed liquid form with various blended solvents. Spirit stains have the advantage of drying quickly. When you use them, a surface can be stained and filled or shellacked and varnished all on the same day. Because they dry rapidly, they are generally not suitable for brushing, but they can be sprayed. Spirit stains bleed—or dissolve into—almost any type of finishing coat, including shellac. Bleeding causes a slight muddiness in the finish. This can be an advantage; since spirit stains will penetrate an old varnish finish, they are often used for refinishing. Other uses include touch-up work and staining sap streaks. Spirit stains fade quickly when exposed to strong light unless well protected with finishing coats. They dry for recoating in 10 to 15 minutes.

Because the average stain of this type dries almost instantly, the best method of application is with a spray gun. If applied by brush, the work must be done rapidly and without backtracking. A small amount of shellac added to the stain will make it easier to brush evenly. Don't apply a coat of shellac over spirit stains, because shellac, which is also soluble in alcohol, will lift the stain, causing a muddy appearance. Wood finished with spirit stain shouldn't be exposed to strong sunlight until coated with varnish.

Pigmented Wiping Stains

Pigmented wiping stains, or stain sealers, are available in a wide range of color tones, which can be intermixed to offer an even wider variety. They are similar to pigmented oil stains, but the pigments are in suspension in a penetrating-resin vehicle instead of an oil. This type of stain, which must be stirred constantly to assure even distribution of the pigments, is effective in making the wood uniform or in staining a piece of furniture made from different woods. Wood should generally be smoothly sanded to ensure a uniform appearance. Soft, porous woods darken heavily, since they soak up more of the color, while harder woods absorb less stain. Pigmented wiping stains generally perform best on white pine and other softwoods. They also furnish a good method by which to create a "distressed" effect in a finish, since they help accentuate cracks, dents, and scratches.

Follow the manufacturer's directions when applying pigmented wiping stains. Be sure to stir frequently and to uniformly cover the entire area. If you are going to use more than one can of stain, mix the cans together in a large container to ensure uniformity of color.

While all stains are wiped, wiping is the most important step in the application of this type of stain. After brushing the material on, allow it to penetrate. Then wait until it starts to dull over or has penetrated to the desired degree. Then wipe clean.

Should the color remain too dark after you have wiped all you can, dampen a cloth with paint thinner as per the manufacturer's directions, and carefully wipe again. You can also use this same technique to blend the wood grain more uniformly; that is, to darken portions of the wood that are too light, like sapwood.

Although staining is usually employed to darken wood, pigmented wiping stains can be used to lighten it or create a "blond" effect. White wiping stain is brushed on, permitted to penetrate the wood surface, and then wiped off. This blond stain, like all pigmented wiping stains, works best on coarse-grained woods. Incidentally, all pigmented wiping stains in a penetrating resin help seal the wood to a degree.

Varnish Stains

These are not often used for fine wood finishes. However, there are occasional quick, cheap, temporary, or repair jobs where a varnish stain may be used to advantage. Varnish stains are simply varnish to which coloring matter has been added in sufficient quantity to produce a decided color, but not enough to completely obscure the surface. Transparent colors are used. These stains fill, color, and add a gloss to the surface, all in one coat. They do not penetrate the surface to any extent, they dry in from 3 to 12 hours, and they do not fade when exposed to strong light.

For really high-grade finishing, skilled craftsmen don't use this kind of stain. When a project is made from the cheaper grades of lumber, varnish stains may be used successfully because they give a uniform coloring to woods streaked with very soft and porous parts. This result is impossible with other stains unless you do a great deal of expensive preliminary work. If varnish stains are made too dark in color, they completely hide the wood grain and give the appearance of an enameled surface. They are applied in the same manner as varnish (see Chapter Six).

Other Stains

Other materials are often used by wood finishers as stains. Following are a few of the more popular ones:

• Warm pine stain is made from plug chewing tobacco. The plug is broken up and allowed to stand in a half pint of household ammonia, then steeped for 15 minutes. Two coats should be applied to give varying degrees of light to dark tones, depending upon the strength of the material.

• Brown stain is often and successfully made from tobacco soaked in water.

• Nut-brown stain is often made by professional refinishers from potassium permanganate, which may be purchased in drugstores. It is violet in color but turns brown when applied to wood.

• The so-called vegetable stains are extracted from roots, bark, and other vegetable matter. At one time they were used extensively but have now been replaced by water-soluble aniline stains. Vegetable stains are mixed and applied in the same way as water stains but have a tendency to fade when exposed to sunlight. Here are some of the vegetable stains: dragon's blood (red), alkanet (red), madder (red), logwood (black), indigo (blue), and fustic (yellow).

USING A SEALER COAT OVER STAIN

A sealer coat should be applied to a wood surface after a stain has been used, unless otherwise directed. It should also be applied before a wood filler (for an ultra-smooth, fine finish) and over the filler before the final coat, as related later in this chapter.

Wood finishers have never come to complete agreement as to the type of undercoat to be used beneath succeeding coats, but it is now generally conceded that the sealer material should be a thin coat of whatever is used for the final finish.

The purpose of the sealer coat is to keep the stain from bleeding into succeeding coats by sealing the pores, to ready the surface for a filler or smooth it for the final finish. The sealer prevents liquids from entering the wood fibers and reducing the stain materials, which often causes a gray cast or light-colored area surrounded by small rings.

Sealer coats should be so thin that they will leave no shine. Only one coat is applied (with a brush) and later smoothed, according to the final finish to be used, as follows:

For a varnish finish (or mixture containing varnish), reduce 1 part of varnish with 1 part of pure turpentine.

For a shellac finish, reduce 1 part of pure white shellac (4-pound cut) with 8 parts of denatured alcohol.

For most lacquer finishes, use two thin coats of pure white shellac, thinned one-half. Another popular sealer for lacquer and varnish is a special product known as sanding sealer. It is made of a lacquer-shellac base, which dries ready to recoat in about an hour. It brushes easily, has a good hard surface, and contains a sanding agent that permits clean, powdery sanding without gumming.

If a filler is to be used on a sealed stained surface, merely knock off any roughness by rubbing very lightly with 3/0 steel wool. If the final finish is to be applied directly over the sealer coat, the surface should be completely smoothed. Do this with worn 6/0 to 8/0 garnet paper or grade 3/0 steel wool. When using either type of material, great care must be taken not to rub too heavily on the edges or the corners, for fear of cutting through the stain. Should this be done, the spots will have to be restained, dried, and a new sealer coat applied.

Sealing Fir and Other Softwoods

Fir and some other softwoods need a good sealer because of the special character of the grain figure, which is made up of alternate hard summer growth and softer spring growth. If you do not use a sealer, the first coat of paint or finish penetrates unevenly and results in a wild, overconspicuous grain.

To tame or quiet this grain, several special types of resin sealers have been developed. (Firzite is one example.) They may be purchased from lumber, paint, or hardware dealers. If the resin sealer is used properly, it allows the stain to soften the darker markings and deepen the lighter surfaces. The finish will be soft and lustrous, and the wild grain figures pleasantly subdued. For application details, follow the manufacturer's directions.

FILLING THE WOOD SURFACE

Certain woods, such as oak, mahogany, walnut, and chestnut, have an open-grained structure with large, noticeable "pores," which make it difficult to achieve a smooth, even finish. With these woods, best results will be obtained if a paste wood filler is used. Filler is sometimes applied to bare wood, and sometimes over stain and wash-coat sealers, depending on the effect desired. Fillers are available in colors to match different woods, or in natural (not colored) types. The natural can sometimes be tinted with oil colors to match the color of the wood (or the stain). It is best, however, to buy the shade you wish, to be sure the filler's color will be permanent. If unusual effects are desired, contrasting colors can also be used. Fillers can be obtained in two forms—paste and liquid.

Paste Fillers

Paste fillers are made with silex, a crushed and finely ground rock, crystalline in character and with no chemical action. Paste fillers can usually be bought at stores selling paints and painters' materials and are usually found in colors to

FILLER MIX REQUIRED FOR VARIOUS WOODS

NO FILLER NEEDED	THIN FILLER	MEDIUM FILLER	HEAVY FILLER
Aspen	Alder	Avodire	Ash
Basswood	Beech	Butternut	Chestnut
Cedar	Birch	Kornia	Elm
Cypress	Cherry	Mahogany	Hickory
Ebony	Gum	Orientalwood	Locust
Fir	Maple	Primavera	Mahogany
Hemlock	Sycamore	Rosewood	(Philippine)
Pine		Tigerwood	Oak
Poplar		Walnut	Teakwood
Redwood		Zebrawood	
Spruce			

approximate those of the wood surface to be filled. In this case, they do not need to be colored.

As a rule, a filler should be at least as dark as, and usually darker than, the wood it is to be used on.

THINNING PASTE FILLERS Commercial paste fillers, as they come in the can, are a thick, heavy paste and must be thinned considerably for use. General directions for thinning and material used will be found on the containers, but they may be confusing, as they often seem to be directed to the professional shop. There they are measured, by the weight of the base stock, to the gallon of thinner. You will also find various thinning materials or combinations of them recommended by different firms.

Manufacturers of paste fillers and authorities recommend as a thinner pure turpentine, benzine, or naphtha. The purpose of thinning is for ease of application, and the medium used must evaporate. You may use any one mentioned above for good results. You should get the best results when the filler is thinned to the consistency of thick cream.

There is but one rule to remember: It is difficult to handle and remove a filler that is too thick. And while, if it is too thin, a succeeding coat of the filler may be applied should there be bare spots, too thin a coat may be injurious to a stain if the stain is not properly sealed.

1.

2.

5-13. Applying wood filler: 1. Before applying a filler to a surface, open the wood pores by rubbing water over the surface with a sponge. It's best to test the finish on a sample piece.

2. In place of wetting the wood, you can rub the surface down with a stiff wire brush. This can also be used in combination with wetting.

PROPORTIONS FOR MIXING VARIOUS QUANTITIES OF FILLER

Heavy Mix (16-lb. Base)

APPROX. AMT. NEEDED*	PASTE	THINNER
2 gal.	16 lb.	1 gal.
5 pt.	5 lb.	2½ pt.
2 qt.	1 qt.	1 qt.
2 pt.	1 pt.	1 pt.
1 pt.	1 lb.	½ pt.
½ pt.	½ lb.	4 oz.

Medium Mix (12-lb. Base)

APPROX. AMT. NEEDED*	PASTE	THINNER
1 gal. 3 qt.	12 lb.	1 gal.
3 qt.	5 lb.	3 pt. 5 oz.
2 qt. 10 oz.	1 qt.	2 pt. 10 oz.
1 qt. 5 oz.	1 pt.	1 pt. 5 oz.
1 pt. 20 oz.	1 lb.	10½ oz.
9 oz.	½ lb.	5¼ oz.

Thin Mix (8-lb. Base)

APPROX. AMT. NEEDED*	PASTE	THINNER
1½ gal.	8 lb.	1 gal.
1 gal.	5 lb.	5 pt.
3 qt.	1 qt.	2 qt.
3 pt.	1 pt.	2 pt.
1½ pt.	1 lb.	1 pt.
12 oz.	½ lb.	½ pt.

*One pint of thinned filler covers approximately 36 square feet.

USING PASTE FILLERS There is a difference of opinion as to how the thinned paste fillers should be applied. If the following method and the correct timing for padding are used, the work should be a success, provided the filler is applied to a surface properly prepared for its acceptance. Have on hand a supply of clean burlap (15 to 18 inches square) and clean rags. It is generally best to seal the wood with a wash coat.

1. Clean dust from the surface with a stiff brush.

2. Apply the filler quickly and generously but to a limited area at a time, with an old, stiff, short-bristle brush, *with* the grain of the wood, rubbing it in a little. Then brush it smooth, with the grain. Stir the mixture thoroughly before each application.

3. Fold a piece of burlap several times to about the size of your hand. When the surface of the applied filler flattens and loses its shine appreciably (usually 5 to 10 minutes), rub the filler into the wood surface with the *cross-grain* and a circular motion and without changing to a new surface of the cloth. This operation pads the powdered silex particles into the wood pores and smooths the surface. The time when this work should start is most important, for, with conditions favorable, the filler sets up quickly.

4. Follow immediately by wiping off the surface, *across* the grain only, with clean pieces of burlap squares, followed by fresh rags, until all the surplus filler is removed and the surface is clean and free from smears. Finally, when you look at the surface against the light and it shines, you

may stroke the surface with a clean cloth *with* the grain, to remove all traces of surplus filler and fingerprints. This must be done lightly, or the filler may be pulled from the surface.

5. Carvings, joints, moldings, etc., should be scrubbed with a small brush packed with the filler. When the surface "flattens," wipe with clean burlap, followed by cloths, etc. Hold a bit of cloth over the point of a wooden meat skewer or a small, sharpened dowel stick to clean out the depressions and corners.

6. A filled piece should dry at least 24 hours in a warm room, but 48 hours or even more would be better. Fillers that have colors added to them take longer to dry.

When the work is correctly accomplished by the above steps, the surface should be smooth and ready for a sealer coat. If the surface shows evidence of the filler, remove the filler and smooth with worn 6/0 to 8/0 abrasive paper dipped in white gasoline.

If the surface has blotches or smears not seen until the filler has dried, moisten with a cloth with the same thinner as used in the filler and wipe the spots carefully to avoid creating a light-covered area. If this will not remove the excess dried filler, the spots or area must be sanded lightly with a worn 6/0 to 8/0 abrasive paper dipped in white gasoline. If the area is then too light in color, dip a rag in the filler and work over that part of the surface until the color is blended. Then allow to dry and use the sealer coat on the entire surface.

If a filled and dried surface is found to lack a sufficient amount of filler, fill the entire surface again by starting at the beginning of the process.

SEALING THE FILLER

Apply a sealer coat to a surface that has been treated with a paste filler. This should be a very thin coat of the same material used for clear final coats. Thin shellac with alcohol or varnish with turpentine as previously directed (see page 130). This coat will penetrate the filler and, being of the same material as the sealer coat applied prior to using the filler, it will have the same adhesion and expanding factors, and assist in leveling the surface. Sand with 6/0 to 8/0 grade abrasive paper to prepare for succeeding final coats after the sealer coat has dried for 24 hours.

Use a varnish sealer coat over paste fillers on wood surfaces when the final coat is to be enamel, as this product is also thinned with turpentine. When a shellac sealer coat is used, it fails to give proper adhesion between the enamel and the filler, allowing the enamel to chip more easily.

six

Applying the New Finish

You were previously advised to plan your work in advance, not only for the type of finish you decide to use, but for the type most suitable for the piece.

The finish best suited for a particular piece depends upon these factors:
- The wood from which the piece is made—pine, mahogany, etc.
- The utility of the piece—chair, cabinet, table, etc.
- The quality of the workmanship or fineness of the piece—a highboy as compared with a cobbler's bench
- The customary finish for the type or period of the piece—as, for example, a crude piece of pine furniture as compared to a mahogany dining room table that has been smoothed with a paste filler

It is just as bad to overfinish as to underfinish, depending on the factors just outlined. There are, however, many cases that are not in the extreme; a worker should use good judgment.

You were also advised to plan any change of color or degree of smoothness desired, in order to decide on a stain to be used (for color), or whether to apply a paste filler (for smoothness). This work must be completed, and a sealer coat applied after each, before putting on a finish coat.

When all work of preparing for a new finish has been successfully completed, you are then ready to apply a previously chosen finish material, to be left in a:

High-gloss finish, the natural gloss left after the application of several coats of finishing material. A finish seldom desired for indoor furniture.

Satin rubbed finish, a finish secured by smoothing a high-gloss finish with abrasive papers or steel wool and then waxing. The most used and preferred finish, it can be closely duplicated without the need to rub by using satin varnish.

Polished rubbed finish, a finish requiring

a paste filler before the final finish. A finish to be used on that type, period, or quality of furniture requiring it.

The most employed clear final finishes are varnish, shellac, oil, penetrating wood sealer, and lacquer finish. The first of the procedures that follow gives full and complete information and instruction for the application of a varnish finish. The balance of this chapter gives information, specific uses, and instructions for the other finishing materials for a high-gloss, satin rubbed, or polished rubbed finish.

VARNISH FINISH

The most satisfactory finish coat for the do-it-yourselfer to apply is varnish. Varnish is available in high gloss, medium gloss, satin finish, and completely flat. A good furniture varnish is resistant to water, alcohol, and other liquids and should be relatively easy to apply. The number of coats determines the "depth" and smoothness of the finish.

A good finish requires at least two and preferably three or more coats with light sanding between each. Avoid working in dusty locations, and never apply varnish when the air is damp or cold. Where possible, lay pieces horizontal to simplify brushing.

Varnish is best applied with a good-quality bristle brush, although a pad of lint-free cloth can also be used.

The Material

Most varnishes today are made of synthetic resins—alkyd, phenolic, vinyl, or urethane—that dry fairly rapidly to form a hard surface coating that is exceptionally resistant to rough wear. Of these types, the alkyds are best for furniture work. Phenolics, often called spar varnishes, are primarily for outdoor use. The urethanes are extremely tough, best suited to such high-wear situations as floors and bar tops. Vinyls tend to be soft and won't rub out well; avoid them. Don't buy a cheap varnish. A small quantity of varnish covers a large area and a cheap grade will never result in a good or lasting finish.

Brushing Varnish

Although brushing varnish is the most difficult of all ordinary brushwork, this should not discourage the beginner. With practice you can master the technique. Meanwhile, rubbing and polishing can remove a host of flaws and help achieve a good finish despite less-than-perfect brushwork.

Varnish should be "flowed" onto a surface with a brush, and with thin, even coats. The process is called laying it on and tipping it off. It's important to have a good brush for varnishing. There are brushes especially made for use with varnish. (For general information regarding brushes and the type to buy, see pages 225–30.)

If workers inexperienced in applying varnish will follow instructions carefully in their first few jobs, they will soon qual-

1.

2.

3.

4.

5.

6.

6-1. How to apply a varnish finish: 1. Sand the entire surface of the furniture. 2. Mix stains to obtain the right color, then test out on a scrap of wood before using it. 3. The stain may be applied by either a cloth or a brush. 4. Hold the brush at this angle for varnishing. 5. Sand lightly after each coat has set. 6. Complete the job with a protective coat of wax over the last coat of varnish.

ify for doing precision work. Instructions for brushing varnish (and similar materials) are as follows:

1. Never varnish in damp weather or on surfaces that are not thoroughly dry.

2. Both the room and the varnish should be 70 degrees F or warmer. There are times when the work must be done in a colder room. In such cases, or if it is desired to use varnish warmer than the room temperature, place the unopened can in a pan of warm water for about an hour before using it.

3. Surfaces to be varnished should be free from dust. Wipe surfaces with a clean, lintless cloth (shaking often), then remove dust from cracks, deep pores, etc.,

with a clean, dry brush, and wipe again with the cloth. Finally, wipe with a tack rag to remove every last particle of dust, lint, etc., before applying varnish.

4. Never shake or agitate varnish before removing the lid, since this will cause the formation of small bubbles that will be detrimental to smoothing out a coat. Hold the can in your hand and rotate it gently back and forth a few times to mix the varnish before removing the lid. When some of the varnish has been taken from the can, immediately place the lid (loosely) back on top so that the vehicle for thinning won't evaporate.

5. Varnish sets very rapidly. When varnish thickens to a point where it does not

6-2. Small artist's brush is a good tool for carefully picking off bits of dust or lint that fall onto a fresh coat of varnish.

flow easily from the brush, it should be thinned as directed by the manufacturer on the label. A little thinner goes a long way, and it should be thoroughly mixed.

6. A brush is prepared for use before starting work by being dipped into the varnish and worked back and forth on clean paper to distribute the varnish evenly through the bristles. Too much varnish on a brush will cause it to drip or run onto the handle.

7. Never dip the brush into the varnish by more than one-third its length, and always apply liberally with a minimum number of brush strokes. Do not remove excess varnish from the brush by dragging the bristles across the rim of the can. This causes tiny bubbles to form in the varnish and will make it almost impossible to achieve a smooth finish. Instead, tap the bristle tips *lightly* against the inside of the container, above the surface of the liquid. Better still, use a "strike wire" for removing excess varnish from the brush before applying it to a surface (see page 239).

8. When brushing varnish, apply only a moderate amount of pressure on the handle. Do not bend the bristles. Apply with parallel strokes, then cross-stroke immediately by brushing at right angles to

6-3. A shallow can fitted with a strike wire cut from a coathanger makes a good varnish cup. The shallowness of the can prevents dipping the brush too deeply into the varnish, and the strike wire lets you gently stroke excess varnish off the brush without creating bubbles.

the original direction. Finish off by stroking lightly with the bristle tips, using an almost dry brush and working parallel to the grain only. This eliminates brush strokes and will assure a coating of uniform appearance. Remember, that first coat of varnish should be "brushed" on very thinly; later coats should be "flowed" on.

9. On horizontal surfaces, the varnish is laid on with very little brushwork. Lay an area only about 6 to 8 inches at a time, working from the unfinished to the finished surface and taking about two strokes. Then tip off the varnish, to smooth it and wipe out any bubbles, by holding the brush straight up and going lightly over the surface with the tip of the bristles. Inspect the surface against the light.

10. On vertical (standing) surfaces, the procedure is different, to prevent curtains (sags) on the finished work. Working an area of about 6 inches square, use short, quick strokes, back and forth across the surface by brushing down halfway and up halfway, so that the brush is lifted from the surface in the central portion. Working on horizontal surfaces is always easiest. Turn your work to avoid working on vertical surfaces whenever possible.

11. Start strokes from a center toward an edge, rather than from an edge toward the center, to avoid wiping the varnish from the brush over the edge, leaving heavy deposits of varnish called "fat edges."

12. On turned parts, such as chair and table legs, brush around turnings but stroke lengthwise on the long, plain sec-tions, tipping off halfway up and halfway down.

13. When varnishing small furniture (chairs, tables, etc.) that may be easily lifted, turn the article upside down, place on a workbench (boards on sawhorses are good), complete the entire understructure first, and then do the upper.

The common causes of varnish problems are as follows:

Pinholes often appear when a varnish has dried because the varnish was applied on a damp surface, a poor thinner was used, or the thinner was not thoroughly mixed with the varnish.

Crawling may be caused by coats being too thick, by atmospheric changes, or by the preceding coat's not having dried.

Chipping or "crackling" may come from using a type of varnish that becomes brittle, or by placing one kind of varnish over another, the two having varying degrees of elasticity.

Sweating usually occurs when a varnish is rubbed before it is thoroughly dry.

Brush marks usually result from using too small a brush or brushing the varnish too long.

Drying a Varnished Surface

Under no circumstances should a varnished surface be rubbed with any type of abrasive (steel wool or an abrasive paper or cloth) until it is *completely* dry. If a surface is rubbed before it is thoroughly dried out, the result will be disastrous, in some cases requiring a complete removal of the finish and a new one to replace it.

For good results, be guided by the general information given herein regarding the time for drying, tests for dryness, the removing of "fat edges," "curtains," etc., as follows:

1. For high-quality work such as a polished rubbed finish, the first (thin) coat should be given a minimum drying time of 24 hours, 48 hours for the second, and 3 to 5 days for the third or final coat.

2. When insufficient time is allowed for drying, an abrasive rubbed on a surface will pick up any little particles of foreign matter (dust, etc.) embedded in the finish and cause them to scratch or wear through the hardened face of the varnish. When this hardened face is damaged, the partially dried under material piles up on abrasive paper or is torn out by steel wool, leaving pinholes or spots on the surface.

3. Make a test with a thumbnail for hardness. If the surface seems hard, then make a test with the ball of the thumb for a print. Wipe the thumb clean and dry. Press it down hard on the surface, wipe the spot with a clean cloth, and examine for a print. If any is noticeable, set the piece aside for further hardening (a warm room is best).

4. It takes a long time for fat edges, drips, sags, and curtains to become completely dry because of the thickness of varnish in them. If an attempt is made to sand such a defect before it is hardened throughout, it will cut through to the bare surface, making it necessary for the work to be done over, as no later coats would cover such a depression. So when you test varnish for hardness, always test where the finish is softest, at thick spots such as sags or fat edges.

5. When such defects have completely dried, they may be sanded down with #320 abrasive paper, well lubricated with water, if great care is taken while doing this work. It is best to cut a thick defect (raised surface) down only partway. Then it should be washed and dried, and set aside to dry for some days. This extra precaution often avoids the necessity of removing the entire finish and starting over again.

Sanding between Finish Coats

When more than one finish coat of varnish is being applied, each dried coat should be lightly sanded before the next one is applied. This sanding is done with #400 waterproof sandpaper used wet. Soapy water is often used as a lubricant.

Remember always to sand the finish by working parallel with the grain and sand with *light* pressure only. Use enough pressure to dull the sheen and produce a uniform, satiny-smooth finish—but be careful to avoid cutting through the finish. Use a padded sanding block. This will help "plane" down high spots in the finish. The smoothness can best be determined by stroking lightly with the fingertips after wiping off the abrasive dust that has accumulated.

When sanding a large surface, such as a tabletop, rub with the grain of the wood toward the ends first and then near the sides, taking extreme care not to sand the finish from the edges or the corners. Then sand the center section with the grain, using long strokes and an even pressure. Never sand cross-grain or in circles.

Avoid cross-grain sanding on furniture parts made of several pieces of wood with the grain running in different directions. For example, it is best to sand a paneled-type door as follows:

1. First sand panel moldings, if any.

2. Then sand the panel, in straight lines, with the grain.

3. Then sand the top and bottom rails, protecting the side members of opposite grain from scratches by holding a piece of stiff paper at the joint.

4. Finally, sand the side members, protecting the top and bottom rails.

When sanding is complete, dust thoroughly by wiping with a tack rag before applying the next coat of varnish.

High-gloss Finish

It is usually preferred that furniture for use in the house not be finished to a high gloss. There are, however, many articles, such as porch and patio furniture, on which you may wish to have a smooth and glossy finish.

In cases such as these, use a spar-type varnish and leave the final coat unsanded and unrubbed. You will probably need three or more coats to get a good smooth finish.

6-4. A tack rag removes lint and dust before varnishing. Store it in an airtight jar between jobs to keep it from drying out.

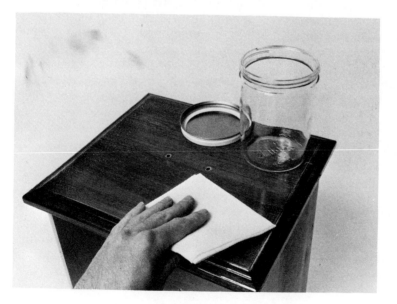

Satin Finish

This finish is the most preferred and used of all the degrees for a final finish. It is a general-purpose finish that is most satisfactory from the standpoint of wear and general appearance. It is adaptable to most types of wooden furniture and other wooden objects and is recommended as a final finish for all antique furniture, except for period furniture and those pieces of fineness or quality of workmanship that have been smoothed with a paste filler and require using a polished rubbed finish.

You can achieve a satin finish by rubbing down a dried glossy varnish or simply by using a satin varnish. The satin varnish will not produce quite so smooth a finish as one that has been rubbed from glossy to satin, but it will come close and requires less work. If you decide to use a satin varnish rather than rubbing, use the satin varnish only for the last coat. Use glossy varnish for all other coats. This will produce a clearer finish.

If you decide to rub a glossy varnish down to a satin luster, here's how to do it:

1. Sand the final coat very lightly with 8/0 to 10/0 wet or dry finishing paper—lubricated with water. This is to remove dust particles, etc., that can be smoothed only by sanding.

2. Rub the surface with 3/0 steel wool, with the grain, until the desired sheen has been obtained.

3. It is best and customary to wax this finish (two coats are best).

Polished Rubbed Finish

This is the pinnacle or acme of all final finishes, except perhaps the French finish, now seldom used. The most sought-for polished rubbed finish is a soft gloss with a high luster. The degree of smoothness of this finish is in direct proportion to the care taken in the application and smoothing of a paste filler and the sanding between coats of varnish.

A polished rubbed finish is seldom used on other than high-quality antique period furniture, or more recently made furniture of fine workmanship and design, made of choice hardwoods. It is customary that such furniture have this finish.

While this finish does require a lot of work, the work is not particularly difficult to master. Care and patience are more important than skill.

In the past, most workers achieved the polished rubbed finish by using materials such as powdered pumice, rottenstone, paraffin oil, and so on. Today these materials are often hard to find. You can do the job more easily using ordinary automotive rubbing compound, such as DuPont number 7, available at all auto supply outlets, many gas stations, and discount-store auto departments.

To achieve the polished rubbed finish:

1. Let the final coat dry thoroughly. This will probably take at least a few days. When it is fully hard, sand it carefully with 400-grit waterproof sandpaper used wet and wrapped around a padded sanding block. Sand carefully until you have knocked all the gloss off the final coat of

6-5. *A high-gloss rubbed finish like this is the ultimate varnish job. It does not require a great deal of skill, just patience and work, as the next two photos show.*

6-6. *A good rubbed varnish job will require several coats of finish. Sand between coats using plenty of water and wet-or-dry paper wrapped around a block. Use 240 grit between coats, switching to 320 before the last coat. When the last coat is dry, sand it smooth with 400-grit paper until it is smooth all over. Then rub with 4/0 steel wool. All this sanding and rubbing will soften the finish slightly, so let it harden for a week before the final step.*

6-7. *After the finish has hardened, rub it with automotive rubbing compound, following directions on the can. This is easier to use than pumice and rottenstone, and available at any auto supply store. Keep rubbing until you get a mirror finish. A desk top may take up to an hour's work.*

varnish, but take care not to sand through the varnish to bare wood.

2. This sanding will probably soften the varnish, so let the varnish harden up again. This will take several days. Do not rush this drying process. If you rub the varnish too soon it will look smooth for a while, then slowly start to show the grain beneath it as the finish hardens and shrinks even further. Then you will have to sand and rub again. This is not only extra work but presents the danger of cutting through to bare wood, necessitating starting the whole process over again.

3. When the sanded finish is completely hard you can begin rubbing. You can use clean rags, but for flat surfaces heavy felt glued to a wooden block is preferred. You can buy this felt—about ¼ inch thick—from Constantine's. To do the rubbing, dampen the rag or felt, place a small blob of the rubbing compound on the surface to be rubbed, and start rubbing. Work with the grain, not across it, and not in circles. As you rub, the flat, dull surface of the sanded varnish will begin to take on a gloss. This takes time, so be patient. Add fresh rubbing compound as needed and keep rubbing until the surface of the varnish is smooth as glass. A small tabletop may require about a half-hour of work before it reaches its full luster. That's a lot of rubbing, but when you see the results you will agree that the work was worthwhile.

4. If you want an even smoother, more polished finish, follow this rubbing with another, using an automotive paste wax containing fine abrasives. When you have finished this final rubbing, the surface of the finish will feel silky smooth and you will be able to see your reflection in it, although it will have not the cheap, flashy gloss of an unsanded gloss varnish but the deep, rich look of quality.

Polyurethane Finishes

In addition to conventional furniture varnishes, there are several other synthetic clear coatings that are sometimes used for furniture. Of these finishes, the clear, oil-modified urethanes, such as the polyurethane finishes, are the most popular, because they are highly resistant to abrasion, scratching, water, chemicals, grease, solvents, food stains, alcohol, and oils.

Polyurethane finishes may be applied to bare wood (new, or wood with its old finish removed) that is smooth and free of dust and grease, or over a varnish finish that has been cleaned and deglossed. Do *not* apply a polyurethane finish over a shellac or lacquer finish, sanding sealer, or a paste wood or liquid filler unless especially formulated for polyurethane finishes.

Despite their toughness, the urethanes suffer from adhesion problems. They do not bond chemically to any other finish, including themselves. Adhesion is based solely on a mechanical bond, best achieved by thorough sanding between coats to provide good tooth for the new coat to grip.

To apply polyurethane finish to bare wood, *follow label directions to the letter*. Pay special attention to recoat intervals:

recoating too soon can cause wrinkling; too late can hurt adhesion.

SHELLAC FINISH

For years, shellac was a favored finish of home handymen because it was quick drying and quite easy to apply. In recent times, the so-called modern finishes—the synthetic varnishes and penetrating wood sealers—have replaced it to a degree, but for many purposes shellac still is a fine finish. For instance, it is perfect for chairs, settees, benches, desks, display racks, picture and mirror frames, clocks, etc. It is better not to use it on such items as tables, stands, chests, cabinets, bureaus, etc., on which may be placed articles that are hot or contain water or alcoholic beverages, since shellac stains easily and white rings develop when wet glasses, vases, etc., are placed on it.

Almost any kind of wood may be finished with shellac, but it is more complimentary to pine and the lighter-colored woods, particularly when white and orange shellacs are mixed to just the right shade to do justice to the wood involved, in which case it intensifies the wood colors.

The main reason why a shellac finish is so easy to apply is that in a correct mixture it is greatly thinned with alcohol. Many amateurs (and some professionals) attempt to hasten the work by applying shellac that is too thick. The result is a botched job, unsightly in appearance. Also, many people apply a succeeding coat before the previous one has dried thoroughly, fail to rub surfaces between coats, and often leave the last coat glossy, instead of removing the shine and applying wax.

The Material

Shellac is made from the secretion of the lac insect. Proper thinning of the shellac purchased in commercial mixtures is a vital part of its correct application.

The concentration of shellac in alcohol is known as its cut. Most shellac on the market is 4-, 4½-, or 5-pound cut; that is, 4, 4½, or 5 pounds of granular shellac are dissolved in 1 gallon of alcohol. The cut is indicated on the label. For almost all purposes, commercial shellac will require thinning with alcohol. The accompanying table shows how to convert one cut to another.

DILUTION TABLE FOR REDUCING SHELLAC TO DESIRED CUT

ORIGINAL CUT	DESIRED CUT	MIXING PARTS* ALCOHOL	RATIO PARTS* SHELLAC
5 lb.	3 lb.	1	2
5 lb.	2 lb.	1	1
5 lb.	1 lb.	2	1
4 lb.	3 lb.	2	1
4 lb.	2 lb.	3	4
4 lb.	1 lb.	2	1
3 lb.	2 lb.	2	5
3 lb.	1 lb.	4	3

*"Parts" refers to liquid volume. Any convenient unit, such as pints or cupfuls, can be used. Proportions given are not precise, since minor variations in the resulting cut will have little or no effect on the final results.

Using the table, you will be able to convert any quantity. That is, the proportions are the same even if you are thinning only a pint of shellac. For example, if you wished to thin a pint of 4-pound cut (the best cut for general use) to a 2-pound cut, you would use ¾ pint of alcohol to 1 pint of shellac. When thinning the cut, use only pure denatured ethyl or grain alcohol—never use acetone, gasoline, benzol, or the antifreeze grade of alcohol.

Before you use shellac, shake or stir it thoroughly. The first two coats should be thinned to 2-pound-cut consistency, whereas a 3- or 4-pound cut is best for final cut.

Shellac is available in three types: orange, bleached (or white), and dewaxed. Orange shellac has a pronounced reddish-brown color and is cloudy in appearance. White or bleached shellac is a similar solution, but it is made from bleached resin. It looks milky in the container, but dries nearly colorless. Dewaxed shellac is usually light in color, but unlike the other two it is wax-free and thus perfectly clear.

The three forms are very much alike. However, white shellac is best for most work and is essential for blond finishes. Orange shellac is used for dark wood or over darkly stained woods. Intermixing white and orange shellac to obtain color effects isn't advisable. Should deeper colors be desired to tone a finish where the stain doesn't seem exactly right, a transparent toner, which can be made by mixing alcohol-soluble powder stain with alcohol and adding it to the shellac as required, may be used. The same method can be used to darken lacquer and varnish finishes, using lacquer- and varnish-soluble powder respectively.

One fault of shellac is that in time it goes stale. About a year after it has been made, a chemical change causes the shellac to become so gummy that it will not dry. For this reason, shellac should be purchased in small amounts as needed, from a store where there is good turnover. Good shellac is usually sold in dated containers so you can judge its freshness.

Satin Rubbed Finish

This finish is ideal for most furniture or other wood articles. It is perfect for the cruder type of furniture and pieces made of pine and other light-colored woods on which it is advisable to use a little orange shellac for added color. Here are some points to remember about applying shellac to obtain a satin rubbed finish:

1. Apply enough coats (usually four or more) of the shellac mixture so that the last one shines. Allow time for each coat to dry thoroughly (the first will dry much faster than the later ones). Test for dryness by trying to make a thumbprint.

2. Sanding between coats is not required for good adhesion, but whenever roughness is felt with the fingertips, rub the surface (with the grain) between coats, using #400 abrasive paper. Dust with a brush and wipe the surface with a cloth after each coat.

3. Allow several hours for the last coat to dry completely (overnight is preferred), then rub it with 3/0 steel wool until there is absolutely *no* shine remaining. It is important to shake the shellac dust from the pads of steel wool and refold them, as steel wool becomes dull with use. Too much rubbing in one spot causes heat from friction, softens the finish, and tends to roll it up. Use great care at corners and edges to avoid cutting through the finish. When many minute bright spots still remain on a surface after the gloss has been removed by rubbing it with steel wool, sprinkle the surface with dry 2/0 pumice stone and brush it lightly. Use a small hand scrub brush with soft bristles on flat surfaces, and an old shaving brush (held by the bristles) on carvings, angles, etc. When the spots have disappeared, give the entire surface another light rubbing with steel wool.

4. Dust and wipe off the surface. Then apply at least two coats of wax. (See "Waxing and Polishing," page 218.)

Polished Rubbed Finish

This finish is for high-grade furniture that calls for extreme smoothness and high polish. Surfaces should be completely smoothed with a paste filler before this finish is applied. Here is how to accomplish a polished rubbed finish with shellac:

1. Apply enough coats of the shellac mixture (usually six or more) that the last coat shines. Allow each coat to dry thoroughly. Test for dryness by trying to make a thumbprint.

2. Rub the surface (with the grain) between coats, using a #400 abrasive paper dipped in a linseed oil mixture (half raw linseed oil and half pure turpentine) whenever the slightest roughness is felt with the fingertips after the first few coats. When you can notice the finish beginning to build up toward the final coat (or to shine), rub the surface between each coat using pumice and the linseed oil mixture. Rub carvings and moldings lightly with a small hand scrub brush with soft bristles, dipped first in the oil and then in the pumice. Turnings may first be rubbed with the steel wool dipped in the oil mixture and then a 3/F pumice.

3. After each rubbing, wipe the surface clean with rags and allow a few hours for it to dry completely.

4. When the last coat shines, first rub the surface (with the grain) with 3/0 steel wool dipped in the linseed oil mixture, taking only a few strokes and gradually working across the area, until you believe the entire surface is completely dulled. Then sprinkle the surface with dry pumice, dip the rubbing pad in the oil mixture, and rub the surface lengthwise (with the grain), taking long, even strokes, until the entire surface is polished. Wipe off and examine for shiny spots. These should be rubbed without addition of more pumice. When the entire surface has been completed, wipe it off with soft rags and allow to dry completely. When a highly polished finish is desired, it may be obtained by a final rubbing with rottenstone and the oil mixture after the surface has been completely cleaned, following the use of the pumice.

5. Apply at least two coats of wax.

French Finish

The French finish dates back at least

three centuries and is the finest finish known—probably the most beautiful of all. This finish is acquired with shellac and raw linseed oil, building up coat after coat. The work is painstaking and tedious. It requires time, patience, and skill. You are here given but a brief outline of how the work is done, from the standpoint of knowledge rather than for practical use, as most refinishers hold this finish in high regard. It is sometimes called the "lost art" of finishes.

The finish must be applied to woods that are extremely smooth, whether or not they are filled, and over a water stain.

Thin shellac with alcohol to the consistency of water and apply with an old nylon stocking made into a ball, squeezing out a little of the material at a time.

Dip the pad in the shellac solution and apply with straight strokes. As soon as it's dry, continue to apply more coats until a sheen or gloss is acquired. If cracks appear on the surface, sprinkle on a little pumice stone and rub. Then apply more coats of the shellac until the cracks are filled.

Allow time for the surface to dry completely. Then put only a few drops of raw linseed oil on the pad, and rub with a circular motion over the entire area, adding a few more drops of the oil as needed. When a high polish is seen, add no more oil, but continue rubbing until the surface is thoroughly dry. Allow to stand overnight, and repeat the rubbing with the oil.

This hard and rugged process will give a high polish. It can't be had by rubbing a surface with so-called French polish.

OIL FINISH

An oil finish is one of the oldest for hard or close-grained woods. It produces a rich color that is considered by many to be the most beautiful of all finishes. It is particularly good for tables and furniture that may be easily spotted or scratched. When this finish is properly applied, the wood is impervious to water, heat, scratches, and most stains. The furniture may be used during the process of finishing, which may take up to a year to complete. The finish requires no waxing when sufficiently oiled and rubbed. The oil finish may overdarken some woods, so test it before finishing.

Applying Oil Finish

The old-fashioned oil finish is accomplished by using a mixture of two-thirds (commercially) boiled linseed oil and one-third pure turpentine. As we will see later, there are modern oils that have certain advantages over linseed oil and that have largely replaced it. But for those who like to do things the old way, here's how to do a linseed oil finish:

1. The wood must be free from any old finish, repaired, sanded, wiped with a dry cloth, and then tack ragged.

2. Apply the mixture (hot or cold) generously with a rag and rub into a limited surface for 10 to 20 minutes. A hot mixture penetrates more quickly but produces a darker color. It should never be applied hot to carvings or grooved parts, as it sets too quickly. When applied hot, the mix-

ture should be heated in a double boiler to prevent ignition.

3. Wipe off all excess oil with soft, lintless cloths, taking care to get it out of all crevices or carvings, as excess oil becomes sticky or hardens quickly. It must then be removed with alcohol or a commercial paint and varnish remover.

4. Rub each surface vigorously (one area at a time) with a hard polishing cloth for 10 to 20 minutes. This rubbing with a hard cloth develops heat by friction and is essential in bringing out a luster.

5. From five to about twenty coats of the oil mixture should be applied as directed above. The process is repeated until no dull spots remain. Allow at least two days between the first two coats (in warm weather), and from a week to a month between later coats. Each coat must be dried before another is applied. If it isn't, the following coat will become sticky. Test a surface by holding a hand on it for several minutes. If the surface is oily, it is not dry enough for the next coat. Repeat oiling once or twice a year to keep the furniture in good condition. Oil table leaves *on the underside* as often as on the top, to prevent warping.

If the grain of the wood is raised with oiling, rub the wood until smooth with 3/0 steel wool. If the oil hardens in the crevices, remove it with a paint remover.

It must always be remembered that oiled rags are easily combustible. To prevent fire, they should be burned or washed soon after being used. Should there be any delay, spread them out flat or hang them on a line. If left too long they will harden. Store the rag that was used for applying the mixture in the container with any unused portion of the mixture.

Quick-Method Oil Finish

Here's a quick, four-coat oil finish that may be employed for those who don't wish the long procedure for the regular oil finish:

First coat Apply one-third *raw* linseed oil and two-thirds turpentine. Allow 24 hours to dry.

Second coat Apply pure *boiled* linseed oil (purchase commercially boiled linseed oil). Dry 24 hours.

Third coat Apply *boiled* linseed oil, and dry 24 hours.

Fourth coat Mix and apply half *boiled* linseed oil and half japan drier.

While applying, watch closely for any tackiness and rub off with burlap. Complete the finish by rubbing with pumice and oil, then with 3/0 steel wool in the manner described on pages 148 and 149.

Modern Oil Finishes

There are several so-called modern oil finishes (Watco is an example) available at paint stores that are easy to apply and offer the following advantages:

1. They resemble the mellow satin luster of old oil-type finishes that required hours of hand rubbing.

2. They accent the beauty of natural grain patterns; finish and appearance improve with age and use.

3. They saturate the wood and fill and

6-8. A modern oil finish is far superior to old linseed oil. It is easy to apply, looks good, and has great durability. It is even easy to repair if necessary.

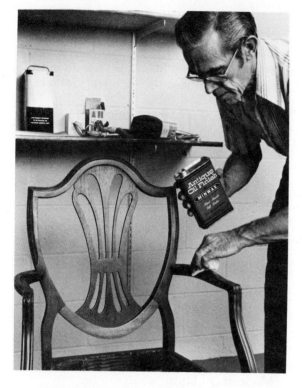

seal pores; therefore, water spots, stains, and even minor burns may be steel wooled away and the spot retouched with the oil finish.

4. They dry and solidify to provide a permanent finish needing only occasional reapplication.

5. They do not gum up in warm temperatures or feel greasy.

To apply these natural wood oil finishes (for wood with beauty in grain and color):

1. Pour the oil as it comes from the can

on the surface and spread uniformly with a lintless cloth or roller; or dampen a lintless cloth with oil and apply to the surface.

2. Allow the oil to penetrate the surface for a few minutes.

3. Wipe the excess off, leaving the surface dry (to prevent dust particles adhering).

4. Allow 6 hours or more between coats. Three coats may be sufficient for most surfaces except dining table tops and chair arms.

5. Allow the final coat to dry 24 hours before using.

PENETRATING WOOD-SEALER FINISHES

Penetrating oil finishes, like linseed oil, have long been used to beautify and preserve gun stocks and other fine woods. Penetrating *resin-oil* finishes are a second generation in this family of finishes and preservers. They actually improve the wood permanently without hours of hand rubbing; a simple application imparts to the surface a lustrous hand-rubbed look that is long lasting, seldom needs replenishing, and never needs resanding.

The exciting thing about this finish is that anyone can do it. It doesn't run, no tell-tale application marks are left behind, and no dirt or bugs can stick and stay in the finish. You get this beautifully rich wood finish by simply wetting the wood, waiting until penetration stops, and drying the surface. Resin-oil finishes withstand stains, watermarks, minor burns, and scratches. Should damage occur, it doesn't necessarily mean ruin, since the finish may be steel wooled, replenished with more penetrating resin oil, and become good as new. Old-style surface finishes cannot be repaired so easily. The use of penetrating resin-oil finishes is surprising to anyone familiar with lacquer and varnish. It is quite an experience.

Besides beauty, the resin-oil finish has other important qualities. Once application has been completed, the wood is ready for immediate use. There is no sticky surface to dry. After about a month, the resin oil will have turned to a tough but flexible solid mass inside the wood that effectively preserves it. The wood will have become harder and will have remarkable dimensional stability. There is less shrinkage or expansion in extremely hot or cold weather and little or no warping, even in unusually wet climates. Wood-boring insects cannot enter, and decay and fungus are kept out.

Choose the sealer to suit your purpose, one resistant to heat and cold for dining table tops, for instance. Read the labels carefully, and follow the manufacturer's directions. The available literature on these products generally states that they are made from a base of synthetic resin or tung oil (obtained from tung trees, mainly found in China but grown in some southern states, and valuable for quick drying, penetration, and hardness). Some of the mixtures contain varnish, others plastics. Read the label and literature and ask the salesperson for the best type for your use. The best all-around types usually contain tung oils plus alkyd resins.

Applying a Sealer Finish

Apply the penetrating sealer within 12 hours after smoothing the wood, or 24 hours after applying stain. Before applying the finish, wipe the surface with a dry cloth, then a tack rag.

Strain the sealer each time it is used by stretching a piece of nylon stocking over the top of the open can. Dip a clean, lintless cloth (rayon or nylon fabric) into the sealer that wells up through the nylon stocking. Apply the sealer to the wood with a cloth.

For the first coat:

1. Apply the sealer with a cloth to one section at a time. Use a circular motion, working across the wood grain. Immediately remove all surplus sealer, wiping with the grain, before applying sealer on the next section.

2. Rub the sealer in and off with your hands. The warmth of your hands helps the sealer to penetrate into the wood. Rubbing removes the air bubbles and ensures even lapping of the finish.

3. Apply the sealer to any rungs on the piece, using another piece of nylon stocking or fabric. Wipe the surplus away immediately with your hands. Remove the surplus sealer from the edges and carvings with your fingers.

4. Don't let a heavy, glasslike coating of sealer build up on the surface. Wipe off any excess that is not absorbed. Allow the sealer to dry 24 hours.

5. Before applying the next coat, and before every succeeding coat, smooth the surface gently with 3/0 steel wool. This removes the bubbles and makes "tooth" for

1.   2.

6-9. *Applying a penetrating wood-sealer finish:*
1. After sanding, apply a quick-dry nonsealing
alcohol- or water-based stain with a clean cloth
or brush. 2. Let the stain dry for about 45 min-
utes, then pour on liberal amounts of the pene-
trating oil-resin finish. 3. Allow to soak for about
30 minutes, or until penetration stops, keeping
the surface uniformly wet.

3.

4.   5

6.

(Figure 6-9 continued)
4. This is the most important step of all. Wipe the surface completely dry, using a soft, absorbent cloth. 5. For more luster, let dry 4 hours, then wet-sand lightly with a small amount of resin-oil finish. 6. After wet-sanding, dry wood thoroughly with a clean cloth, then polish briskly with another cloth.

the next coat. Wipe the surface with a dry cloth and then with a tack rag.

For the second coat, apply the sealer as for the first coat. Rub the sealer on, in, and off. When smoothing and for extreme smoothness on dark woods, use crocus cloth. (Crocus cloth is coated with jeweler's rouge—iron oxide—which tints light woods a reddish color that cannot be removed.) Wrap the crocus cloth around a smoothing block for wide surfaces. Crocus cloth may be obtained from hardware stores.

For succeeding coats, apply the sealer as for previous coats. Apply several coats to the undersides of table leaves and the insides of drawers. Allow each coat to dry 24 hours in good drying weather—36 hours or more if humidity is high. Then rub the surface lightly with 3/0 steel wool. Wipe with a dry cloth, then a tack rag.

Continue to apply finish coats until no dull spots appear. For an even, satinlike smoothness and a hard finish, apply three to five coats on chairs or legs of a piece. Apply nine to twenty-one coats of finish on dining and coffee table tops, depending on the degree of smoothness you desire and the intended use. Let the final coat dry 1 week. For extreme smoothness on dining table tops and similar surfaces, rub the surface when thoroughly dry with 500-A silicon carbide abrasive paper and a mild soap (not detergent) solution. Dip the 500-A silicon carbide abrasive paper in the warm soap solution and wrap around a smoothing block. Smooth gently with the grain, but not on the edges. When the abrasive begins to drag, dip in the soapy water again, then proceed with the rubbing as described.

For a handsome satin finish, you can eliminate the rubbing. Simply wait about 4 hours—preferably overnight—after drying the surface of excess resin oil, then, using a small amount of resin-oil finish or carnauba (palm oil) stain wax as a lubricant, wet sand lightly with superfine paper, wait about 10 minutes, and wipe clean and dry. Polish with a soft cloth.

If you have trouble finding a good resin sealer, you can easily mix your own. Use 1 part *boiled* linseed oil or tung oil, 2 parts alkyd varnish, and 3 parts turpentine. Mix and let stand overnight before use.

LACQUER FINISH

Lacquer has generally replaced varnish and shellac as finishes in the furniture-making field as well as in custom finishing because it is easy to spray and dries quickly for fast production. But for the home handyman, the lacquer system of finishing isn't widely used because spray equipment is necessary. Several so-called brushing lacquers are available, but even these are a bit tricky to brush on smoothly.

Lacquer offers a hard, durable, waterproof surface that is able to withstand high heat without becoming sticky. A lacquered surface is transparent, enhances the colors over which it is laid, and brings out the beauty of the wood grain when a natural finish is desired. It also tends to darken woods less than other types of finishes. Some varieties of lacquer are resistant to acids and alcohol—ideal for bars and tabletops.

Lacquer is the fastest-drying finish ever developed. The drying time is 1½ to 2 hours, as compared with the quick-dry paints, varnishes, and enamels, which require at least 4 hours. But due to its speed in drying, the best way to apply lacquer is by spraying. This produces an even coat unmarred by brushmarks. When applied with a brush, the lacquer must be "slowed up" to prevent marking and sagging.

Before applying lacquer, the wood surface must be perfectly smooth and ready for the final finish. But before discussing the application of lacquer, two words of warning:

1. Lacquer is extremely flammable, and all precautions should be taken to prevent fire and explosion. Make sure there are no lighted cigarettes, pilot lights, etc., in the room.

2. Dust in the air from sanding, floating lint, etc., will ruin your work. Clean up well before you begin to apply lacquer.

Spraying Technique

The best spraying method requires a pressure of 30 to 40 pounds. As a rule, with a spray gun of this pressure a single coat will suffice. When the air pressure is lower, the lacquer must be thinned to a point where two or more coats will be necessary.

Before beginning the spraying job, be sure the equipment is clean, and make sure it works properly by trying a test pattern on waste material. A heavy-centered pattern indicates too much liquid weight, which is corrected by thinning or increasing the air pressure. A "peanut"-shaped pattern results from clogging of the gun. Rotate the tip of the gun, and if the pattern rotates, clean the air cap. If the pattern remains the same, clean the fluid line. Too much air pressure sometimes results in a split pattern.

Handling a paint sprayer is an art that comes quickly with practice. Apply the spray in even lines across the surface, moving the sprayer parallel with the work rather than turning the spray head from side to side in an arc, which will produce an unsatisfactory wavy surface. Some common errors in spraying with lacquer are dry spots from holding the gun too far from the work; sags from too heavy a fluid mixture in the gun, or from lack of speed in applying, or from holding the gun too long in one place; and pinholes produced by holding the gun too close to the work or by using too much pressure, which blasts the area already covered. More on spray-gun techniques can be found in Chapter Ten.

Furniture-finishing lacquer is now available in aerosol pressure cans. For full details on operating these cans, see pages 234–38.

Brushing Technique

As stated earlier, there are a number of slower-drying lacquers prepared especially for application by brushing. However, with a bit of skill, and by cutting down on the quantity of thinner, almost

6-10. *Applying a brushing lacquer:* 1. *The first step after preparing the surface is application of the desired color stain. Apply along the grain and wipe off excess with a cloth.* 2. *After the stain has dried, apply the first coat of lacquer. A large brush is best, as lacquer dries rapidly. Apply along the grain.* 3. *Rub each lacquer coat lightly with fine steel wool wadded into a ball and frequently turned inside out. Use even pressure.* 4. *Rub the final coat of lacquer (and there may be from three to five coats) with blooming oil and fine-grit waterproof sand-paper.*

1.

2.

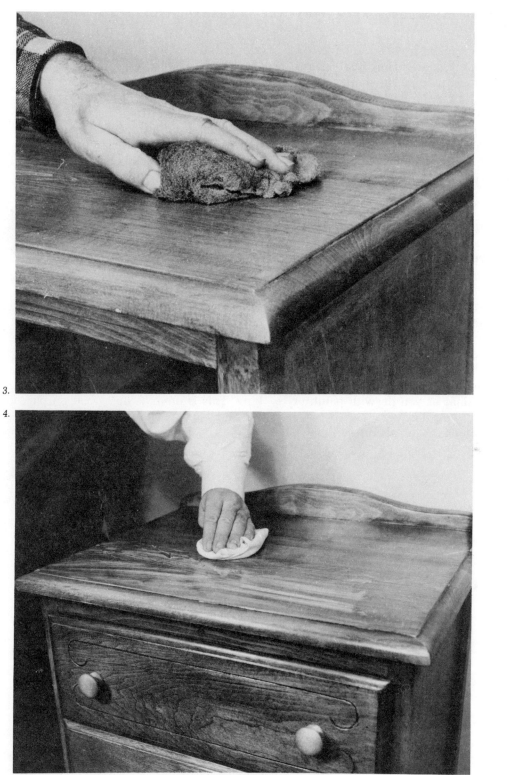

3.

4.

any lacquer can be brushed on. Just remember that you are using the fastest-drying finish available. The more thinner used, the quicker the drying process becomes. Speed in application is essential, and mistakes are hard to correct.

With that thought in mind, first look to your brush. A cheap one won't do. If bristles drop out, they are hard to retrieve from a lacquer surface without marring the work. Nylon bristles can sometimes dissolve in lacquer thinners, so avoid them. A good brush is a must.

When you buy lacquer, buy twice as much thinner. Some will go to thin the lacquer for application. More will be needed to keep the brush in shape, and still more for "mopping up" spots and sticky fingers.

To apply, fill a container half full of the lacquer. Add your thinner. Then soak the ends of the brush thoroughly in the mixture, but do not rub off excess on the rim of the container as you do with paint, or the quick-drying lacquer will become sticky and foul the brush on successive trips to the container. Instead, squeeze off any excess against the inner side of the container.

Make your brush strokes bold and rapid. Carry each stroke as far as you can go without running out the lacquer into thin, separate lines. Overlap prior strokes slightly. If the surface is large, work from opposite ends, blending the strokes in the center.

When putting lacquer on uneven surfaces, such as beading and carving, take care not to allow the lacquer to accumulate in the hollows. Pick up the excess with the tip of the brush.

Once you've finished the lacquer application, let the work stand for 24 to 48 hours. Then for the final process—rubbing.

The lacquered surface upon drying is hard, brilliantly glossy. Most people prefer it reduced to a satinlike quality by rubbing. This is done as described on pages 148 and 149.

seven

Painted Finishes for Furniture

During the past three centuries, many styles or pieces of furniture were painted rather than finished with oil, shellac, lacquer, varnish, or wax. In some instances, however, lacquer and varnish may have been colored to give a painted appearance. Painted finishes made it possible to obtain a uniform appearance from woods of different color, grain, or unequal quality used in one piece; they also helped to preserve the wood, and they provided a background for such ornamentation as freehand painting, stenciling, and gilding.

Painted furniture in America was influenced by English cabinetmakers and architects, French monarchs, designs from ancient Greece and Rome, lacquerwork from the Orient, and the creative ability of early American cabinetmakers and individuals. Today it's not necessary to be a professional or experienced person to paint furniture. But the furniture should be worth the energy, patience, and time spent in applying the painted finish.

In general, there are three reasons for painting furniture:

1. Some furniture styles were painted originally and may need repainting. Such styles include variations of the following: Louis XV and XVI furniture; Italian seventeenth- and eighteenth-century furniture; Sheraton fancy chairs; Windsor and Hitchcock chairs and rockers; and Pennsylvania German furniture.

2. Many new unfinished pieces of furniture are available, but may lack beauty of color and grain and look better painted than they do with a natural finish. Such pieces are made of pine, poplar, or beech and come knocked down or assembled.

3. The appearance of some furniture may be improved by painting. Such furniture may include Mission-style and late Victorian pieces, and furniture that has been damaged by stain or wear.

PAINT SELECTION

Alkyd resin-base enamel is the most satisfactory paint for wood furniture. It provides a hard, durable finish that is resistant to wear, water, marring, and chipping. Do *not* use latex-base paint and polyvinyl acetate-base paint on wood furniture. Water in these paints raises the grain of the wood, making it difficult to achieve a smooth finish. Also, water-base finishes often remain slightly soft and tacky for weeks or even longer.

There are two basic types of paints used in furniture work:

Undercoat, which may be labeled undercoat, flat, or primer, depending on the brand. It should have no gloss and is used as the undercoat for the final finish. An undercoat used alone won't provide adequate wearing qualities.

Finish coat, which may be a high-gloss, semigloss, or satin enamel. High-gloss enamel has a high luster and gives the hardest and most durable finish. Check the brand label for specific wearing qualities. Semigloss or satin enamel gives a low-luster finish, usually less durable than a high gloss.

A beautiful enameled finish may be obtained by rubbing down the last coat to a fine and soft polish with pumice or rottenstone and water or with automotive rubbing compound. This is accomplished by the same method as used for varnish. (See "Polished Rubbed Finish," page 149.) This finish may be obtained only after several thin coats of enamel have been applied and sanded lightly after each coat with #320 waterproof abrasive paper. The use

of a paste filler before the undercoat also helps give a perfectly smooth finish.

When selecting paint for small children's furniture, make sure that it contains no ingredients that would be harmful if chewed or swallowed by them. If a paint contains even small amounts of lead, antimony, arsenic, cadmium, mercury, selenium, or soluble barium, it is not advisable to use it on children's furniture. These poisonous elements are no longer allowed in modern paints but may be present in old paints kept on hand from years ago. If in doubt, buy new paint.

Color Selection

When selecting paint color for a piece of furniture, look for one that will harmonize with other furnishings in the room and with the room interior. The color may be chosen from a picture, the draperies, rug, wallpaper, or other accessories. But, when selecting color from paint chips, remember that most colors are lovely in small areas. Applied to large areas, these same colors may be too intense, dull, dark, or light. Also, paint colors change in intensity or value when they dry. Flat paints dry lighter than they were when wet, and enamels dry darker.

Also consider the size of the furniture, its location, and the background provided by the wall. Furniture painted the same color as the wall will seem a part of the background; if painted a contrasting color, it will stand out and attract attention.

Select the paint of a reliable manufacturer and buy from a reputable dealer. Colors are available as follows:

Ready-mixed paints can be purchased in a variety of colors to harmonize with interiors. If these are unsatisfactory, many dealers will mix paints from formulas supplied by paint companies.

Formula-mixed paints can be purchased in large paint stores. The formulas are prepared by manufacturers on paint chips. After the customer selects the desired color from the paint chip, the dealer mixes it at the store on a special machine.

Mix-your-own paints begin with a base coat of white or a color. To obtain the desired tint or shade, use colors in oil; these may be purchased at paint or art stores. Keep a record of the amount of each color used for each sample chip. Look at each paint sample where it will be used—both by sunlight and incandescent or fluorescent light.

Be sure to purchase enough paint for at least two coats each of undercoat and finish—especially if the color is mixed at the store. Four coats may not be necessary for every piece of furniture, but sometimes it is difficult to match paints if they are specially mixed. Be sure to remember that, if mixing paint colors, use one brand, one kind, and one type. Each manufacturer has his own formula. Never mix different brands or kinds of paints.

SURFACE PREPARATION

The surface of furniture (or other articles) to be enameled is one of three classes, namely:

1. Bare wood that has never been painted.

2. An old finish in good condition.

3. An old finish that is cracked or damaged.

Hardware should be removed, if possible, before applying the remover or paint. Its removal will prevent possible damage to the hardware and alleviate tedious work during the paint removal, smoothing, and painting processes.

Old finish, if cracked, chipped, sticky, rough, or too thick, should be removed with paint and varnish remover. Small chipped areas can be smoothed with abrasive paper and/or carefully touched up with undercoat several times. If the old finish is in good condition but very soiled, wash the surface with detergent and water. Use mineral spirits or gum turpentine on a cloth to remove grease and old wax. Allow the piece to dry 24 hours before applying new paint.

New wood should have the hair grain removed or controlled to obtain a smooth surface for painting. Wipe the entire surface with a cloth dampened in clear water. Dry for 24 hours, then smooth with very fine and extra-fine-grit abrasive papers folded over a padded smoothing block.

New unfinished furniture, especially pine, needs sealing to prevent knots and sappy spots from bleeding through painted finishes. Follow the subsequent directions for sealing. If these methods do not stop the sap, the wood is improperly cured and will continue to bleed until it dries out over a period of months.

Knots, sappy spots, mahogany-stained varnish, inks, and other stains often bleed through painted surfaces, if not sealed.

Sealer Method

Apply two coats of clear modified or white-pigmented shellac-base sealer (such as BIN) with a brush to resinous or stained areas. Follow the directions on the can for drying between coats. Smooth lightly between each coat. White-pigmented shellac sealer also serves to prime and mask the wood. Clean the brush with alcohol solvent or ammonia.

Filling Holes and Cracks

Holes and cracks should be filled with filling compound such as wood dough, plastic forming wood, surfacing putty, or spackling compound. Automotive body filler is another good material for filling under paints. The two-part polyester sets up in minutes, does not shrink, and sands well. Do not use water-base fillers in large holes and gouges. The water in the filler may cause the wood around the filler to swell and expand, and when the wood dries it will shrink and pull away from the filler. Apply the filler with a spatula or putty knife. When dry, smooth level with fine-grit abrasive paper.

Coarse- or open-grained woods—such as oak, chestnut, and ash—need filling before paint is applied. Mix a small amount of paste wood filler with gum turpentine to thin, if necessary. Apply across the grain with a stubby brush. As the filler starts to dry, giving a dull, flat appearance, rub off the excess filler with a piece of burlap, going across the grain. Don't rub with the grain, because this will pull the filler out of the open pores. Dry for 24 hours. It may be necessary to repeat this process two or three times to completely fill the open grain to a level surface.

Removing Dents and Bruises

Dents and bruises can be removed from bare wood by putting several layers of damp woolen cloth over the surface and pressing with a hot iron. Moisture causes the wood to swell and rise to normal height. It may be necessary to repeat this process. If the dent can't be removed, fill it as you would a hole or crack. Do not use this method on veneer.

If no surface repairs are necessary before applying the first coat of paint, smooth bare wood or previously painted surfaces with #220 abrasive paper and a sanding block. Always smooth in one direction. Use steel wool on curved surfaces. Remove sanding dust with a tack rag.

STEPS IN ENAMELING

An enamel is actually a pigmented varnish, so its application procedures and brushing techniques are basically the same as described in Chapter Six on varnishing.

As with all finishes, plan the order of painting so that the piece may be picked up and turned without marring the fresh enamel. That is, when painting furniture always do the hard-to-reach parts first— legs, cross spindles, and the back of the chair—then proceed to accessible parts.

To finish a chair, proceed as follows:

1. Begin by turning the chair upside down and placing the seat of the chair on a table or box. Paint all bottom surfaces of the seat, legs, and back.

2. Then stand the chair upright on its legs and do all the top surfaces, finishing with the seat.

To finish a table, proceed as follows:

1. Begin by turning the table upside down and painting the bottom and its edges.

2. Then paint the legs, doing the inner sides first.

3. Finish the legs with smooth strokes lengthwise.

4. When enameling turned or round legs or braces, brush around them; do *not* attempt to finish with smooth strokes lengthwise.

5. Now turn the table right side up and do all the top edges.

6. Finish the tabletop last, applying the enamel across the table width. Smooth the entire surface with light brushing along the table length, using only the tip of the brush to achieve an even finish.

To finish a cabinet or a chest, proceed as follows:

1. For dressers, buffets, and cabinets that have drawers, remove the drawers. Take off handles and knobs. Do the drawers separately.

2. Paint the molding (if any) surrounding the panels, then paint the panels, picking up any runs or sags at the corners.

3. Paint the frame and top. Finish the top and panel surfaces with cross brushing.

4. Begin the drawers by enameling a side about 6 inches back. Do all the edges. Then finish the front panel (do the interior of the drawer first, if desired). Stack until dry.

First Coat:
Undercoat

Thoroughly mix the undercoat. It's a good idea to tint the undercoat to approximately the same color as your final finish. To keep the paint as free as possible of dirt and dust, pour a small amount into a container for immediate use.

Dip the brush in the paint to about one-third of its bristle length. Work the paint through the bristles by brushing back and forth on clean paper. Dip the brush in the paint again and wipe off the excess. Apply the paint to the surface, brushing in all directions. Then "tip off" by removing excess paint from the brush. Hold the brush at a right angle to the surface. Brush in one direction only—with the grain—gently skimming the freshly painted surface to remove any excess paint and to level the painted surface. Do not paint too large an area at one time. Dry 24 hours or more.

Between First and Second Coat

Smooth lightly with 320-grit abrasive paper and a smoothing block. Waterproof abrasive paper and water may be used on painted surfaces for more rapid smoothing. Dry.

Second Coat:
Undercoat, Semigloss, or Gloss

Sometimes it is necessary to apply a second undercoat to dark surfaces. But if this is not necessary, the surface is now ready for the first coat of satin, semigloss, or high-gloss enamel.

Semigloss and high-gloss enamels should not be stirred rapidly, because bubbles form that are difficult to remove from the painted surface. Stir the paint slowly but thoroughly. Apply the paint in the same manner as for the undercoat. Do not overbrush. While wet, enamel will "level" itself. Do a small section at a time and work rapidly.

Between Second and Final Coats

Let the surface dry, then smooth. The gloss must be cut to make "tooth" for the next coat of paint. Use the same smoothing method as before.

Final Coat

Follow the directions as for the preceding coats. Drying and thorough curing may take several days to two weeks, depending upon the weather and the paint used.

Final Rub

If a satin or low-luster finish is desired rather than a high gloss, use a satin enamel. For a high-quality gloss finish,

1.

2.

7-1. Steps in enameling furniture: 1. All finishing work starts with sanding, by either hand or power. 2. Apply both undercoat and the enamel from the inside out, starting with hard-to-reach points, then the sides, then the top, and edges last.

3.   4.

5.   6.

(Figure 7-1 continued)
3. *The wide brush is held at an angle, enamel being applied with even strokes. Always follow along the grain lines of the wood.* 4. *Most important—the stroke should continue out past the end of the surface. Hold the brush at a near-right angle, and move in steady strokes.* 5. *Excess enamel should be picked up by the brush to keep it from filling grooves or other recesses in the piece being finished.* 6. *Removable trim: knobs and hardware are removed and enameled separately.*

use a glossy enamel and rub it. Use the same procedures you would to rub varnish.

ANTIQUED FINISH

Antiquing over enamel is a glaze or toner coat used to obtain a mellow or soft appearance that will simulate great age. The finish is achieved by a glaze coat colored with oil colors applied over a basecoat enamel in a lighter value. When the glaze coat is sparingly and carefully applied, a pleasing effect should result.

A glazed finish is more effective when applied to furniture with carved surfaces, moldings, and turnings rather than to a piece that is entirely flat in design.

A new, unfinished piece of furniture or a piece that has all the old finish removed will require the following applications for a glazed finish: an undercoat or primer, two coats of enamel, a glazing liquid, and a protective coat. Some pieces, with the old finish in good condition, will not require the undercoat and need perhaps only one coat of enamel. Some commercial glazes do not require a protective coat over the glaze coat.

Glazing kits may be purchased complete with all of the necessary products and supplies for refinishing an article. The supplier may also have each of the products and needed supplies for sale separately. Compare the convenience, quality, desired colors available, and the cost of the kit with separate unit purchasing. Some kits may contain items you already have on hand.

The furniture piece to be painted is prepared in the same manner as a piece that will not have a glazed finish, with the exception of the final rub. Make "tooth" for the glazing liquid on the final coat of enamel by lightly rubbing with 3/0 steel wool. Then wipe the piece clean with a clean cloth or tack rag. The piece is now ready for the glaze application.

Glazing Liquids

You may prepare your own glazing liquid or purchase one that is ready mixed. Prepare a glazing liquid by mixing 3 tablespoons gum turpentine, 1 tablespoon varnish, and 1 teaspoon of the desired oil color(s). Stir well until uniformly mixed.

Examples of glaze oil colors to use over ivory or off-white base enamels to achieve a mellow look are raw umber (grayish tone), raw sienna (reddish tone), burnt umber (brownish tone), and burnt sienna (reddish-brown tone). Other hues are equally effective, depending upon the enamel color and the color scheme of the room in which the finished piece will be used.

Applying the Glaze

Wipe the enameled undercoat surface with a tack rag to remove all traces of dust and dirt. Then mix the glazing liquid and oil colors thoroughly. If using a commercial glazing liquid, stir it thoroughly with a wooden paddle and read the label instructions carefully.

Apply a thin coat of the glazing liquid with an oil paint brush, painting one side of the piece of furniture at a time. Long, even strokes with the grain of the wood will produce the best results. If the piece has prominent legs, turn it upside down and paint the legs first, then the top, working downward. Pay special attention to carved trim and crevices, painting them first to allow more absorption of the glaze.

Let the color glaze set for 10 to 30 minutes before beginning to rub or wipe.

Wiping the Glaze

Once the glaze has set enough to be slightly tacky, use cheesecloth to wipe lightly at first and then more heavily in those places where you want more highlights—usually the high points of carving and the center of panels. Wipe in long, straight lines in the direction of the grain (usually the long way to your piece).

Blend further by patting the surface with clean cheesecloth, and finish blending with a dry paint brush. Work the brush from the center toward the edges. Wipe the brush off on a cloth to remove excess glaze. Wiping off and blending are not at all difficult when only a small amount of glaze material remains on the surface. They give a slightly noticeable but most effective appearance.

Rub large, flat areas in long, even strokes, beginning with a light touch and applying more pressure as you go along. If you find that you have allowed the glaze to set too long, simply dampen your rubbing cloth with mineral spirits. If wiping shows that you haven't allowed the glaze to set long enough, simply apply another coat and wait again.

For carved surfaces, moldings, and turnings, proceed as for flat surfaces. Remove excess glaze material from depressions with a dry paint brush. Wipe the brush off on a cloth. Highlight by wiping the glaze off the raised areas with a clean cloth, leaving the glaze in the depressions for contrast. Difficulty in rubbing intricate carved trim can be overcome by using a cotton tip in those hard-to-reach areas.

Other materials may be used for wiping to get still different results. Try the texture of Turkish towels or paper towels, for instance. For extra-fine grain, try wiping with fine 3/0 steel wool. Experiment—just apply a layer of imagination.

For example, dry brush is the one most often used by professionals for furniture antiquing. It gives a more "grainy" texture than wiping. If your piece seems to lack interest after wiping, try the dry-brush technique right over it. First, wipe your brush dry and spread the bristles by pinching so that they will deposit the color in irregular separate lines. (Here is where a cheap brush works better than a good one.) Instead of dipping your brush in the paint can, spread some glaze on a saucer or sheet of aluminum foil. Pick up the glaze with the tip of your brush. Apply the glaze in long straight but irregular lines with this almost dry brush. Work in the direction of the grain. For beginners it may be easier to get the "dry-brush" effect by wiping with coarse material of some kind—a Turkish towel, paper towels, even a square of carpeting.

If you use the steel-wool method to achieve a wood-graining effect, don't try to copy the wood grain. If you follow the simple straight-line wiping directions that follow, you will be surprised at the ease with which a close-grained, fine hardwood effect reveals itself without any special effort to imitate or copy the grain of the wood. Remember that grain usually runs the length of the piece or part. So, wipe the long way of each section in long, straight lines—remembering that wood grain lines are straight, but not mathematically straight.

With your 3/0 steel wool, wipe lightly with a long, sweeping motion. Don't start your wiping motion from a still position—rather, have your hand in motion before the steel wool touches the surface. Pick up lightly on the finish of each stroke with a follow-through of motion. This gives a light, brushing attack to the job that lets you blend one stroke into another without depositing smears of glaze at the beginning or finish of each stroke. To touch up rough or unsatisfactory areas, use a light whisking motion.

To avoid "directionalism" in wiping and to get the natural random look of wood grain, *walk around* your piece as you wipe. Attack it from both front and rear. If you stand in the same place throughout the wiping, the piece will get an unnatural *slanting* appearance. Working from both front and back cancels out the slant and results in a blend that is more natural looking.

Inside corners are difficult to get at with steel wool. It's generally best to start the wipe from the corner with a dry brush, continuing with steel wool.

On tabletops, dresser tops, etc., finish wiping with an outward sweeping motion that continues out into the air at the end of the piece. In this way you can maintain the illusion of continuing grain.

The steel wool will fill up with glaze quite quickly. When glaze begins to "ball up" on the surface of the wood, remove excess glaze by pressing the steel wool against cheesecloth or paper towel—or change the steel wool to another position. You may need to do this every two or three strokes if you are working on a large surface. It's a good practice to unroll the steel wool and cut it with scissors into short pieces—about 6 inches long. This gives you a number of good handfuls, each of which can be turned several times as it fills up. After cutting, shake each piece several times to free it of loose particles.

Glaze and wipe one area at a time. This method allows you to work in an unhurried manner. If interrupted, you have only to finish wiping the glazed area and then resume work at your leisure. Also, stop to judge the effect frequently while wiping; maybe you're finished and don't know it. Don't overwork your piece, but try to get a fresh, free feeling. While you are busy working, you are "too close to the woods to see the trees" and thus a poor judge of the effects you're getting. You may be underrating them—getting too "fussy." It is advisable to work quickly (but not hurriedly), without going back over your work too much. Relax! Tell yourself, "If I don't like this I can wipe it off and start over." Now go away and leave it for a while. When you come back, your transformed piece will surprise you. You may decide that this is exactly the effect you want.

When you've finished wiping, allow enough time for the paint to dry thoroughly, usually 24 hours. With some commercial antiquing systems a second coat of glaze is required, applied in the same manner as the first.

A glazing liquid you have prepared yourself should have a protective coat for greater wear and durability. When the glaze is completely dry, apply a coat of *water-clear* varnish. (Do not use regular varnish, as it has a yellowish color.) Allow one week for the varnish to dry. If the surface is too shiny, rub carefully with automotive rubbing compound until a satin finish is obtained. Wipe the surface with a clean, dry cloth to remove the rubbing compound.

A commercial glazing liquid may also require a protective coat. The label will state if a protective coat is needed. If it is, then purchase the protective coat in the same brand as the glazing liquid.

With either commercial or homemade glazing liquid, if you wish to wax the surface, it is best to allow the paint to dry for at least a week before applying.

Special Effects

While applying the glaze there are a few tricks that can be used to achieve interesting special effects:

SHADING To get a shaded effect, glaze more thinly in the center of large areas such as door panels, dresser and tabletops, end panels, etc. The lightest area of your shading should be roughly oval in shape. Shaded areas will curve softly around the oval, dissolving into deepest shadows at the corners. For shading, use slightly more glaze to start. Then, with cheesecloth, wipe out some glaze from the center oval area. Before wiping with steel wool, "feather" the hard edges of the wiped-out oval by brushing back into it with an almost dry brush.

FROSTING If the work is delicately done, beautiful effects may be achieved by using white to glaze over furniture enameled light opaque colors, resulting in a "frosted" effect. White primer material or enamel is used in the glaze mixture in place of the oil color. This is applied, wiped off, and finished in the same manner as for antiquing.

SPATTER (A SPECKLED TEXTURE) The spatter technique requires a stiff brush. Try an old toothbrush for small areas or a small whisk broom—or any other stiff household brush—for larger surfaces. Flip the glaze off the bristles in a coarse spray. Bend the bristles with your fingers or a stick to get a spring action that will throw the spray. To avoid blobs, don't overload the brush. After reloading the brush each time, try out the spatter on a newspaper to get rid of blobs and to judge your "aim."

Spatter makes good imitation worm holes on antique furniture. It is a good finish procedure because it will blend patterns together. Because spatter is a "chancy" method, apply it after the glaze coat has dried overnight. Then you can wipe it off and try again, if necessary.

SPATTERN (SPATTER WITH A PATTERN)
While the glaze is still wet, spray mineral spirits using the spatter technique just described. The mineral spirits will cause the glaze to "crawl," pushing it back into little circles or "star" patterns, revealing the undercoat.

Spray once, then watch! The clear droplets will "flower" slowly on the surface, which should take several seconds to a minute.

Spattern should be applied only to a flat horizontal surface. If applied vertically or on a slanting or rounded surface, the mineral spirits may run and streak your work. Remember that the addition of mineral spirits may slow the drying time.

WATER-STAINED WOOD This traditional and interesting look can be achieved by first rubbing the toned surface, then splattering it with mineral spirits. The toner will spread out in the spots where the liquid has fallen, creating an authentic water-stained look.

STIPPLING (FINE TEXTURE) One of the best stipple patterns is made with a piece of carpet cut to fit your hand. (The "twist"-type carpet is fine.) Apply glaze with a brush and then, holding the carpet in a flat position, pounce lightly over the surface. To pounce, pound with a bounce. This makes an even-textured pattern not unlike a leather finish.

The more usual method of stippling is done with a brush. Using the tip end of a dry brush, pick up paint from a shallow surface. (Use a paint-can cover, a saucer, or a sheet of aluminum foil.) Apply stipple

with a pouncing motion, holding the brush at right angles to the surface you are painting. For a uniform pattern, turn your brush this way and that with each pounce.

For a mottled effect, pounce more in some spots, less in others. For shaded effects, start at the darkest point with a freshly loaded brush and work out toward lighter areas as the glaze in the bristles is used up.

CRUMPLE (COARSE TEXTURE) This is a method of applying coarse texture with a pad of crumpled material. You can use almost anything that will crumple—paper, cheesecloth, burlap, to name a few.

Plastic is best of all because it is non-absorbent. It will not get soggy and change shape. Cut up a plastic bag or use sheet plastic. Crumple the plastic to fit the hand and press it lightly onto a previously glazed surface. If the surface is thinly glazed or wiped, add more glaze with the crumpled plastic, picking it up from aluminum foil or some other shallow surface. Pounce, turning your hand with each motion to assure a random pattern. If your first try doesn't please you, redistribute the glaze by brushing it in one direction or start over. For a different effect, give the plastic wad a slight roll or twist each time you touch the surface.

MARBLELIKE TEXTURE For a marblelike texture, crumple a sheet of plastic and shake it out. Spread it out over a freshly glazed surface. There should be some air bubbles under it. If not, give it a twist and turn or push it together in some places. Pat with cheesecloth to get good tight adhesion in several spots. Now, pick it up quickly but carefully (without dragging it across the surface). The resulting texture is very much like marble veining, or travertine marble. Spray "spattern" over this texture for a fine marbleized surface.

A similar marble effect can be achieved by using a sponge, burlap, a feather, or a combination of these.

VEINING The classic tool for marble veining is a turkey feather. Drag it across the glaze to make a straight, thin line; twist and turn the feather a little to vary the width of the line. Occasionally change direction—but at an angle, not with a curve—and keep veining lines straight. A string saturated with glaze and dragged across the surface several times at different angles makes a fair imitation of veining.

BEGINNERS, NOTE: Allow the piece to dry overnight before attempting veining. This allows you to wipe it off and try again. Also, with a dried surface, it is possible to obscure the veining line if it becomes too dark. Pick up excess glaze by laying a paper lightly over the surface and lifting it gently.

THE RANDOM EFFECT The random or chance effect is most important to successful marbleizing. Planned irregularity is more difficult than an ordered arrangement because almost from birth we have been trained to arrange things in an orderly manner. To "think random," reverse this training—check the following points:

Avoid:

• Lines or configurations that start from a corner or from the center of any side.
• Concentration of interest in the exact center.
• Lines parallel to each other or to the outer edges of your piece.
• "Directionalism"—that is, a slanting effect, like handwriting. This comes from working always from the same position. Offset this by walking around the piece. Work on it from different angles.

TORTOISESHELL This effect is best created by working on one small area at a time. Apply a heavier than usual amount of toner glaze, then tap the surface lightly with your fingertips, changing the angle of your hand each time. For a random effect, walk around the piece—let each tap be from a different angle. For bigger shells, use heavy rubber gloves. For a less-distinct shell pattern, put your hands inside a plastic bag.

A similar appearance is achieved by tapping the surface with a short bristle brush, beginning in the center of the area and working toward the edges.

HIGHLIGHTING After the glaze coat has dried thoroughly (overnight) you can increase and heighten the light-and-dark effect by highlighting. The object of highlighting is to emphasize the shading you achieved in the wiping step. With highlighting you reveal the full gamut of color from the clear, unglazed paint to the depths of the glazed shadows. These touches are still different from those achieved by wiping—and should be explored. Try them in an inconspicuous place. The highlight step also makes it possible to correct some deficiencies of wiping.

With the finest sandpaper or steel wool, rub lightly all over to flatten any nibs, dust particles, etc. Rub in the direction of the grain. Avoid corners and edges because paint will wear away very quickly at these points. For spindles and other rounded or curved surfaces, use steel wool.

With medium sandpaper, sand more vigorously in the center of panels and large areas, bearing down just enough to remove some of the glaze. Always sand with the grain, and leave a heavier coat of glaze around the edges. Gently "feather" edges of highlights so as not to leave an abrupt and obvious line between highlight and shading.

As you sand, the glaze will disappear first from atop the ridges formed by the brush strokes of the undercoat paint. These brush-stroke lines will lend additional interest to the texturing. Add highlights gradually. Stand back and judge the effect from time to time.

Work on the following areas:

1. Highlight the centers of panels and of all areas large enough to reach with the sandpaper.

2. Highlight high points of carvings and spindles. (Use your finest sandpaper or steel wool here, proceeding carefully. Paint wears off quickly.)

3. Highlight normal wear spots on chairs—that is, arms, front of seats, center of back, etc.

Don't worry about "chalking" or the light powdery look that first results from the sanding step. It will disappear in the finishing process. If you find that too much

glaze has been removed, simply dry brush on more fresh glaze, wipe, and let dry overnight.

STRIPING For really professional striping, get a long-bristled sign-painter's striping brush, available at any paint or art store. Before striping, let the piece dry overnight. This will allow you to rest your hand on the piece to guide your brush and also to repair the stripes by wiping the edges, or to wipe them off and try again.

To stripe, dip your brush deep into the glaze, coating the full length of the bristles. Remove excess by drawing each side of the brush against the edge of the can. Your brush should be loaded but not dripping. To stripe effectively, use the brush with a careful, slow, dragging motion.

For a wide stripe or border, lay the brush flat along the stripe line with the full length of the bristles in contact with the surface. Drag the brush in the direction of the stripe. When you run out of glaze, reload and resume the line, overlapping a little.

For a narrow stripe, turn your brush to the side of the narrow edge and proceed as for a broad stripe. The width of line is a little harder to control in this position.

The easiest kind of striping is where you have a beveled edge or the concave indentation of a molding to act as a guide for the brush.

Where there is no such guide, more skill and practice are needed. On a tabletop or border where you want a line to represent a panel on a door or drawer, draw one light guide line with a pencil. Keep your brush to the right of the line (if you are right-handed). Keeping your eye on the line, draw your brush along it with a motion swift enough to keep the line from wavering. Do not go back over it. The grain of the line will give it a finished look.

GOLD EFFECTS Some pieces look better with the addition of gold, others don't. If you're not sure, try adding gold touches to a small area or one corner and then think about it awhile. In general, gold will be applied to formal period furniture, such as English and French eighteenth-century pieces. Gold is used less often on French Provincial designs, and very little gold appears on early American and Victorian.

Use gold powder and bronzing liquid (available at any art supply department or paint store). Mix the powder with the liquid only as you need it. When you become much more expert, try gold leaf for striping and larger gold areas.

For gold striping, see the preceding directions for striping.

For gold highlighting, with a dry brush (see page 169), touch high spots lightly. If too much gold is deposited, wipe lightly before the gold sets.

For gold wipe, apply gold lightly with a dry brush (see page 169). Wipe thoroughly and quickly before the gold sets. This distributes the gold in small amounts over the entire area, to create gold *glints* rather than gold spots.

For gold spatter, see "Spatter," page 171. This is still another way to achieve gold glints.

For gold in wax, a now quite widely distributed paste form of gold may be rubbed on with the finger or a cloth, dried, then buffed to a fine sheen that resembles gold leaf. Use very small amounts—a little goes a long way. It is excellent for striping a concave molding line that may be traced with the finger. For flat or textured surfaces, thin with turpentine and apply gold, using a dry-brush technique. Thin with turpentine to spatter or for use with a striping brush. To repair or remove gold in wax, use turpentine.

DISTRESSED Distressed wood is one of the most popular antiquing effects, and if your piece of furniture isn't naturally worn, the effect can be simulated. Make your own scratches and mars by beating the surface with a heavy tool or a burlap bag filled with chains. Sand the scratches and apply artist's oil paint, using the color raw umber, straight from the tube. Rub off excess oil paint vigorously.

DISTRESSED PAINT This effect can be achieved by applying two layers of contrasting colors to your furniture, allowing each to dry thoroughly. Then take a coarse sandpaper and lightly sand the surface, until the initial color is in evidence. Do this only in the spots where normal wear would occur.

PAINTED-ON WOOD FINISHES More often than you know, those furniture finishes that look the most mellow and shaded are completely painted on. They are the ones that seem most to glow with "the patina of age." The new painted-on wood finishes show only a subtle indication of grain.

Three separate color coats (one opaque, two transparent) assure color variation and a remarkable illusion of "depth" of wood grain. The first coat is paint; coats 2 and 3 are two different glaze colors.

Painted-on wood finishes are particularly effective on traditional cabinets and doors with decorative detail. Panels, carving, and molding trim can be shaded and distressed with spatter to give a mellow "old" appearance.

Painted-on wood finishes are useful for "matching" radiator covers, baseboards, or other metallic or nonwood surfaces to surrounding wood color to maintain a continuous wood effect, as in a paneled room.

EBONY FINISH Any close-grained wood may be given a good imitation ebony finish with a black stain made by pouring 2 quarts of boiling hot water over 1 ounce of powdered logwood extract. After the extract has been dissolved, add to it a solution made by dissolving 1 dram of powdered potassium chromate in a few drops of hot water. Combine these two solutions and allow to cool before using. If the first coat does not produce a sufficiently deep black, apply a second and a third coat. The water stain has a tendency to raise the grain of the wood. It is a good idea, therefore, to sand the surface after each coat has dried. The last coat will usually not cause any noticeable raising of the grain. Protect the ebonized finish by applying a thin coating of shellac after the stain has dried. Rub lightly with extra-fine sandpaper to remove the gloss of the shellac.

FROSTIQUE This is a relatively new textured look in a light, bright key. It is paint plus glaze, but not traditional antiquing. Six sharp modern pastel colors are each modified with a white glaze to make a series of soft flowery tints. They are excellent for dressing rooms, baths, kitchens, feminine-looking bedrooms, and girls' rooms. They can be wiped in the traditional antique method or textured for a modern look.

MODERN PAINT TREATMENTS The "wet look," strong, bright colors with a high-gloss finish, are in great demand now for ultramodern treatments of cabinets, bookshelves, and built-ins. But there are not a lot of high-gloss colors to choose from—only a few ready-mixed enamel colors.

For a "wet look" custom color, first paint the color coat, using a flat-finish high color. Give it the "wet look" with a high-gloss water-clear varnish. This makes a color that is ever so much brighter and stronger than a semigloss of the same color.

DÉCOUPAGE

You've admired those museumlike pieces in antique stores and expensive gift shops—those small furniture items and plaques decorated with art prints preserved in clear lacquer or varnish finishes. An artist created them with découpage—an art that dates back to the seventeenth century—and you can practice the same art easily and economically.

Actually, découpage means to decorate surfaces with cutouts of favorite art prints, unusual designs, photographs, old maps, documents, wedding and birth announcements—any collection of designs, stamps, or cherished printed mementos you want to preserve and display.

The steps in découpage are as follows:

1. The surface of the object to be découpaged must be completely clean and smooth. Sand carefully, fill cracks and holes with wood plastic or filler, and sand smooth. If the furniture piece or object was previously painted and can't be sanded smooth, remove the paint with paint remover and then sand smooth. Wipe clean with a soft cloth. Apply an undercoat or wood stain base coat in the desired color (which should complement your selected print). Allow to dry thoroughly.

2. Choose a cutout (print) of suitable size to cover the object or to be centered attractively as desired. Cut out the print by feeding the paper into the scissors, rather than cutting along the edges as you would normally do. Some artisans prefer to tear around the print following the shape of the picture, creating a ragged edge. If you tear the print, sand lightly on the reverse side to smooth out the torn edges. NOTE: If the print or picture has printing on the back, you must seal it by coating the back with white glue slightly diluted with water; allow to dry thoroughly. This prevents the printing from showing through on the surface of the print.

3. You are now ready to glue the print to the object. Apply some slightly diluted white glue to the surface on which the print is to be placed and also to the back of the print. Place the print on the object and press out all air bubbles with your fingers, or with a roller. Place waxed paper over the print and, using a roller, press out all excess glue, and wipe clean with a damp cloth. Now, brush the print with the diluted white glue to seal the surface of the print. Allow to dry thoroughly.

4. Brush on the first coat of lacquer, varnish, or découpage coating. Allow to dry. If you desire an antique effect, apply antique glaze, wipe lightly with a soft cloth for graining effects, and allow to dry. Continue to apply coats of lacquer, varnish, or découpage finish, sanding lightly and wiping with a soft cloth between coats—until the print is completely submerged in the clear lacquer, varnish, or découpage finish.

5. The final step achieves a deep, rich finish. Using very fine steel wool or fine sandpaper wet with water, rub the object until the finish is uniformly dull. Apply one or two coats of a good-grade paste wax, polishing vigorously with a clean, soft cloth. Your masterpiece is now completed.

FABRIC OR WALLPAPER FINISHES

Fabric or wallpaper is sometimes used to cover furniture, the inside of drawers, and other surfaces. The fabric or paper should be carefully cut to size with a razor blade, wallpaper knife, or similar cutting device. Then apply wallpaper paste to both the area to be covered and the paper or fabric.

The paste should be mixed and applied according to the directions on the package. Always smooth the paste out well, covering all areas so there will be no loose sections. Smooth the paper firmly in place, working the strip down gradually so no air bubbles are left under the surface. Wipe smooth with a clean, dry cloth, but use a damp cloth to remove any paste that has smeared over the edges. Remove these spots before they have a chance to dry. After the paper or fabric has dried, it may be treated to a surface coating of special wallpaper wax (wallpaper wax *only*), or it may be painted or sprayed with a thin coat of clear shellac, lacquer, or varnish.

FIR PLYWOOD FINISHES

One of the most popular and most economical types of plywood is made of fir. Fir plywood needs a good sealer, because of the special character of the grain figure, which is made up of alternate hard summer growth and softer spring growth. Without the use of a sealer, the first coat of paint or stain penetrates unevenly, resulting usually in a "wild," overconspicuous grain.

To tame or quiet this grain, several special types of sealers, which may be purchased from your neighborhood lumber, paint, or hardware dealer, have been developed. If the sealer is used properly, it allows the stain to soften the darker markings and deepen the lighter surfaces of the fir wood, minimizing the wild grain figures.

To obtain a light natural finish, first sandpaper the wood smooth with fine sandpaper, then apply an even coat of resin sealer. Lightly sand when dry and follow with a thin coat of pure white shellac. It is suggested that the shellac be reduced to 2-pound cut. Sandpaper again when dry and apply either a satin-finish lacquer or a gloss varnish. If a flat finish is desired, a flat or dull varnish may be substituted. After drying thoroughly, steel wool and complete with white wax.

For a painted surface on fir plywood, the sealer will provide a smooth, even base that will enable the paint to take evenly. The paint may be applied directly over the sealer, but, for the best results, the surface should first be made smooth with sandpaper.

HARDBOARD FINISHES

Hardboard is reconstituted natural wood fabricated by reducing natural wood to fibers and then pressing the fibers together into panels of various thicknesses and surface dimensions. It is often used as a tabletop surface, in drawers, and on other furniture parts.

When painting hardboard, both surface preparation and the application of a good primer-sealer are essential for a smooth, uniform finish. The hardboard should be clean and dry. All grease and dirt should be removed with a suitable cleaner, and nail heads should be countersunk and puttied.

Good sealing by the primer is required to prevent absorption of the top coat. Good water-thinned and solvent-thinned primer-sealers are available for this purpose. Factory-primed hardboard is ready for painting unless the primer has been damaged. Damaged areas should be spot primed or given another coat of primer-sealer to ensure proper sealing.

After the hardboard has been properly sealed, the top coat can be applied. A smoother and better-appearing finish will be obtained if the sealer is lightly sanded to remove irregularities before the top coat is applied. This is especially true if a gloss enamel is used as the final coat. Usually, two coats of paint—semigloss or gloss enamels—are a good idea, with a light sanding between coats.

PARTICLEBOARD FINISHES

Particleboard is the newest member of the family of synthetic wood panel products used in furniture and cabinetry. Because it is competitively priced and offers certain woodworking and performance advantages, particleboard is one of the fastest-growing segments of the wood products industry.

In general, all particleboard surfaces within habitable spaces that are not covered with finished adhesive-bonded laminates should be painted. Unpainted, exposed particleboard is easily soiled, difficult to clean, and may sometimes develop an odor when used extensively within confined spaces.

When painting particleboard doors or other free-moving units, it is especially important to finish both sides of the door with an equal number of coats. As with other wood products, particleboard will gain or lose moisture with changes in the atmospheric conditions, so, unless both sides are finished equally, the less-finished side will gain or lose moisture faster than the other side, and the panel will warp. Tops and bottoms of doors should be well sealed with paint to reduce moisture intake.

The edges of particleboard have the same tendency to absorb paint as the surface, usually, in fact, to a greater extent. When edges are to be exposed to view, they should be filled with water putty. After the putty has dried, sand it smooth. Then prime all surfaces of the particleboard with an alkyd primer. *Do not use water-based primers.* They will raise the individual chips of wood and create a rough-textured surface. Once primed, particleboard can be finished just like any other wood. Best results on edges are achieved by applying the filler with a putty knife.

PAINTING LAWN FURNITURE

A lawn chair or table's life is a rugged one—exposed to rain, sunshine, moonshine, and even passing birds! You can't halt the weather, but you can make a protective shield for your furniture with paint. You will want a durable finish, one that will withstand the weather and that will take to soap and water cleanups.

Is your lawn furniture metal? Keep a sharp eye open for cracks in the old finish where moisture is apt to sneak in and promote rust and corrosion. Remove cracked paint with a wire brush, and sand away all traces of rust or corrosion with steel wool. After spot coating these problem areas with a protective anticorrosive primer (such as zinc chromate), the entire surface can be painted with colorful exterior enamel. Unpainted iron or steel furniture *must* be painted for protection. Galvanized steel will give its best performance when a primer such as a zinc dust–zinc oxide type is used. Other special primers specifically developed for coating galvanized steel will also give satisfactory protection. Apply the primer, dry overnight, and then apply one or two coats of a good exterior metal enamel for best results.

Aluminum furniture, shiny bright when new, may develop unsightly pitting when left outdoors or in a corrosive environment. To restore a dazzling appearance, and to assure adhesion of the new coating, use a phosphoric acid cleaner or sand the surface to remove all dull film. Wipe clean with turpentine to remove dirt and grease, and then apply a clear, nonyellowing exterior acrylic or butyrate lacquer. Incidentally, if this lacquer is applied to new aluminum furniture (which you have wiped with solvent), you'll be rewarded by a shinier, longer-lasting finish.

Wood furniture is vulnerable to moisture attack from above and below. Moisture from the damp ground can ruin the legs and undersides of furniture. To avoid this problem be sure to protect the entire piece of furniture with a good-quality exterior enamel. First remove all loose paint by sanding or by using a chemical paint remover, and apply a good exterior enamel undercoat before applying the enamel.

Metal fittings on wood furniture need special attention. They should be protected from rust and corrosion by the same methods used for metal furniture. If the wood has been finished to accent the natural beauty of the wood grain, you'll want to use a spar varnish, a rough-and-ready urethane varnish, or a clear exterior lacquer to keep the furniture beautiful.

Exterior enamels come in exciting decorating shades. Why not turn your attention to exterior decorating and color-coordinate your lawn furniture with your patio or the outside of your home.

eight

Applying New Seating Materials

One of the major repair jobs that must be done on many antique chairs is to replace the seating, which may be cane, rush, splint, or webbing. Let's see how to go about replacing these materials.

CANE SEATS

Cane for chair seating is made from a palm called rattan. The plants come from the Indian archipelago, China, India, Sri Lanka, and the Malay peninsula. They grow in dense forests and frequently reach tree height, then fall over and form a matted undergrowth. The stem, which is covered with beautiful foliage, grows in length from 100 to 300 feet and is seldom more than 1 inch in diameter. For export, these stems are cut in 10- to 20-foot lengths. The outer bark is stripped in widths varying from ⅟₁₆ to ³⁄₁₆ inch and is cut in strips. Then it is tied in hanks of 1,000

feet and is ready for the weaver. One such hank is enough for four chairs with medium-sized seats.

Seating cane differs from domestic sugar cane and from the cane known as bamboo, which grows in the southern states. Bamboo, which is shorter, straighter, and thicker, is used for furniture, walking sticks, poles, and the like. Neither bamboo nor sugar cane is suitable for chair seating.

You can buy cane at chair-seating and craftsman's supply houses, at mail order houses (such as Constantine's), and at department stores. Buy long, select cane (from 15- to 18-foot lengths) for medium or large chair seats. You can use shorter lengths but they have to be tied more often. Good cane is smooth, glossy on the right side, tough, and pliable. The "eye," or lump where the stem of the leaf grew out, should be smooth and unbroken. Poor cane has rough and imperfect spots, does not weave easily, and is likely to split.

Plastic cane is also available. It weaves easily, does not require soaking, is strong, and costs slightly less than other cane because little is wasted. Its smooth, shiny texture is suitable for painted chairs; real cane is preferable for fine old furniture.

Binder, to finish the edge of the seat, is cane one width wider than that used for weaving and is included with the weaving cane.

The widths of cane to use depends on the size of the holes in the chair seat and the distance between them. The table below is a guide to the size of cane to buy.

SIZE OF CANE TO USE

CANE SIZE	SIZE OF HOLE IN SEAT (INCHES)	DISTANCE BETWEEN HOLES IN SEAT (INCHES)
Carriage (narrowest)	⅛	⅜
Superfine	⅛	⅜
Fine fine	³⁄₁₆	½
Fine	³⁄₁₆	⅝
Medium	¼	¾
Common (widest)	⁵⁄₁₆	⅞

Getting Ready to Weave

Cut away the old seat, using a keyhole saw. Clean any pieces of broken cane or dirt from the holes and the seat rails. Pull out old nails and tacks. Be sure you can get cane through all the holes. If any are filled, bore a hole through them. Use a file to round the inside of the frame so no sharp edges will cut the cane. If you need to refinish the wood, do this before the seat is caned.

To prepare the cane, pull one of the strands of cane from the looped end of the hank, near where it is tied. As you pull, shake the hank so that the cane won't tangle or tear. Roll the strand, right side out, to fit in a 5- to 6-inch-wide bowl. Fasten the ends with a clamp clothespin.

Fill the bowl with a 10 percent solution of glycerine (drugstore item): about 1½ tablespoons of glycerine to 1 cup of water (warm water hastens the process). Let the cane soak for about 20 minutes or until soft and pliable.

Plastic cane, enough for one chair, is sold in a bunch with strands cut 6 to 7 yards long. If you buy it in quantity on a spool, cut it in strands of similar length. Do not soak it.

How to Weave Square or Oblong Seats

The usual form of weaving is called seven-step weaving: weave from the upper side of the seat; first, from back to front, then from side to side, again from back to front, and from side to side, and then on the two diagonals. If you begin in the center of the back, you will find it easy to make sure the rows of cane are straight. Add the binder last.

STEP 1 Count the holes in the back rail. If there is an odd number of holes, put a peg in the center hole. If there is an even number of holes, put the peg in one of the holes nearest the center. Do the same on the front rail, pegging the same side of the center as at the back.

Take the roll of cane from the bowl and wipe off excess water with your fingers or a cloth. Put another strand in to soak while you work.

Weave the eye whenever you can to keep from roughening or breaking the strand. Pull out the peg from the back rail. Push about 4 inches of an end of cane down through this hole and fasten it with a peg. Bring the cane to the front rail, right side (smooth side) up; take out the peg there and push the cane through. Leave the cane slack, because the mesh tightens as weaving continues. Then replace the peg. Push the cane up through the nearest hole on one side of the center. Pull it across the chair and down through the opposite hole at the back.

As you weave, hold the cane so that it sags a little below the level of the wood seat frame. Weave large seats and plastic cane tighter. If the chair has a scoop seat, press the cane down as far as the bottom of the wood frame. Continue weaving toward the side as long as you can weave in opposite holes. Don't use corner holes unless you are sure there will be room for the diagonal and binder canes that must also go through these holes. Leave the rest of the strand to use later. Fasten it with a clamp clothespin to keep it out of your way.

For seats wider at the front than at the back, weave separate pieces of cane, as shown in Figure 8-1. Canes must not be carried across on the underside of the frame to block holes that must be used later. As you continue weaving you can keep the cane in position without using pegs, except to fasten the ends.

Weave the other half of the seat.

STEP 2 Start at the back on the right side rail as you face the chair, in a hole next to the corner. Pull the cane up through the hole and across the seat over the weaving you have already done. Continue weaving back and forth. If the front rail is curved, weave with separate pieces of cane.

STEP 3 Weave as in Step 1. Keep the strands slack as in Steps 1 and 2. Weave in line with, and on top of, the first and second weaving and to the right of the cane you wove in the first step.

Fasten the ends of cane on the underside of the frame by tying them to or twisting them around the cane crossing from the next hole. Trim the end wherever you can before starting Step 4 and then tie as you go along, so the pegs won't be in your way. Moisten the ends of cane if necessary so they can be tied without breaking.

STEP 4 Real weaving begins, here, as you weave from side to side. Start at the back on the right as you face the chair and in a hole next to a corner. Weave over the canes on top and under the canes underneath. As you work, straighten the canes you wove in Step 2 to help keep Step 4 canes in place. When you are a third or halfway across, pull the length through that far, being careful that it does not twist or break. As you pull, keep your hand

8-1. For seats wider at the front than at the back, weave the pieces of cane as shown at the left. Pull the cane up through the hole and across the seat over the weaving you have, as shown at the right.

8-2. Continue weaving back and forth, as shown at the left. Fasten the ends of the cane as shown at the right.

level with the chair rail. If you lift up, the weaving cane may cut canes already woven, especially if the cane is plastic. Continue weaving across the row. This draws together, in pairs, the canes from front to back and from side to side. When you reach the opposite side, put the end of cane down through the hole and peg it until you weave the next row. Pull the cane up through the nearest hole and weave back across the seat so that the cane passes over the same canes and under the same canes as it did the first time across. If you find it easier, weave with the end of cane.

Repeat for the other rows. At the sides, be sure the canes in Step 3 are on top and at the right of the canes in Step 1. Soak the woven cane with a wet sponge or cloth. Using two pegs, straighten the rows and force them close together in pairs with hollow squares between.

STEP 5 Diagonal weaving begins in this step. Start at the back corner hole on the right side as you face the chair, and weave the first row toward the left front corner. You will weave the cane diagonally *over* the pairs from front to back and *under* those from side to side, keeping the cane straight from the corner holes. First lay it in position to decide how to start. Weave with one hand on top of the seat and the other underneath. Pull the cane through when you are a third or halfway across. Be careful not to lift it and cut the strands already woven. The cane must lie flat and be so woven that the edges do not bind. The cane should pull through easily; it helps to moisten it with a damp cloth.

Weave the *back section* of the seat first, using holes on the left and back rails. For the second row, weave from front to back, going over and under the same rows you did before.

Weave canes in each corner hole, making a "fish head" or a V. You may complete the fish head on the back corner or finish it when weaving the front corner. Sometimes canes can be kept straight only by weaving a single cane in part of the corner holes. Keep the canes right side up. Don't skip holes on the underside of the seat.

Weave back and forth until you have reached a place near the center of the left side. If the seat is round or definitely curved, weave only a few diagonals and then begin to skip holes or double in holes. Keep the rows straight. If there are more holes on the sides than on the back, skip holes, usually not more than three on the side. If the seat is round, you may double in holes across the back as well as skip holes on the side. Make the canes lie straight across the back corner. Check to see that you have skipped enough holes so that the same number are left on the back as on the side. Use a new piece of cane when you need to; or you may use an end left from previous weaving if you can do so without crossing holes on the lower side of the seat. Experienced weavers use all ends of cane so that there will be fewer knots to tie.

The rest of the seat must be woven according to the pattern started on this section.

Since the first diagonal was woven from back to front, weave the first row on the

8-3. The canes should lie straight across the back corner, as shown at the left. At the right, one end is tied and the other cane out of the same hole can be tied to the same strap. Those from the other hole can't be tied until more straps are formed.

front section from front to back, using holes on the front and right rails. Use a new piece of cane.

Check to keep the rows straight. Canes may curve slightly near the rail. Put them in the holes where they will curve the least. To make the pattern alike on the two sides, weave twice (fish-head) in the hole or holes corresponding to those skipped on the left side of the chair. To prevent cutting the cane, you may fish-head in the hole above or below that directly opposite.

On the front rail, double in holes on the left and skip holes on the right. Note the four pegs. Tie ends as you go along, wherever there is a nearby strap to which to tie.

STEP 6 This is the second diagonal, woven in the opposite direction. Start at the back corner hole on the left side as you face the chair and weave toward the front right corner. Weave diagonally *under* the pairs from front to back and *over* those from side to side.

Weave the *front section* of the seat first. Complete the pattern started in the first diagonal, so the corners and the two sides correspond. Each half of the front and back rails must also correspond. On the left side rail, weave twice in holes skipped by the first diagonal. Do the same on the front rail, right side. On the left side, skip those holes used twice before. Don't carry cane across holes on the underside of the seat. Instead, cut the cane if necessary.

For the *back section*, continue the weaving, using a new cane to weave from front to back; double in the back corner hole to match the opposite corner. Weave to the front and double in that corner hole. On the side rail, skip holes woven in twice by the first diagonal. On the back rail, skip any holes already used twice.

STEP 7 The binder cane is the next size wider than that used for weaving. It is used to cover the holes and to finish the edge of the weaving. If the seat is curved, use one strip long enough to go around. If corners are square or turns are sharp, cut separate lengths, each 6 to 8 inches longer than the side of the seat where it will be used. Keep both binder and weaving cane wet and pliable. Lay one of the pieces of binder flat over the holes on one side of the seat, with the center of the piece at about the center hole. Push one end through the corner hole and hold it there with a peg.

Use as long a piece of weaving cane as you can handle easily. Or use a piece left from previous weaving, crossing the corner underneath if you wish. Fasten the binder at each hole or, if the holes are close together, at every other hole. Begin at the end where the binder is pegged. Pull the weaving cane up through the next hole, then pass it over the top of the binder and down through the same hole. Bring it up through the next hole on either side of the binder and repeat. Keep both canes right side up, flat and tight. Use an awl or a bone knitting needle if you need to force an opening for the cane.

If a continuous piece does not lie flat around the corner, start the second side by taking out the peg and pushing the end of the binder through the corner hole. Replace the peg, hammer it tightly, and file the top level with the chair frame. Repeat around the chair. When the cane is dry, it should be tight enough to ring when you snap it sharply with your fingers. The mesh should be level with the seat frame.

How to Finish the Seat

Tie and cut off any loose ends on the underside of the seat. Trim off rough places or hairs with a razor blade.

Cane has a hard, glossy surface that does not need a finish. If you want, however, you may apply a thin type of penetrating wood sealer (to both sides) to prevent drying and cracking. To blend the color of a new cane seat with the finish on the chair, apply a chair seat stain, available where you buy the cane. Rub the stain on the underside first, with a soft cloth or brush. Wipe off the surplus, and repeat on the upper side. When the stain is dry, apply a second coat if you want a darker color.

Cleaning

Cane seats can be cleaned with a cloth wrung from a solution made as follows: Place 1 quart of boiling water in the top of a double boiler (or two old basins). Add 3 tablespoons of (commercially) boiled lin-

8-4. Finish the caning operation.

seed oil and 1 tablespoon of turpentine. Put boiling water in the bottom of the boiler to help keep the solution hot. Do not place the mixture directly over a flame. Clean both sides of the seat.

RUSH SEATS

Chairs with round rails can have seats woven either of rush or of splint; the original seat usually shows which to use. Rush can be employed for chairs of simple design, such as the very early American ladder-back type. It always should be chosen for more elaborate chairs, such as the later Hitchcock type and the Sheraton. Rush can be used if seat rails are of the same height, or if side rails are slightly higher than those at the front and back.

Rush is available in two types—real rush and fiber rush. Real rush or cattail is more authentic than imitation fiber for chairs of good design, although more skill is required to weave it.

The kind of rush used for chair seating is known as cattail. Cattails grow in shallow fresh water, wet swampy places, along the banks of streams, and in lowlands and marshes. They are found commonly in most parts of the northern states. They can be gathered easily and with little or no expense. Rush also may be bought. Stock ordered from a reliable dealer usually is well cured. Fiber rush comes in continuous lengths and is easiest of all rush materials to handle.

How to Collect and Dry Rush

You can tell cattails from other plants by their round spikes of flowers—the "bobs" or "cattails." The leaves are in two rows, with their flat sides back to back. There are two kinds: the broad leafed (about 1 inch wide) and the narrow leafed. The broad leafed is more common; the narrow leafed grows in lowlands and has much longer leaves. Choose the narrow, long leaves (about 7 feet) for chair seating.

Gather the rush when the leaves are full grown, when the stalks are still green, and the tips are beginning to turn brown. Late July, August, or early September is the usual time. Select perfect leaves and those from the stalks that do not have "bobs." Cut the stalks just above the surface of the water or ground. Gather an ample supply. Leaves lose at least one-third of their weight as they cure; there is waste in weaving as well.

Pull the leaves from the stalks. Sort the leaves, placing together those of about the same width and length, and tie them in loose, flat bundles. Be careful not to bend or break the leaves. Dry them thoroughly for at least two or three weeks in a dark, airy room. An attic or storeroom floor is a good place for drying. Do not put the leaves in a damp room, such as a cellar, where mildew might form on the leaves, or in a hot sunny room where leaves might become brittle.

Rush carefully dried and stored should be usable for a year or more.

Getting Ready to Weave

Take out the old seat and remove all old tacks or nails from the rails. Smooth any uneven places in the wood and round the edges if they are sharp and likely to break the rush.

DAMPEN THE RUSH Dampen the rush until it is workable enough to twist and weave without cracking or breaking. This may take 1 hour in warm water in a trough or 8 to 12 hours if spread on the floor and sprinkled.

Fill the trough about three-quarters full of warm water. Add glycerine until the water feels soft, about 1 cup. This solution helps to prevent the rush from drying out. Soak the rush, about a handful at a time, in the solution. You may have to change the solution once before you finish weaving a seat.

You can use plain water if you dampen the rush on the floor.

CHOOSE AND PREPARE THE LEAVES Choose long, unbroken leaves of about the same length, width, and thickness. The number of leaves to use in each strand depends not only on the leaves but on the size of strand you want. Usually, two leaves are twisted together; sometimes, if they are narrow or thin, three may be used. A thin strand is best for a graceful, delicate chair, but many strands are needed to fill the seat. Thick strands, although fewer would be needed, are too coarse for such a chair. It is important to decide what size strands will look best on your chair.

Select and prepare the leaves and make them into strands as you work. Run the leaves through a wringer to take out air from the cells and to make the leaves workable. Set the rollers tight so that the leaves make a sharp crackling noise as

they are run through. Good rush, well prepared, seldom stains the rollers. Draw
each leaf quickly over the edge of a metal
surface, to take out any air left in the cells.

PRACTICE MAKING TWISTS Cut off about 1
yard of cord and loop it around the back
rail of the seat. Tie the ends of cord in a
square knot; keep the loop about 5 inches
long. Arrange two leaves with a butt end
and a tip end together and the flat side of
one next to the rounded side of the other,
like stacked spoons. Put one end of the
pair through the loop of cord for about 3
inches. Fold it toward the front rail and
use the ends of string to tie around the
bunch, making a square knot near the fold
of rush. Tie the string temporarily around
the side rail. Twist the leaves together,
away from you and in such a way that the
strand is smooth, even, tight, and of good
color. Usually the thumb and first two fingers of one hand are used to make the
twist, and the thumb and fingers of the
other hand hold it. Keep the separate
leaves straight and smooth as when making a braid; make long but firm twists, with
the thumbs about 2 inches apart. Practice
until you can make a smooth, even strand
that is of a good size for your chair. Then
untie the string around the side rail and
take out this practice strand before starting to weave.

8-5. How to make the twists

How to Weave

The weaving of a firm, smooth seat
takes much skill and practice if you
choose true rush. How you do it depends
on the way you like to do it and how you
want it to look. One satisfactory method
(not the simplest) is described in the following paragraphs. The simplest technique for using fiber rush is described
later.

SEATS WITHOUT CORNER BLOCKS With a
carpenter's square as a guide, make a
square of stiff cardboard, with the long
side about 15 inches. Use this to mark off
a square center opening. Place the short
side of the cardboard square parallel to
either the front or the back rail and the
long side against the inner edge of the corner of the back rail. Using a pencil, mark
the edge of the square on the front rail. Do
the same on the other side of the seat. The
two corner measurements may not be the
same, but the distance between pencil
lines on the front rail must be the same as
between posts on the back rail.

Weave the corners first until you reach
the marks on the front rail and then weave
as for a square seat. To do this, face the
front of the chair and push the loop of
string that was used for the practice twist
close to the back post on the left side of
the seat.

Begin with 4 leaves, each long enough
to reach around three sides of the seat.
Make 2 pairs, each with a butt and tip end
together and the flat side of one leaf next
to the round side of the other, as indicated
in Figure 8-6. Place one end of the pair

8-6. By numbering rails with pencil (at center), you can follow the steps without error. A short loop makes the fiber easier to handle in this work.

through the loop of cord for about 3 inches. Fold it toward the front rail and use the ends of string to tie around the bunch, making a square knot near the fold of rush.

Choose one pair of leaves, bring them almost to the front rail, and twist them into a strand. Turn this twist away from the post; keep all other twists in the same direction like a rope. Draw the strand over rail 1, close to post A, up through the opening of the chair, over the side rail 2, again close to the corner post A, and up through the opening again, thus holding the beginning of the twist. Lift up the strand from the underside of the seat to shorten its length and thus help to make the seat firm. Lay the strands in position to make a square crossing and

a seam straight from the corner of the seat.

Pull the strand, without twisting the leaves, across the front of the seat. At post B, twist the leaves, bring the strand over side rail 3 close to post B, up through the opening of the seat, over front rail 1, again close to post B. Arrange the strands as at post A.

Pull the strand, without twisting, to the back and fasten it firmly by winding the ends around the back rail and tying them together, or by holding them with a clamp clothespin.

The strands should be twisted only over the rails where they will show, not on the underside of the seat.

Weave the second pair in the same way. Loop the ends tightly around the back rail and fasten them with a clothespin to the first strand. Tie more leaves, one pair at a time, in the same loop of string. About 5 twists fill 1 inch. Use a piece of rush or the cardboard square every 2 or 3 rows to make sure that the corners are square and the rows straight. Use the hammer and block of wood to force the strands in place. Keep the seam straight from the corner toward the center of the seat. Make a square crossing; add from 4 to 6 inches of another leaf, if needed, to fill the space.

After the corners are woven as far as the marks on the front rail, fasten the ends on the right-hand side: tie with a square knot a piece of string about 18 inches long around all the ends of rush. Loop the ends around the back rail and tie another knot. Pull the strands taut and keep the rows straight and close together. Remove the clothespin and cut away the rush that extends over the rail.

8-7. Weaving seats without a corner block is shown above, while square seat weaving can be seen below.

If the rush breaks, replace it with another piece.

PAD THE SEAT After the front corners are filled in, pad them. The padding is put in the pockets on the underside of the seat at each side of the corner seams. Butt ends and short lengths of rush are folded the length of the opening and forced in flat bunches from the center toward the corner posts. To do this, turn the chair over. Use a wooden stuffer and poke a bunch of rush into the pocket on the underside of the seat, from the center to the seam. The finished seat should be hard and flat, or slightly rounded, but not overstuffed. Rush shrinks as it dries, so put in enough padding to make the seat firm but not "fat." Both front corners should be of the same thickness.

As you continue to weave around all four corners, add padding about every 3 inches. Back corners take less padding than do front corners. When you have finished the weaving, add the last padding by poking in bunches parallel to the last strands.

Square Seats

Seat frames may be square or have corner blocks that make the opening square. Weave these seats and seats that are wider at the front, after you have filled the corners, as follows:

Weave the first strand, corner A. Use the same loop that you had for seats wider at the front, or make a similar loop if you are just starting to weave a square seat. Tie in the butt ends of two leaves, one of which is long and the other short. Twist and weave around post A. Loops of string never have to be cut; weaving covers them.

JOIN THE RUSH As you leave corner A, add a new leaf. Place between the weaving and the strand, with the butt end hanging down below the underside of the seat for about 6 inches, or the amount of the stiff end of the leaf, and with the curved side toward you. Twist this new leaf (about twice) with the other two, to hold them together. The butt ends make a seam on the underside of the seat and should hang down rather than be caught in the weaving. That is, always add a new piece of rush after you finish each corner so that when you are ready to weave the next cor-

8-8. As successive rounds are placed, a pocket is formed between the top and bottom layers. Pack the pocket with wadded brown paper to form a bulge. Tie on new lengths of fiber with a square knot.

ner the rush will be securely fastened and you will have enough to go around that corner.

ADDING RUSH Occasionally you may need to use a third piece of rush to fill out the strand, as when crossing twists at the seam. Weave the first strand to corner B. If the strand is too fat, drop the end of the shortest leaf. This can be cut off or folded in for padding. Twist and weave around corner B. As you leave this corner, again add a new leaf. Then continue to corner C and weave, as shown in Figure 8-8. Add a new piece of rush, and proceed to and weave around corner D, again adding a piece of rush.

SPLICING If the rush breaks or you don't have enough to finish weaving the corner, another piece may be spliced in. After you weave the first half of the corner, add a new leaf at the seam with the butt end extending about 6 inches below the seat. Twist the old leaves once around the new to lock it. Then arrange the leaves parallel and twist all three together. If the strand is too thick, pull out the shortest leaf. Continue weaving the second half of the corner. On the underside of the chair these butt ends will stick down, but at an opposite angle from those used for joining, and will be cut off later.

WEAVE THE REST OF THE SEAT Go on weaving, as for the first strand around post A to posts B, C, and D, until there is space for only two more rows on the side rails. Continue to make the rush workable by running it through the wringer and zipping it with a metal tool. Smooth the twists. Join a new piece of rush after each corner. Pad the seat as you weave. Keep the strands taut, and rows straight, by pounding them with the block of wood, seams straight and the opposite sides of the chair alike. Check as you go along to see that the opposite openings measure the same and that you have the same number of twists over each rail. Occasionally force the metal tool quickly between the rows to straighten them and to smooth the strands. Also occasionally, and before the rush dries out, roll and polish the strands with the round end of the stuffer until the seat is smooth.

If the sides are shorter than the back, fill the sides and then weave from back to front in a figure eight. To help prevent holes near the center, weave around the right side rail twice for the last two strands, then proceed to the left rail and weave around it twice. Then weave in a figure eight over the back and front rails until those rails are filled in. Sometimes this process is reversed. Join the rush at the center after weaving the front rail, or after weaving around both rails.

Pull the last few strands through the small opening with a hook made of wire. Weave in as many rows as possible; when you think the seat is filled, add one more strand. Fasten the last strand on the underside of the chair by separating the ends, winding each one around a nearby strand, and tying them firmly with a square knot.

If the unfinished seat is left overnight, fasten the last twist to the seat with a clamp clothespin. Then cover the seat with wet cheesecloth, in order to keep the rush from drying out.

8-9. Use a small block of wood or metal to force the strands tightly against previously laid strands. This prevents a loose weave. Draw the free end tight after the new strand is tapped into place.

Seats Wider than Deep

Weave until the sides are filled as directed for a square seat. See that the opening measures the same on one side as the other and the front the same as the back. Complete the filling of the back and front rails by weaving the twists in a figure eight, going over and under the front rail, up through the opening, over and under the back rail, and again up through the opening. Don't cross the rush; that is, if

8-10. Left: *For rectangular seats, make both ends as you did the square seat, then fill in the center with the back-and-forth weaving technique.*
Right: *For irregular-shaped seats, fill in the front corners, then continue on the corner-to-corner technique.*

you finish weaving the corners on the left-hand side of the seat, weave from there in a figure eight until the opening is completely filled. You may finish weaving the sides in such a way that you would reverse this, weaving from the right side or the back rail first.

Just before making the figure eight, you may weave twice around the side rail as directed above, instead of singly as shown in Figure 8-10.

How to Finish the Seat

After you have completed the weaving and padding, trim the butt ends on the lower side of the seat to about 1 inch, so that they do not show as you face the chair. Trim any loose ends with a razor blade or shears. Use the rounded end of the stuffer to pound and even the seat. On the upper side, trim the loose ends, straighten the rows, and pound with the stuffer to mold and polish the twists. You may also use a piece of leather for polishing.

Immediately after you finish weaving, apply a protective coating both to the top and to the lower side of the seat. One treatment is as follows: Apply a mixture of half turpentine and half raw linseed oil (4 tablespoonfuls each) to both sides of the seat. The next day, when this is dry, apply a second coat (about 3 tablespoonfuls of each), and when this is thoroughly dry, apply a coat of dull varnish. Add coats of varnish until there are no dull spots on the rush.

When first and second coats are still tacky, smooth and even the strands so that when the varnish sets they will be held in place. Shellac may be used instead of the above mixture.

Be sure no one sits in the chair until the finish has dried thoroughly—at least two weeks after the weaving is completed.

FIBER RUSH SEATS FOR CHAIRS

Fiber rush is made from a very tough grade of paper twisted into a strand to resemble rush. It may be purchased, in dark brown, in widths of ⅜₂ inch, ⁴⁄₃₂ inch, ⁵⁄₃₂ inch, and ⁶⁄₃₂ inch to resemble antique rush seats, and, in multicolored strands, in a width of ⁶⁄₃₂ inch to resemble new seats.

Getting Ready to Weave

Prepare the chair, as before (see page 189). Buy the fiber in one-pound or two-pound lots or in quantity on a large reel. That sold in pound lots costs a few cents more; that in reels takes time and patience to unroll and rewind. Handle that on a reel as you would wire; that is, roll and unroll it rather than pull it. Take off about 25 yards to work with at one time. Tie the end to a nearby strand and wind it in a roll about 6 inches across. Twenty-five yards of ⁶⁄₃₂-inch-width fiber weighs about ½

pound. Tie string in a slip knot around the roll so that it won't unwind or untwist.

How to Weave

Use one strand and weave as you do real rush, except that the fiber is already twisted. You may dampen the fiber by dipping the roll in and out of warm water. Don't overdo this; if wet, the paper softens and cannot be used. Fasten and join the fiber, and pad the seats as in the following directions. Cut separate lengths for each time that you weave around the two front corners.

To begin weaving, fasten the ends of the fiber as for real rush, except alternately hooking and tying ends to a nearby strand to make them less bulky. Each time you weave the corners, tighten the preceding strand.

Join the fiber by one of three methods: 1) Fold back the ends of fiber and wire them together; or 2) overlap the ends for about 3 inches and tie them together with very fine wire, fish line, or heavy thread; or 3) tie the end with a square knot on the underside of the seat.

PADDING Heavy corrugated cardboard is desirable for padding. Other cardboard or heavy paper can be used but may rattle as the chair is sat in. Begin padding after 4 or 5 inches are woven on the front rail. If the rails are of even height, cut 4 pieces of cardboard, one to fit exactly each section of the seat. It may help to number them. Force them under the weaving from the upper side of the seat. If the rails are of uneven height, two pieces of cardboard may be used in each section. More padding may be added underneath and between. A hole about 2 inches square must be left in the cardboards at the center of the seat to get the fiber through. If brown paper is used, cut it in squares and fold it in triangles.

To fasten fiber ends after weaving is completed, pull each one to the underside of the seat, untwist the paper, cut it in half, wind it around a nearby strand, and tie. Unfasten joinings that are conspicuous, overlap the ends, and glue or wire them together.

Seats are finished with the oil and turpentine mixture used for real rush and then with a sealer or shellac.

SPLINT SEATS

Splint chair seats are made of wood that has been cut in long thin strips and interwoven in various patterns. The chair on which splint can be used must have seat rails so the splint can be wound around them. Such chairs may also have seats of splint-type materials (reed or wide binding cane) or of rush; the original seat usually indicates which to use.

Splint is suitable for chairs simple in design, with few turnings, such as early American ladder-back chairs. Often it is used when side rails are higher than front and back rails. If side rails slant so the front of the seat is more than 3 inches wider than the back, choose rush or a material no wider than ⅜ inch so the strands will stay in place easily. Splint and flat reed are used for indoor furniture, while flat oval reed and wide binding cane are used for outdoor furniture.

Splint is obtained from native ash and hickory and from tropical palm trees, the source of rattan, cane, and reed. The native splint is cut from selected second-growth timber with a straight grain. Ash splints, machine cut to a uniform width, wear well. Hickory splints often vary slightly in width, giving a pleasing effect.

Splints are sold either in bunches containing enough for one chair or in quantity lots. Costs per seat are about the same. Real splint makes a better-looking seat than does flat reed, but reed may be easier for beginners to weave.

The widths of splint vary, as can be seen in the table.

The width you need depends on the style and size of chair and on the place the

SPLINT WIDTHS

SPLINT	FLAT REED	FLAT OVAL REED	WIDE BINDING
½-inch, ⅝-inch, and ¾-inch Buy 1 pound of ⅝-inch width for a seat of average size (16 inches across the front).	¼-inch, ⅜-inch, and ½-inch Buy 1 pound of ⅜-inch width for a 16-inch seat	³⁄₁₆-inch and ⅜-inch Buy 1 pound for a 16-inch seat; 1½ pounds for an 18-inch or larger seat	About ³⁄₁₆-inch cane Buy 1 bunch of 500 feet for an 18-inch seat

chair is to be used. Narrower widths take longer to weave than wider ones, but wider ones may look heavy or bulky.

Fiber (paper) splint is less durable than other kinds of splint and isn't recommended.

Prepare to Weave

Cut the old splint away from the seat. You may find padding between the layers, but it can be omitted; shaped seats without stuffing are usually more comfortable than padded ones. Pull out all nails and tacks, and clean any dust from the seat rails. If you need to paint or refinish the wood, be sure the wood is dry before you begin weaving.

THE SPLINT Pull one of the strands of splint from the looped end of the hank, near where it is tied. As you pull, shake the hank so the splint will not tangle or roughen. Bend the piece between your fingers. The right side is smooth; the wrong side splinters. With the smooth or beveled side out, roll the strand to fit the pan or bowl in which it is to soak. Fasten the ends with a clamp clothespin. Prepare 3 or 4 strands in the same way.

Soak the splint in a solution of glycerine. This helps to shape the splint and retain moisture and keep the splint from drying out and cracking. To hasten the soaking process, use warm water in the solution. Lay the roll in the appropriate container and let it soak until it is soft and pliable—about 30 minutes for splint and about 20 minutes for flat reed, flat oval reed, and binding cane. Each time you re-

move a roll from the pan, put another one in to soak while you work.

How to Weave

Weaving is done in two directions; the first, called warping, is the wrapping of the splint around the seat rails. Usually this is done from the back to the front of the chair, or the long way of the opening, so that the second step, called weaving, can be done across the open rails, from side to side or the short way of the opening. Both sides of the seat are woven so that they look alike when finished.

All splints woven one way on the top of the seat are at right angles to those woven the other way. If the front of the seat is wider than the back, weave the center first and fill in the corners later with short lengths.

WARPING Mark a center rectangle or square the following way: Using a carpenter's square, cut a cardboard pattern of a size that will fit within the chair rails. Fit this close against one back post, parallel with the back rail. Mark the front corner of the square on the front rail. Repeat on the other side of the seat. Check to see that you have enough space for the width of the splint. If the two sides vary, adjust by marking a slightly greater allowance on the shorter side and less on the long side. On the front rail, mark the center between these two marks. Mark the center on the back rail.

Take the roll of splint from the bowl in which it is soaking and remove the excess water with your fingers, sponge, or cloth.

Put another strand in to soak while you work.

Work with the full length of the strand. Tie one end to the left side rail with string, with the right side of the splint next to the wood, so that you are working with the grain. Pull the strand under, then up and over the back rail, close to the post, in the exact position and shape you want it to dry. Pull the strand to the front rail, with the outside edge exactly at the pencil mark. Pull the strand over and under the rail and then return it to the back rail.

Continue until you have used all the strand. Force the wet warpers close together so they will not slip on the rail—splints are apt to shrink more in width than in length—and keep them equally taut. Hold the end temporarily with a clamp clothespin.

To join strands on the underside, place a new piece under the old, with the right side down. Lay a stick of soft wood across the rails, under the strands, and staple the strands together in three places, 1 to 2 inches apart, so that at least one of them can be covered when you weave the other way. Pull the strand away from the stick and use pliers to flatten the sharp ends of the staples. Leave enough of the old strand to support the new, but cut off any that would make a double thickness around the rail. Pull the new strand under and around the rail.

Continue wrapping strands. When you reach the center mark, count the warpers to make sure you will have the same number on each half of the seat. When you reach the pencil mark on the right side of the chair, use a clamp clothespin to hold

the warper. If the work is interrupted, sprinkle the seat and dampen the end to keep the splints pliable.

You may want to use the old seat as a guide in deciding the pattern of the weave. Or you can use scraps and ends of splints to try out different designs, or work out designs on squared paper, using one square for each warper.

Count the number of warpers on the back rail. This number may be evenly divisible by the number in the design you want to use; for example, 20 strands and a mesh of 2 over and 2 under, or 21 strands with a mesh of 3 over and 3 under. If the number is not evenly divisible, you may use the same design if you:

1. Plan from near the center of the opening and begin weaving accordingly.

Example: If there are 23 strands and a mesh of 3 over and 3 under, weave over 1 to start the row, continue across until you have used 21 strands, and then weave the single strand as on the first side.

2. Plan to use a diagonal design. Emphasis then will be away from the side rails, where the design may or may not be completed. A diagonal design also is desirable if the side rails are uneven.

The second row determines how you use the design. You can move one or more strands to the left for a diagonal design from the right back to the left front of the seat, or you may reverse the direction. For a geometric design, weave alternate rows alike.

Weaving that makes the design frequently is:

over 2 and under 2

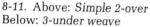

8-11. Above: *Simple 2-over*
Below: *3-under weave*

With finer mesh, strands are difficult to push together closely.

Other designs are:

> over 2 and under 3
> over 3 and under 3

Large seats or seats using narrow strands, ⅜ inch or less, may be woven:

> over 4 and under 4
> over 4 and under 2
> over 5 and under 3

These combinations may be reversed, such as over 2 and under 4. Coarser mesh may be used occasionally if long strands will stay in place and wear satisfactorily. See page 202 for other weaving designs and the method of planning elaborate designs on squared paper. The design you choose depends on the size and shape of the seat opening, the width of splint you are using, the number of warper strands, and whether the number is even or odd.

WEAVING   Be sure the strand of splint is long enough to weave across the top of the seat and to join on the underside. Loosen the last warper over the back rail, remove the clothespin, and bring the warper from the front under and over the back rail and under the preceding warper. Then bring the strand diagonally in front of the back post, under the side rail, and turned so the right side is down. Pull all the strands tight and then weave across, from right to left.

Pull the weaver over the side rail and weave the underside like the top, going over and under the same warpers.

When you join strands, staple from either side, if you know the staples will be hidden under warpers. Or you can cover staples with short lengths of splint tucked under nearby strands. Flatten the sharp ends of staples with pliers, as before. Continue weaving, cutting the old strand inside the rail, even if you waste some of it, and forcing the joining in position. You can't use the wrapper strand you tucked under until you get nearer the front.

The second row is over 2 and under 3, but one warper to the left of the first row. Or weave to the right if you want the diagonal in the same direction as on the top of the seat. Use a stick or a screwdriver to force the strands together. At the same time, pull the strand across the rails so the seat will be firm.

On the underside, plan from near the center of the opening—where the design is established—how to begin the row and so continue the design used on the top. In this way you will weave over and under the same strands as you did on top.

When you have woven far enough to see the design, and have space, cut off a length of splint for a warper in the corner of the seat. Hook about 3 inches over the weaver that will continue the design, near the back of the seat, or just push the strand in rather than hook it over a weaver, if it fits snugly. Bring this warper to the underside of the seat and hook it over a weaver there also. The strands may be joined on top of the seat, under the warpers, to save splint.

If the joining is secure, cut off the old strand so two thicknesses do not show. Also cut the string holding the first strand. The weaving will hold this end in place.

Add other short lengths in the corners of the seat, as you have room for them. Warpers should also be cut so the ends can be concealed under weavers. One or two staples and the weaving will hold the joining. Use a screwdriver or similar blunt tool to help with the weaving as you get near the front of the seat.

Continue weaving to the front rail. Finish the underside by weaving as far across as you can and tucking the end under a warper. If the back of the chair is to be woven, wrap strands the long way (up and down). Weave across from the bottom up so that you can push the strands in place easily.

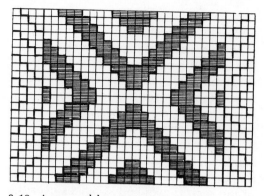

8-12. A more elaborate weave pattern

OTHER WEAVING DESIGNS Elaborate designs should first be planned on squared paper. Count the number of warper strands over the back rail. Estimate the number of rows from front to back by measuring with a piece of splint on one of the side rails. Allow one square on the paper for each strand across the back, and for each strand from back to front.

For a geometric design, choose as square an opening as possible or a design that can be adapted to a wider front rail. Begin in the center and work toward the sides and ends. The side sections indicate that the design can be continued if there is space for added rows.

Weaving with Other Materials

Flat reed is thinner and more pliable than splint and consequently is easier for beginners to use. It is not as smooth, as sturdy, or as fine in quality as splint. The right side of reed is smoother than the wrong side. Follow the directions for weaving splint seats.

Flat oval reed is used mostly for porch furniture. The right side is beveled and the other flat. Strands can be rolled smaller than splint, to fit in a bowl about 11 inches in diameter for soaking.

How to Finish the Seat

Trim off hairs or rough places with a razor blade or sharp knife. Splint that has a hard, glossy surface can be left without a finish. Or you may apply 2 or 3 coats of a thin type of penetrating wood sealer to both sides of the seat. Apply the first coat as soon as you finish weaving. Let each coat dry thoroughly before applying the next. If you want the seat darkened to blend with the color of the chair finish, apply one or more coats of seat stain, which you can obtain from the dealer from whom you buy other seating supplies. A sealer can then be used over the stain. Wax can also be used, but it may stain clothing and collect dust.

WEBBING SEATS

Webbing seats can be used to modernize old chairs, benches, and stools. Webbing also looks good on contemporary indoor and outdoor furniture.

The chair on which you plan to use webbing should be sturdy and simple in line and design. Chair seat frames should be straight, rather than noticeably curved. The front of the frame should be no more than 3 inches wider than the back so the webbing will stay in place without slipping on the side rails. The wood of the frame should be 2 to 3 inches deep to support the webbing underneath. There must be enough space between the seat and back to bring the webbing through the opening.

Webbing can be used on round seat rails as well as on flat ones. For large openings, the frame must be sturdy and the wood able to hold tacks well so the webbing can support the necessary weight. Usually, wooden chairs with small seat openings are neither comfortable nor attractive with webbing. If webbing is to be used on the back of the chair, the wood in the crosspieces should be thick enough to take tacks without splitting.

Select the Webbing

Webbing is available in both plastic and cotton, 2 inches wide, in a variety of colors. It can be tacked or stapled to wood.

Plastic webbing can be cleaned easily with a damp cloth and used on both indoor and outdoor furniture. Cotton webbing stays in place better than plastic webbing but is not as easy to clean or as satisfactory on outdoor furniture. You can buy webbing at chair-seating and craftsman's supply houses, and at certain mail order houses and department stores.

How to Weave

Before beginning the weaving process, the old seat should be removed and the chair refinished or painted. Then the new webbing can be applied.

SEATS WITH FLAT RAILS Measure with a stiff ruler and mark the center of the front rail. Do the same on the other three rails. Place short strips of webbing loosely on the chair, to plan the number of strips you will need to use each way, or fold a long length and estimate the number of strips. As you plan, avoid the legs and the lower part of the back posts. Use tacks and clothespins to hold the webbing temporarily in place. Arrange crosspieces to see how the mesh will look. Allow space between strips so the seat will not look solid or bulky.

The right side is usually on the outside of the roll, is smoother, and has more sheen than the wrong side. Cut the number of strips you'll need back to front. Allow enough webbing for each strip to extend across the top of the seat, down the rails to the underside, or to the inside if there is room to hammer the tacks, and to turn under ½ inch.

Tip the chair so you can tack easily. The place you begin tacking is determined by the shape and construction of the chair. Tack only temporarily until you are sure the strips are where you want them.

Fasten strips first on the straighter of the two rails or on the one with a crosspiece, where you have less room to hammer. Then you can stretch the webbing and tack it on the more open rail. If the back of this chair is curved, fasten the strips first on the front rail so they can be stretched taut from the straight edge. Fasten the webbing on the inside of the frame so that the lower edge of the front rail will look smooth rather than bumpy. Fasten the outside strips first, with the webbing close to the chair leg. Or you may find it easier to start in the center.

Put the tape over the end of the strip to prevent raveling. Turn the end under about ½ inch and fasten with 5 tacks, staggered to help keep the wood from splitting. Tack the center strip next, or those on each side of the center if you have an even number, and then the strips between. When you are sure the strips are evenly spaced and properly placed, pound the tacks all the way in. On the curving rail at the back, tack the center strip first so you can be sure it is straight. Tape the end.

Cut cardboard strips, one for each webbing strip, about ¼ inch narrower than the webbing and the wood. Turn under the taped end and insert the cardboard to help make the edge smooth. Pull the strip taut and tack it on the bottom of the seat rail, since this edge shows least. Or, if the wood splits easily, tack it on the inside of the frame.

When pulled tight across the top, the outside strips will be on a slant underneath the rail. Cut the end parallel with the rail. Tape the end, and tack the strip temporarily in place. Do the same on the other side, then fasten the strips between in the same way. The strips will be closer together on the back rail because it is shorter than the front rail. When you are sure the strips are placed correctly, tack them permanently.

Measure and cut all the side strips at once. (If you want to save webbing, you may find it more economical to cut each one as you work.) Fasten them together with a clamp clothespin, in the order in which you will use them from front to back.

Weave the front strip over and under to determine how you want the design and how the mesh will best be held in place. Weave the next strip under and over, and alternate the rest.

Fasten the strips on alternate sides. Since the side rails slant, the ends of the webbing will slant. Tape one end of each strand and tack the front strip, bringing the edge close to the front legs. Tack on the inside, if you have space, because the wood splits less, or tack on the bottom edge. Tack the back strip close to the back leg, then the center strip and those between. Pull the strips taut and tack them. When the strips are all in place, evenly spaced and equally taut, pound all the tacks all the way in.

SEATS WITH ROUND RAILS Webbing can also be used on chairs with round rails. Paint the chair or refinish with a natural finish. Be sure the chair is thoroughly dry before you weave the seat.

Mark the centers of the four rails as directed on page 182. Plan the number of strips you will use each way and cut those for back to front.

If both back and front rails are straight on this chair, first fasten the strips to the back and stretch them toward the front. The wood neither takes nor holds tacks easily, so use a heavy stapler gun to fasten the strips. Use 3 strong ⁵⁄₁₆-inch staples across the width of each strip of webbing. There is little room for cardboard strips on round rails, so omit them and turn the

8-13. Stapling plastic webbing to a round rail

webbing under a generous ½ inch. Otherwise, the seat is woven in the same way as the one with flat rails.

BACKS OF CHAIRS Webbing may also be used for the backs of chairs. Mark the centers, and plan and cut strips as for seats. Allow enough length so the laced webbing will shape to the back of the person using the chair as well as to the back of the chair. Strips are first fastened up and

down, then other strips are woven from side to side.

Tack the end of the strip first on the front of the lower crosspiece. Then pull the strip over the top of the crosspiece down the back, under the crosspiece, and then up the back of the chair and over the top crosspiece, tacking the end on the underside.

The tacking of both ends of side-to-side strips is more difficult to conceal. Figure

8-14. Two methods of finishing webbing on backs

8-14 (left) shows tacks fastening the upper two strips. The two lower strips are stapled to the chair and are less conspicuous than tacks.

In the illustration above right, two fastenings are covered by folds of webbing. Weave the strips first. About 2 inches in from one end, tack near the front of the post. Turn the end under and insert a strip of cardboard. Use three ¾-inch wire brads to hold this fold. The top of these brads can be concealed by forcing apart the mesh of the webbing. The cardboard pre-

vents the brads from going all the way through and also keeps the edge of the fold smooth.

Fasten the other end of the strip to the opposite post in a similar way.

FURNITURE UPHOLSTERY REPAIRS

Upholstered furniture consists basically of a frame, strip or cleat webbing, padding, and cover. Some furniture also has spring upholstery. Repairs needed on upholstered furniture generally include recovering; replacement or redistribution of padding; replacement or refastening of webbing; and regluing, reinforcement, or replacement of frame parts. With spring construction, replacing, anchoring, and retying springs may also be necessary. Loose cushions may also be repaired; for this information, see pages 209–16.

Recovering

Replace the entire cover if the covers on seat, back, or arms are torn, soiled, or worn beyond repair. Even with fairly new furniture it is usually impossible to match new material to worn or faded fabric, so all sections must usually be recovered when one is damaged.

Procedures for recovering upholstered furniture vary with furniture design, but the following general procedure applies to almost all types:

1. Remove the old cover carefully, taking out all tacks.

2. Using the old cover as a pattern, cut a piece of new material to the approximate shape and size.

3. Smooth out and replace any lumpy or torn padding and lay the new cover in place, making certain all four sides have the same amount of surplus material.

4. Tack the center of the opposite sides, stretching the material lightly but firmly. Don't drive the tacks all the way in. Work from center to edges, stretching the material evenly. If wrinkles develop, remove the tacks and work the wrinkles out. Note how the old covering was folded and fitted at corners and around legs and arms. If this was satisfactory, fit the new cover the same way. When the covering fits smoothly, drive the tacks all the way in.

5. After the covering is tacked to the side of the frame, cover the tack heads with an edging or gimp. Fasten the gimp with large-headed upholstery nails spaced about 2 inches apart.

Replacement or Redistribution of Padding

Padding tow, cotton batting, excelsior, or moss is used over the springs in the case of spring construction, or on the webbing in the case of padded construction. When padding shifts or becomes lumpy, remove the cover and redistribute or replace the padding. To replace padding:

1. First, remove all old padding and tack a piece of burlap smoothly over the entire surface to be padded.

2. Spread padding evenly over the burlap, forming a compact cushion about 1½ inches thick.

3. Cover this with a second piece of burlap or muslin, tacked down securely, and place a 2-inch layer of cotton batting on top. Pull off surplus cotton around the edges; don't cut the cotton, since this will make a ridge under the cover.

4. Tack a cambric cover over the frame bottom to keep the padding from working through to springs or webbing and falling out.

5. Replace the cover as described previously.

8-15. Method of attaching webbing to a framework

Repairing the Frame

Tighten loose frame joints with glue blocks, pins and screws, or angle irons. Repair any frame damage. Full details on this type of work may be found in Chapter Two.

Repairing Webbing

Check strip or cleat webbing for signs of wear or breakage whenever the cover is removed. Replace damaged webbing and refasten loose strips. To ensure that webbing will hold securely, double it over at the ends to give the tacks more gripping power, tighten, and tack so that stress is at right angles to tack length. Run the webbing in two directions, at right angles to each other. Closing the entire bottom with

webbing is not necessary, but too much webbing is better than too little. If springs are to be anchored to the webbing, space the webbing to support the spring bases. Similarly, anchor metal strips or wood cleats securely and space them for springs.

Adjusting Springs

Springs may shift, bend, or become otherwise damaged. Reanchor and retie loose springs; replace those that are damaged.

Springs are usually attached differently on webbing, on metal strips, or on wood cleats. Fasten spring bases to webbing with heavy flax cord about ⅛ inch in diameter. Anchor springs to metal strips with clamps. If the clamps loosen, rerivet them. Fasten springs to wood cleats with staples or metal straps and nails.

After the springs are anchored, retie them with heavy flax cord like that used to anchor springs to webbing.

1. Nail the cord to the center of one side of the frame. Pull it over the top of the springs to an opposite anchoring nail. Allow enough cord to tie two double half hitches to each spring and cut to this length.

2. Bring the cord up to the top of the first coil spring and tie it with a double half hitch to the nearest rim of the first spring. Before drawing the knot tight, pull the spring down to shape the seat or back. Continue to the opposite side of the top on the same spring and tie it.

3. Continue in like fashion, tying two points on each spring and finally anchoring the cord to the nail on the opposite

8-16. Left to right: Tying a spring to webbing, fastening a spring to a metal strip, and fastening a spring to a wood cleat

8-17. 1. A spring tied lengthwise
2. Crosswise and diagonally in place

side of the frame. Run cords in both directions (side to side and front to back) at right angles to each other, until all springs are tied in two directions.

4. Tie springs diagonally in the same manner, beginning at one corner of the frame and anchoring the cord on the opposite corner.

5. Repeat with the cord at right angles to the first set of diagonal cords. Tie this cord to the spring with two double half hitches and also tie it to the other three cords at their junction in the center of the coil. Each spring is now tied in eight places, and the crossing cords are tied together as well.

6. Replace the padding.

Repairing Innerspring Cushions

A sagging or lumpy seat cushion with an innerspring unit can be repaired in a few hours. With a new case for the springs and a little extra padding, you can make the cushion look as good as new.

Place the cushion on a table, top side up, with the front toward you. Insert a safety pin near the front. Using a stiff rule, measure and write down the height of the boxing between the seam cords.

Open the outside cover by ripping the back and side seams of the bottom of the outside cover to within an inch of the front corners. Throw back the loose flap.

OPEN THE PADDING Manufacturers use different methods to lay the padding around an innerspring unit. Examine the padding of the cushion, disturbing it as lit-

tle as possible, to find out how the cushion has been padded.

If the padding is wound several times around the innerspring unit, usually the springs can be pulled out through one of the easily opened ends of the padding.

If the padding is badly torn, take out the springs through a hole in the top. When the old padding is in this condition, usually most or all of it has to be replaced with new padding.

REMOVE THE SPRINGS Before taking the springs from the padding or before tearing the unit apart, count and write down the number of springs from back to front and from side to side so that they may be placed in the same order in the new case. Then take the springs out of the padding. If some of the rows of springs are crushed together so the count can't be made in this way, lift out the springs and, if they can be seen, count the number of circles on the bottom padding. But if the material covering the springs is badly torn and all the springs are tangled, pull them apart, count them, and determine the number that should be in each row.

All springs should be the same height and should stand erect. If they are not the same height or don't stand erect, pull the bent ones into shape. To shorten them, hold the top coil down with one hand and pull the next coil upward. You may need to follow this procedure at both ends of the spring. To straighten the spring, use one or more of the following methods:

1. Pull sideways, toward you on one

wire and away from you on an adjacent wire.

2. Or twist the coils around and bend them, if necessary.

3. Flatten the spring and then twist the coils between the palms of the hands. Test each spring to be sure it stands erect from both ends.

MEASUREMENTS YOU NEED

	SAMPLE CUSHION	YOUR CUSHION
Height of the boxing in the cushion (inches)	3½	_____
Number of springs from back to front (case)	6	_____
Number of springs from side to side	4	_____
Total number of springs	24	_____
Diameter of the widest part of the springs (inches)	3	_____

MAKE THE CASES The new innerspring unit is made of several long cases of firm, nonstretching material, such as muslin, feed bags, or burlap, in which are stitched the pockets for the springs. When these cases are filled, the springs and cases are tied together.

Make one case only, to test your measurements before making the rest of the cases. Tear or pull a thread across the material to get a straight cutting edge. Pull the material if necessary to get it straight and to make it lie flat.

See the table on page 212 for measuring width and length of one case before proceeding.

Cut off this measured strip on the grain of the material and fold it in half lengthwise. Draw pencil lines ½ inch in from each end, then stitch on these lines. Make a test pocket before stitching all the pockets. Differences in quality and weight of the cloth may make the pockets too loose or too high for the springs. Starting from the seam, mark off the width of one pocket, draw a line from that point parallel to the seam, and stitch along this line, backstitching each end for about 1 inch. Now fit a spring in this pocket, inserting it sideways and turning it upright after it is in the pocket. The spring should fit the pocket easily. If the pocket is too tight or too loose, the material will wear out quickly. Make the necessary change in measurement now if it is necessary and restitch the pocket. Starting from the line of the first pocket, measure and mark accurately as many other pockets of the same width as are needed, drawing parallel pencil lines from top to bottom and stitching all the way through on these lines.

Next test the pocket for height. Insert the spring sideways and turn it upright

For the width of one case (cut on the width of the material), add together:

	SAMPLE CUSHION	YOUR CUSHION
The diameter of the widest part of a spring	3 inches	_____
The height of the boxing	3½ inches	_____
Seam allowance	½ inch	½ inch
Total	7 inches	_____
Multiply by 2 for the width of one case	× 2	
Total	14 inches	_____

For the length of one case (cut lengthwise of the material), add together:

	SAMPLE CUSHION	YOUR CUSHION
The diameter of the widest part of a spring	3 inches	_____
One-half of this diameter	1½ inches	_____
Total	4½ inches	_____
Multiply the above total by the number of springs in one row from back to front:		
4½ inches × 6 springs	27 inches	_____
Add 1 inch, for ½-inch seam at each end	1 inch	1 inch
Cut the case this length	28 inches	_____

as before. Then put a row of pins along the top of the pocket ½ inch down from the open edge. Measure the height of the spring as it stands in the pocket; if it is higher than the height of the boxing of the outside cover (measuring from seam to seam or between the cordings), lower the pins for the distance needed to make the measurement the same as that of the box-ing. Mark this pinned line at one point and remove the pins and the spring. Measure from the bottom or folded side of the case up to this point to determine the height the pockets should be. Using this measurement, from the folded edge mark the height of all the pockets, then draw a line.

Make the rest of the cases like the first

8-18. *Cases tied together*

so there will be one case for each row.

INSERT THE SPRINGS Press the springs flat and insert them sideways into the pockets, pushing each one to the bottom. If there is a poor spring, place it where the cushion has least wear. Hold the springs down by placing a pin in the cloth close to each spring, and hold the two sides of the case together by inserting two or three pins at right angles to the edges. Stitch on the line. Remove the pins and turn the springs upright in the pockets, with the seam running through the middle of the spring tops.

SEW THE CASES TOGETHER Arrange the filled cases with the long sides together,

8-19. *How to sew together the pinned edges of the cover*

squaring them up against the corner of a table. Insert a few pins to hold them in place. Fasten them by tying the tops and bottoms of the springs right through the cloth as follows: Cut a length of mattress twine a generous 1½ times the distance to be sewed. Thread a curved or straight needle with the length of mattress twine. Insert the needle through the cloth and under the top wire of an outside spring. Tie a slip knot. Then continue by passing the needle through the material and under *two* top wires of each pair of springs, using the knot shown in Figure 8-18. End the row with a square knot. Tie the front row next, in the same way, and then the other rows from side to side. Repeat the tying from back to front. Turn the unit over and tie the bottom side in the same way.

SEW THE UNIT INTO THE CUSHION   To replace the finished spring unit in a cushion that has an open flap, lay the spring unit back in the padding in its former place without crushing the side pads. See that this side padding is pulled up around the sides of the spring unit and that it is of the same thickness all the way around, that it fills the corners, and that it is smooth on the outside. Draw the loose top padding back over the spring unit. To insert the spring unit into a cushion that has padding wound around it, bend the sides of the unit inward, push it through the hole at the end of the padding, then flatten the unit.

In both types of cushion, make the corners square and well filled. Cover any holes in the padding by laying pieces of upholsterer's felt under them, or place a new layer over the entire top and bottom. If this material is not available, use layers of cotton batting, or cut pieces from an old blanket, smooth quilt, or mattress pad large enough to fit over the top and bottom of the old padding. With such pieces the cushion will not be so soft or look so good as when the upholsterer's felt is used.

If all-new cotton padding is to be used, lay 2 or 3 thicknesses of the upholsterer's felt in the bottom of the outside cushion cover. Use pieces large enough to come up to the top of the side walls. Then lay the spring unit in place on the bottom, usually a little nearer the front of the cushion than the back, and bring the padding up around the sides. Cover the top of the unit with the same amount of felt, tucking it over the sides down to the bottom. This makes two or three thicknesses of cotton over the top and bottom of the unit and four or more in the space between the sides of the unit and the side walls of the cushion cover. Add more if needed, particularly in the corners. There should be

1.

2.

3.

4.

8-20. Steps in covering a leather or plastic seat

5.

enough padding so that you cannot feel the springs on the outside when you press the cushion with your hand.

Pull the loose top of the cushion cover back into place. Make sure that all raw edges are turned in and that the cording, if the cushion has cording, is stitched securely to the edge of the cushion-cover top. Pin the open edges together first at the corners, then at the middle of the back and the middle of the sides. Continue to pin first from a center and then from a corner on each side of the cushion. Pull all the seams into their proper places on the cushion.

To sew the pinned edges together, use a linen thread matching the color of the cushion. First fasten the end of the thread into the material, then run the needle straight upward through the two open edges. Insert the needle again a little ahead, and push it diagonally through. Insert the needle again and repeat the sewing procedure. The completed cushion should look flat, should have sharp corners, and be firm and comfortable.

nine

Care of Furniture

Today's miracle furniture finishes have new and desirable qualities and characteristics. They are more durable and more resistant to scratches, stains, and extremes in temperature. Coatings industry research programs have made it possible to bleach and apply uniform color finishes to even lower-price hardwoods—something that was impossible a few years ago.

However, even these amazing new finishes need to be cared for properly. There are right and wrong ways for even the simplest care of furniture, and the following hints will help you in protecting the beauty of *all* your furniture.

Of course, the patina of furniture, which develops a mellow richness of color and texture, is purely a surface condition and a great asset in antique furniture. Unfortunately, it's not only the surface of furniture that needs to be dusted regularly, and occasionally washed or polished, and perhaps waxed or treated with oil; it is

also important that the wood should not become too dry or absorb too much moisture, thus causing it to shrink or swell.

It's not difficult to keep furniture in excellent shape, provided it is not neglected. Frequent care will help to keep wood furniture in good condition.

DUSTING

Furniture should be dusted frequently. Unless fine particles of dust are removed often, they will act as abrasives and become ground into the finish. Always follow the grain of the wood while dusting—wiping across the grain is likely to cause scratches, since dust contains grit. A few drops of quality furniture polish on your dustcloth will help pick up the dust, instead of just pushing it around the surface.

For dusting, use soft cheesecloth or chemically treated dust mittens or cloths.

WASHING

Furniture sometimes acquires a coat of grime that dusting won't remove because its home is in a smoky city, or because it is exposed to greasy fumes or smoke from a fireplace or kitchen. The furniture is then best cleaned by washing or using materials prepared for cleaning. Furniture should also be washed when waxes have gradually built up and have created a thick film. This film streaks, smudges, and hides the natural beauty of the wood grain. Additional waxing can only add to this accumulation, and you will only be polishing the old wax, not the finish.

Wash a section at a time, dipping a cloth (such as toweling) into a sudsy solution of warm water and a good detergent or soap flakes. Rinse the cloth often and again follow the wood grain with your strokes. More than one washing may be needed to get down to the original finish. When the furniture surfaces have dried thoroughly, they are ready to be properly waxed or polished. Furniture finished only with oil should never be washed. More on washing furniture can be found in Chapter Three.

WAXING AND POLISHING

It's the belief of many professional refinishers that an occasional rubbing with furniture polish is beneficial to a finish but that excess use of oil polishes should be avoided, since they have a tendency to cause a dull and lifeless surface that collects dust more rapidly.

When using commercial furniture polishes, follow the directions on the container closely. In using most polishes, it is best to saturate a piece of cheesecloth with hot water and wring it out. When the cloth is cold, shake the polish thoroughly, apply sparingly to the cloth, and clean the furniture by brisk rubbing. Turn the cloth as it becomes dirty. When the piece is clean, rub the surface with a soft dry cloth until a fingerprint will no longer show on it.

A mixture of 1 part commercially boiled linseed oil and 1 part turpentine makes an excellent polish for use once or twice a year on varnished and highly polished surfaces. This polish brightens a dull, foggy finish and helps either to stop surface checking or make existing checking less obvious. The oil feeds the finish, and the turpentine loosens dirt and helps the oil to penetrate. Apply the mixture with a soft cloth, wipe off excess with a dry one, and polish with the grain of the wood until no fingerprint will show on the surface.

Waxing furniture properly with a quality product has a more lasting and softer effect than does treating it with furniture polish. Once wax is correctly applied it lasts a long time, and its polish can be revived by rubbing the surface with a soft and lintless cloth. Additional wax should be applied only when needed. This is indicated by the refusal of the surface to polish, after a firm rubbing with a dry, soft cloth. Applying wax thickly, or building up too many coats, is a detriment to a good finish, causing surfaces to become slippery and to have too high a shine, instead of the desired soft, mellow appearance, and, under damp conditions, to become sticky. The same conditions prevail when wax is used as a floor polish.

DO'S AND DON'TS WITH WOOD FURNITURE

DO
• Dust furniture regularly—lift lamps, ashtrays, and other objects, too
• Rub with the grain of the wood when dusting, polishing, or waxing
• Carefully read and follow the label instructions on all furniture-care products
• Use a pad under bowls and platters to prevent heat damage on your dining room table
• Use coasters or pads under drinks, flower pots, and other containers for liquids that are placed on furniture

DON'T
• Use self-polishing floor wax on furniture
• Wet any of the glued joints on furniture
• Use rubber mats or coasters unless there is a felt pad beneath them. (Some rubber compounds and vinyl films may stain or soften furniture finishes.)
• Wash furniture finished only with oil

UPHOLSTERED FURNITURE

Sofas and upholstered chairs are among the most frequently used pieces of furniture and are therefore subject to constant wear, tear, and soil. Upholstery will look better and last longer if given frequent light cleaning; once soil is deeply embedded, cleaning becomes difficult if not impossible. Remember that upholstery fabrics can be cleaned only on one side, so water and chemicals that soak into the upholstery must be avoided. The best insurance against future soiling is to have all upholstery fabrics processed with one of several chemical materials to repel spots and stains.

There are two kinds of dirt that plague the home. There is dry dirt, particles of dirt that are in the air, a problem generally solved by vacuuming. Then there is the dirt produced by cooking fumes, heating, and floor and furniture wax. This kind of dirt produces an oily film on upholstered furniture and must be removed by wet or dry cleaning.

For weekly care, go over upholstery to remove surface dirt and dust. Use a whisk broom or vacuum cleaner brush attachment on the entire piece, giving special attention to arms, headrest, and crevices. Clean cushions the same way, unless they are stuffed with down. In that case, use only a cloth or brush; the suction of a vacuum cleaner may pull out the down if the cushions don't have down-proof ticking. Seat cushions will keep their shape better if they are turned frequently. Down pillows and others without spring construction should be plumped daily.

Remove all spots as soon as they occur. The longer a spot is permitted to sit on a piece of furniture, the harder it will be to get off. Before attempting to remove spots, however, check with the furniture manufacturer for special instructions. There are special upholstery spot removers available, but read the instructions carefully and always test them on a concealed area of your furniture. In some cases, spots and stains on delicate fabrics should be treated by an experienced dry cleaner.

Fresh grease spots and lipstick stains can often be successfully removed with absorbent powders, such as cornstarch or talcum. These powders are safe on all fabrics.

Heavy grease stains can be treated with a commercial dry-cleaning fluid. Use in a well-ventilated room and follow the safety precautions on the label. Incidentally, tar, paint, machine oil, furniture polish, chewing gum, ice cream, shoe polish, and similar stains may be removed with these commercial products. But dry cleaners and solvents must never be used on foam rubber upholstery; they cause the rubber to disintegrate. Use only foamy or liquid cleaners.

Food spots, urine and perspiration, mildew, and cosmetic marks can be removed with a solution of light-duty detergent and water or a commercial upholstery shampoo. Apply the cleaner sparingly with a clean cloth. Work from the outer edge of the spot toward the center so that the stain does not spread. Use a clean part of the cloth for each application.

Never use soap on upholstery fabrics. Since it cannot be properly rinsed, it forms a film that attracts dust and soil. In general, woolen and silk fabrics require a lighter-duty detergent than synthetic or cotton fabrics.

Vinyl plastic upholstery materials re-quire proper care for maximum service. Clean deep-embossed patterns regularly with a damp, soapy brush. Wipe leather-like finishes with a damp, soapy cloth. (Use mild soap and avoid abrasive cleaners.) Rub off lipstick, crayon, or ink with cloth dampened with rubbing alcohol. Rub off shoe polish, paint, or tar with kerosene or a similar agent.

Vacuum or dust the furniture thoroughly. Check the label for fiber content and special cleaning instructions, then prepare your cleaning solution and test an inconspicuous spot of the furniture. A "dry" foam made from a detergent and water (use only the foam) is a simple cleaner you can make at home.

Apply the foam to a small area with a soft brush or a sponge. Work in a circular motion and wipe immediately with a dry towel. The process should go quickly with as little moisture as possible. Excessive moisture can cause shrinkage and mildew. As you begin each area, overlap the previous one so that the entire piece will dry evenly. It's a good idea to begin with arm rests or other heavily soiled areas so you can go over them again, if necessary.

Dry as quickly as possible. Furniture can be dried out of doors in the shade, indoors with the windows open, in the draft of an electric fan, or in a heated room. The furniture may feel damp for a day or so, depending upon the atmospheric conditions.

ten

Furniture Repairing and Refinishing Tools

It is surprising how much can be accomplished with only a few simple hand tools. However, these should be of the best quality. It is difficult and often impossible to accomplish good work with hand tools that are cheaply constructed, are made of poor materials, are out of balance, or won't retain a cutting edge.

Good tools are the delight of every mechanically minded person, and to use them is a fascinating, often profitable, hobby. You realize a profit when you construct a needed article in spare time, or when repairs, which you complete in a satisfactory manner, would otherwise have had to be done by a professional.

In practically every household can be found a hammer, saw, screwdriver, pliers, rule or yardstick, and perhaps a chisel and plane. These are fine for a starter if they are quality tools that can be used for good workmanship.

This chapter will give you a list of those hand tools that are deemed adequate for the work you will first attempt. When purchasing tools (hand or power), it pays to buy those of a size, weight, or kind suitable to the worker or the work to be done. Don't hesitate to ask for information from a knowledgeable salesperson. Buy tools of a good brand with years of reputation behind them. A friendly carpenter or cabinetmaker can often be of great assistance.

In the list that follows, the tools are shown singly or in groups, according to the type of work for which each is to be used. Referring to the classification will make it easier to select a tool for a specific purpose.

BASIC TOOLS SUGGESTED FOR PURCHASE

Boring
Bit brace, 8-inch ratchet type
Auger bits, ⅜-, ½-, ¾-inch
Countersink
Electric drill
Twist drills (drill bits), straight shank,
⅛-, ³⁄₁₆-, ¼-inch

Clamping
Mechanic's bench vise
C (screw) clamps, 2 each, 3- and 6-
or 8-inch
Clamp clothespins, 6
Pliers, combination step-joint,
6- or 8-inch
Pliers, long-nose, side-cutting,
5- or 6-inch
Screwdrivers, 6- and 8-inch or 10-inch
Screwdriver bit, to fit brace, ⅜- or
½-inch

Cutting
Pocketknife (Scout), with strong,
pointed blade
Old knife, blunt
Razor-blade holder, with blades
Diagonal cutting pliers, 7-inch

Filing
Half-round wood rasp, 10-inch
Smooth mill file, 8-inch
Shoemaker's rasp
Nail file

Hammering
Carpenter's nail claw hammer
Tack hammer, claw-type, lightweight
Nail-set, ³⁄₁₆-inch
Mallet, rubber-headed

Marking
Center punch
Pencil

Measuring
Rule, steel roll-type, 6-foot
Rule, straight, wood, 6- or 12-inch
Try square, 6- or 8-inch

Painting
Paintbrushes, 2-inch
Paintbrushes, artist's, for touch-up

Removing Finishes
Putty knife, stiff blade, 2-inch
Toothbrushes, old
Meat skewers, wood

Sawing
Handsaw (panel), crosscut, 26-inch,
8 points per inch

Sharpening
Grinder
Oilstone

Shaving
Plane, "block," 7-inch
Chisels, ½-inch plain type (straight
edges) and 1-inch beveled edge

Miscellaneous
Ice pick, for marking and holding
Oil can, small
Dusting brush and pan
Teaspoon and tablespoon,
dime-store type
Clothesline, cotton and strong

ADDITIONAL TOOLS SUGGESTED FOR PURCHASE

Boring
> Auger bits, ⅜-, ⅞-, and 1-inch
> Bit depth gauge, adjustable
> Expansion bit, ⅞- to 3-inch capacity
> Twist drills as needed

Clamping
> Woodworker's bench vise,
>   quick-acting type
> Hand-screw wood clamps, 2 each,
>   5- and 12-inch jaws
> Furniture bar clamps, 2 each, 3 and
>   5 feet long

Cutting
> Scissors or shears, 6- to 8-inch
> Tin snips, combination type
> Cold chisels, ¼- and ⅜-inch

Filing
> Rattail file, slim and tapered
> File brush

Hammering
> Mechanic's ball-peen hammer,
>   13- to 16-ounce
> Nail-set, ⅛-inch

Marking
> Wood-marking gauge
> Scratch awl

Measuring
> Carpenter's combination square
> Slide **T** bevel square
> Steel square (framing), 16 by 24 inches
> Rule, 2-foot, folding
> Spirit level, 18 to 24 inches long
> Calipers, both inside and outside types
> Dividers

Painting
> Putty knife, 2 inches wide,
>   flexible blade

Sawing
> Portable circular saw
> Ripsaw, 26-inch, 7 points per inch
> Dovetail saw, 8-inch,
>   17 points per inch
> Keyhole or compass saw
> Coping saw, 6½-inch
> Miter box
> Backsaw, 12- to 14-inch, 13 or
>   14 points per inch
> Hacksaw, type adjustable to length
>   of blades

Shaving
> Plane, smooth, 8- to 10-inch
> Plane, junior jack 11½-inch,
>   or jack 14-inch
> Plane, fore or joiner, 18-inch
> Spoke shave, 2 cutters, blades
>   curved and straight
> Drawknife, medium size
> Cabinet scrapers

Miscellaneous
> Carpenter's bar, gooseneck 18-inch
>   (commonly called a wrecking bar)
> Electric soldering iron
> Staple gun and staples, ¼-inch size
> Spatula, artist's or druggist's with
>   flexible 3- or 4-inch blade
> Spirit lamp
> Cutter and chisel grinder
> Combination oilstone

CARE OF TOOLS

The care of tools is of great importance in keeping them in proper working order. Those with cutting edges may become dulled easily by careless handling or by being stored in the wrong manner, or they may become rusted, which can be prevented. Instruction on the proper care of tools can be divided into four parts.

Handling Tools

More tools with cutting edges are dulled or damaged by the way in which they are handled (or stored) than through actual use.

Example: Many workers lay a plane on a surface with the cutting edge down, instead of on its side. If they stopped to reason, they would realize that the blade will not cut unless it extends below the bottom of the plane. When it is laid on that surface, the blade is dulled.

Also, chisels, saws, cabinet scrapers, knives, etc.—in fact, all tools with a cutting edge—should always be handled with the utmost care when being laid down, for fear of damage.

A good rule to follow before any work is done with a cutting tool is to examine carefully all wood for hidden pieces of metal, such as broken nails, screws, etc.

Storing Tools

Saws should seldom be laid down, because of dulling the offset teeth, but rather should be hung on a peg or nail, immedi-ately after use. If they must be stored by being laid down, the cutting edge should be protected by wrapping the saw blade in paper, or by placing a narrow U-shaped strip of wood over the teeth and tying it in place with a string. This strip may be made on a power saw in a few minutes.

If there is a chance of damage to chisels, make a small hood for the point by folding a piece of thin cardboard and tying it with a string, so that it may be slipped on and off easily.

Sharpening Tools

Many workers are careless about keeping their cutting tools sharp and their other tools in shape to do good work. Quality work is largely dependent on properly sharpened, edged tools, together with the manner in which they are handled.

A worker should learn how to sharpen chisels, plane irons, and cabinet scrapers, since they need attention often, but sharpening saws is a very difficult task. A saw, made of good steel and correctly sharpened, will remain sharp a long time unless abused, and should never be sharpened by an amateur, unless he is trained to do the work properly.

Oiling Tools

Tools become rusty from being stored in a damp place and from being handled. This may be prevented by cleaning and oiling them before they are stored away. And while there are products especially made for this purpose, a mixture of 1 part of #10-grade motor oil and 1 part kerosene works perfectly. Keep some in an oil can and apply with a piece of cheesecloth. Wipe the tool with this cloth and then lightly with a dry cloth, thus leaving a thin film of oil. Spraying with a product such as WD-40 is simpler and neater. Whichever treatment you use, the tool shouldn't rust under normal conditions. No tools should ever be stored in a damp place.

Slight rust on the surface of a tool can often be completely removed by rubbing it with a pad of 3/0 steel wool dipped in kerosene. Care should be used not to injure the cutting edge. When a tool is badly rusted, it is impossible to remove all the rust by this method, but try to remove as much as possible.

PAINTBRUSHES

Paintbrushes play an important part in restoration work. Here are several thoughts with which many experienced workers in this field may not agree, but which have proven practical and may save time and money.

Selection of Brushes

A good brush is one that picks up a good amount of paint and lays it on smoothly with almost no drag, pull, or brushmarks remaining in the paint film. A good brush is one that doesn't lose hairs or wear out after a few paint jobs and repeated cleanings. It is also one that works with less arm weariness, gives better coverage, is more fun to use, and saves you money.

Paintbrushes are made of pure bristle, or a mixture of bristle and horsehair, or pure nylon or other synthetics. As a general rule, use bristle brushes for varnish, oil paints and stains, lacquers and shellac, but not for water-based finishes. The water will make natural bristles swell and become soggy. A good bristle brush will do a better job of varnishing than a synthetic brush, but truly good bristle brushes are expensive and hard to find. A good synthetic brush can be used with any type of finish.

If you look at any brush, you will see that the bristles are combined in several sizes. It is the thickness, length, mixture of filament or bristle shape of the end, and soft flag or split ends that make a good brush and determine its cost.

Larger brushes may have two or three wedges, or dividers, where the bristles are seated in the ferrule. But the total wedge thickness should not be over half the thickness of the brush at the ferrule. Very cheap "giveaway" brushes usually have thick wedges and thin layers of bristle, in addition to short bristles of inferior quality.

When you go to buy a new brush, check the total thickness of the bristle, the length, and the general shape. Separate the bristles down the center with a knife or stick and inspect the size and placement of the block insert. Hold the brush by the handle and feel the bristle ends against the back of your other hand. A good brush will feel elastic and springy, and the bristles will not fan out excessively.

Look next at the tips of the bristles to see that they are both tapered and flagged. Flagged ends will show tiny splits and shoots very similar to those of a young plant. Stay away from brushes with blunt-tipped bristles. Finally, check the setting by reading the manufacturer's label or guarantee. It is impossible to see the vulcanized setting in a good paintbrush without breaking it apart. If you can see the rubber base below the edge of the ferrule, it is a poor brush.

It is seldom that any brush other than a 2-inch width is used in most wood finishing. The only real occasion for the use of ½-inch and 1-inch brushes is for the application of stains to a small area. Turnings and carvings can often be worked over better with a 2-inch brush than with a narrower one. It is also necessary to have one or two sizes of small, fine-pointed artist's brushes for touch-up work, especially for stains.

Any type of old and worn brush is satisfactory for applying paint and varnish removers.

It is an excellent plan to mark a letter on both sides near the top of the handle of each brush to indicate a single use for that brush. This letter may be made by hitting a screwdriver lightly with a hammer, making straight-lined letters. Having the letter near the top of the handle makes it easy to identify when the brushes are stored with paper wrapped around the bristles. (See pages 228–29.) Typical markings could be as follows:

V—Varnish
Z—Shellac (Z looks like S)
N—StaiN
L—Lacquer
P—Paint

(It is not necessary to mark brushes used for paint remover, since they are hung on a nail.)

There are other single-purpose brushes used in a well-equipped shop:

1. A large scrub brush to be used with lye as a remover.

2. A small hand scrub brush for abrasive powders on finishes.

3. A long brush with a horizontal handle, used for removing dust (with added wiping) before finishes are applied. A standard product in most paint stores.

4. A brush for cleaning workbenches. A cheap 7-inch paintbrush with coarse bristles is perfect for this work.

5. A shoe brush for use in applying paste furniture wax.

Preparing Brushes

A new paintbrush almost always has some loose hairs that should be removed before the brush is used. This may be done by rolling the brush rapidly between the hands, then beating it lightly across spread fingers. This also removes any dust.

Many professional painters prepare their new paintbrushes for use by suspending the bristles in raw linseed oil for 12 hours. The surplus oil is squeezed out with the fingers, then brushed on a clean, lintless cloth and the brush is ready for use. It is said that this preparation keeps paint from sticking to the bristles too much.

Using Brushes

Standard paintbrushes are composed of three parts: the bristles, the ferrule, which binds them into shape, and the handle. This type of brush should be held by the handle and near the ferrule, very much like a pencil, for ordinary use. When applying varnish or similar products, it is better to hold the brush farther down, so that the fingers and thumb rest on the upper part of the ferrule.

Most brushwork should be done with a short and quick, easy motion of the wrist, and with little movement of the arm. The reason for the lower grip on the brush, when applying varnish, is to take advantage of the V shape of the special varnish brush. Varnish should literally be "flowed" onto a surface with very little brushing, except to smooth it out and pick up snags or runs.

A brush should not be used unless it is clean, the bristles flexible and free from dust. The bristles should never be dipped more than one-half their length into a material, and, before it is applied to a surface, the brush should be wiped lightly on the edge of the container. When using materials that are difficult to work with, it is best to get the brush shaped, and the material flowing properly, by stroking the wet brush a few times on a dust-free newspaper.

Cleaning Brushes

By cleaning a brush thoroughly immediately after use you will avoid the necessity of using a solvent at a later date after the material has hardened, which weakens the bristles. (See note 3 following.)

Under no circumstances should a furniture-finishing brush be left or stored in a container filled with water. This makes the bristles soft and flabby, destroying their spring and resiliency, and often swells and splits the ferrule. It is a common habit in households and is the result of carelessness, want of time, or lack of knowledge of brush cleaning. (It would save time and be better to throw away the brush after use than to store it in water.)

Cleaning a brush immediately after use is a simple matter; it is easy to do, takes little time, and, when completed, the brush can be stored. The brush will then be ready for future use and will be as good as ever, except for ordinary wear.

The method for cleaning a paintbrush is as follows:

1. Wipe the brush on the top edge of the container to remove as much of the paint material as possible.

2. Remove more of the material from the brush by stroking it on clean newspaper.

3. Then clean the brush in the type of solvent recommended for the paint material used. Fill three containers about one-third full. For this purpose the larger-sized cans (about 2 quarts) in which fruit juices are sold are ideal when their tops have

been so removed as to leave a perfectly smooth edge.

4. First hold the brush in one hand and manipulate the bristles with the fingers while submerging the brush in the solvent in the first can.

5. Then remove the brush from the can and continue to manipulate the bristles, while holding the brush upward at an angle of about 45 degrees, so that the solvent fluid will flow from the bristles at their juncture with the ferrule, bringing with it any paint material that has worked deep into the bristles.

6. Repeat operations 3 and 4, *using the same can*, until the bristles and metal on the ferrule are relatively clean. Then repeat those operations in the *next* can, until the metal and bristles are thoroughly clean.

7. Finally wash the brush in the *third* can to remove any paint material remaining. Then shake the brush to remove surplus solvent. Many careful workers follow up with a wash in warm water and detergent, then a water rinse.

The solvents to be used for the cleaning of paintbrushes are listed in the table on page 229.

Sometimes the solvent recommended will not take the stickiness out of a brush completely. This often happens when attempting to clean a brush that has been used with a material (sometimes synthetic) that doesn't indicate on the label what thinner to use. (A proper thinner for a paint material will always clean a brush.) In such cases, experiment either with other solvents or try to complete the cleaning with warm water and detergent.

Paint that has hardened on brushes may be removed by the use of products sold for the purpose.

Storing Brushes

The simplest way of storing brushes is to wrap a few thicknesses of newspaper around the bristles and ferrule, fold it back so that the bristles will not be bent, tie with a string, and lay the brush away in a clean place where there is free circulation of air.

Paintbrushes that are frequently used are often stored by being suspended in a container partly filled with either raw linseed oil, painter's thinner, or a mixture of the two. It is best that only enough of the material be used so that the bristles alone are in the liquid. A brush should never touch the bottom of the container.

There are several ways of adapting a container for this purpose. Painter's thinner will evaporate, so that when the mixture is used the container should be covered. A mason jar is best for this purpose, since it is transparent. Cut a hole in the lid the size and shape of the brush handle. Drill a small hole through the brush handle, put the handle through the hole in the lid, and insert a nail through the hole in the handle to hold the brush suspended in the jar, which should then be filled to the proper level with the solvent. Another method is to use a tall tin can with a lid. Drill or punch holes through the sides of the can at a height where a wire can be inserted through the holes in the can and in the brush handle.

Many professionals who wish to store a

Solvents for Cleaning Paintbrushes

MATERIAL	SOLVENT
House paints, enamels (varnish base), and varnish (oil type)	Turpentine, painter's thinner, or mineral spirits
Synthetic varnish and other similar materials, including plastic	As directed on the can for thinning or, if questionable, try turpentine or mineral spirits
Shellac	Denatured alcohol, ammonia
Lacquer and lacquer sealer	Lacquer thinner (sometimes benzol may be used)
Oil stains	Turpentine, painter's thinner, kerosene, or naphtha
Spirit stains	Denatured alcohol
Water stains	Warm water and detergent
Paste wood fillers	Mineral spirits
Paint and varnish removers	Denatured alcohol
Latex paint	Warm water and detergent, then lacquer thinner, then warm water and soap

number of their frequently used brushes make containers from gallon paint cans. For a closed-top type, a thin disk of plywood is cut to a size that will just go through the can opening. Another is cut but slightly larger. The two disks are temporarily tacked together, and several holes, slightly larger than the width of brush handles, are bored through the disks. The disks are then taken apart and a piece of rubber (an innertube is good),

cut to the size of the smaller one, is placed between them, and the disks are secured together with screws. Slots are then cut through the rubber at the holes. When a brush handle is inserted through the hole from the underside, the rubber holds the brush suspended in the lid.

A way of using a gallon can with an open top is to drive short nails or screws through the sides of the can, near the edge, on which brushes are hung by holes in their handles. Another method is to suspend brushes from a stick in which several oval-shaped notches have been cut to fit the brush handles where they are narrow. These elongated holes are cut along both sides of the stick and are shaped in such a manner that there is a narrow opening on the stick edges to permit the brush handles to pass through.

With these open-can methods, only the raw linseed oil should be used, and the cans should be covered with a piece of cheesecloth to prevent dust from getting into them.

SPRAY GUNS

Whether finishing new furniture or refinishing older pieces, you can get professional results with the spray method by following a few simple instructions.

The basic equipment needed for spray painting is a gun, air compressor, and hose. There are two types of spray guns to choose from, suction or pressure feed. The pressure-feed gun will spray heavy materials, such as varnish and paint, with a low volume of air and is ideal for use with a small compressor. However, the suction-feed gun is best suited for the lacquers and light synthetics used in furniture finishing, since it is easier to clean and allows quick changes of color and materials.

If you expect to do a great deal of high-grade finishing, you may require an oil and moisture separator that filters water, oil, and other particles out of the air supply.

It is always a good idea to get the feel of

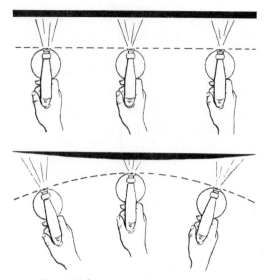

10-1. Top: *Right way—moving the gun parallel to the work surface, keeping the wrist flexible. Hold the gun 6 to 10 inches from work.* Bottom: *Wrong way—keeping the wrist too stiff causes arching and poor distribution of the finish.*

the gun before doing any actual finish spraying. Practice with some inexpensive finishing material until you have adjusted the gun properly and mastered the techniques explained below. Use old cartons or sheets of newspaper tacked to a carton or box for practice spraying.

The spray-gun stroke is made by moving the gun parallel to the work and at a right angle to the surface. The speed of stroking should be about the same as brushing. Gun distance from the work should be between 6 and 8 inches. Each spray stroke should overlap the previous one by one-half to assure a full wet coat without streaks.

Never tilt the gun up or down away

from the surface or angle the gun at the end of the spray strokes. Both of these practices result in an uneven spray pattern that coats some areas heavier than others.

The fluid flow is regulated by the fluid-adjusting screw on the gun. You start with the adjusting screw nearly closed, then gradually open it until the spray seems right. A distorted spray usually indicates a dirty air cap. To remedy the situation, take the cap off and wash it carefully in clean solvent. If it is necessary to ream the air-cap holes, use a matchstick or a broom bristle—never an instrument that is hard or sharp.

It is a proven fact that 90 percent of spraying ailments can be traced to lack of cleanliness. Clean your gun immediately after use. If the paint dries in the gun, it will be almost impossible to get out.

Triggering the spray gun is the heart of spray technique, since proper triggering prevents excessive overspray from being deposited on adjacent surfaces and conserves material. To "trigger" the spray gun properly, start the stroke with a dry gun, pull the trigger when the gun is opposite the edge of the work, release the trigger at the end of the work, and continue the dry stroke a few inches before reversing for the second stroke. The main point to remember is hitting the exact edge of the work, maintaining full coverage without undue overspray.

An important factor in spraying furniture expertly is setting up the job beforehand to get it done with the least effort and without overspraying parts already coated. Work on such parts as legs,

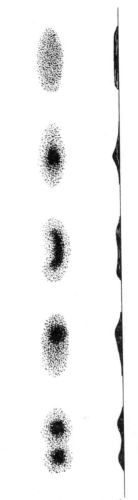

10-2. *The correct pattern is shown at the top, while poor fan patterns—the result of incorrect pressure, a dirty spray gun, etc.—are also detailed.*

stretchers, and other slender members is best done with a small spray pattern 3 to 5 inches wide. This small pattern is dense at the edges, permitting close control of overspray.

Chairs and tables are easily handled if mounted on a pedestal turntable. If you have an outboard turning stand for your lathe, it can be used as a base. Chairs are usually turned over for the legs to be sprayed, especially if you use the bench setup shown in Figure 10-8. Some sprayers also work on table legs upside down since this position gives the best spray angle.

There are three common methods of painting chair and table legs. Most beginners like the four-square method, in which the operator stands opposite each of the four sides in turn and sprays everything facing him.

A faster method is the diagonal system, which employs two work positions. The operator faces the corner of the chair or table and aims the gun at the corner of each leg, covering two of the facing surfaces with one stroke. Then the table is turned and the other two surfaces of each leg are sprayed in the same manner. If the work has round legs, the usual system is to spray the inside of all legs first and then spray each leg completely.

To spray an entire table, use a vertical fan pattern and spray all the inner sides of the legs first. With the insides of all legs sprayed, the general procedure is to spray four-square; that is, you spray all of the other outer surfaces and edges facing you in a systematic manner. The top is sprayed last. If you are using lacquer, take care not to overspray surfaces already coated. If you like the faster system of spraying legs two sides at a time, use a horizontal fan for good coverage. In this case, spray the legs inside and out and then change to the

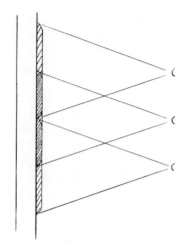

10-3. *Spray bands at each end.*

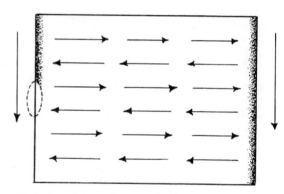

10-4. *Overlap strokes one-half.*

vertical fan required for the rest of the job.

In casework and cabinet jobs, the inside is always sprayed first. Then the outside is worked four-square, the right end first, followed by the front, left end, and top. On some jobs it is practical to leave draw-

10-5. On level surfaces, start at the near edge to avoid overspraying on coated work. Any overspraying then falls on uncoated work.

ers in place, although the usual practice is to remove them for spraying separately.

Any brushing material for furniture finishing can be applied by spraying. However, the gun is at its best when used with quick-drying materials. Both non-grain-raising and pigment stains can be obtained in quick-drying products, which can be recoated in from 10 to 30 minutes.

Good quick-drying fillers can be obtained that dry for recoating in 2 hours. In top coats, nothing beats lacquer for speed—you can finish maple natural with a double coat of lacquer and the work will be dry to the touch in a matter of minutes. Spraying synthetics, too, are fast, with many good 1- and 2-hour air-dry products available.

A final word on finishing materials: always strain them through fine screen or cheesecloth before spraying. Also, if you're using a spray gun to apply the paint, add 2 tablespoons of mineral spirits to thin the mixture enough to ensure an even flow of paint.

SPRAY-CAN PAINTING

From a modest beginning, aerosol paints have grown to a sophisticated line of products. Today you can buy aerosol paints in flat, semigloss, or high-gloss finishes, in frosted finishes, in antique glazes, in metallic finishes, and in specialized primers. These will do a good job on small items but are slow and expensive on large work.

There are four basic components in aerosol paints: the container, the valve, the propellants that produce the pressure, and the paint itself. The principle that makes aerosol painting work is a simple one. With the injection of the propellant, the pressure within the container becomes greater than that in the atmosphere. Thus, when the valve is opened, the pressure produces a fine spray of paint.

Most aerosol paints are stirred by the movement of small balls within the container. When you shake the can, you cause the balls to move and stir the contents, mixing in any pigment that may have settled at the bottom of the can. Remember that this pre-painting "shake-up" is a very important step. Without a thorough shaking, the paint may come out too thin, or you may use up the pressure before you use up the paint.

Here is another important suggestion. When you have shaken the container well, hold the can at its top and swirl the container around until the ball is at the bottom. This trick will ensure blending of the pigments, which often settle at the bottom of the container.

Here is a worthwhile precaution: try your hand at spray painting on a piece of scrap cardboard or newspaper. Once you get the hang of it—which you will in no time—you'll find how simple spray painting can be.

Application

Place the piece on a horizontal surface when possible to avoid running and facilitate even distribution of paint. After the preparations are completed, and your aerosol paint is completely shake blended, you're ready to go. Hold the container at least 10 to 12 inches away from the surface you are painting, keeping the nozzle parallel with the piece. Press the button all the way down and move the can evenly over the surface. Release pressure on the button before you end each stroke—the trick is to follow through. That is, work across the piece starting before its left edge, beyond its right edge. Overlap the first stroke with at least one-third of the next. Always keep your distance equal—the angle 90 degrees. Be sure to use rapid, smooth strokes as you spray. If you stop the movement of the can, or go too slowly, drips will result.

If you've never used aerosol paints before, you are likely to hold the valve down too long, as if you were using some other aerosol product. This "freezing on the button" will cause dripping and running. Don't forget to turn the can upside down when you are through painting. Press the trigger once or twice with the can in this position. It clears the nozzle and keeps it clear for the next job.

If you are painting cabinets with drawers, it's a good idea to open the drawers ¼ inch so that the spray will cover the sides, top, and bottom to that distance. Spray chairs upside down first, working along legs and rungs, then reverse it to spray the top.

Only when spraying openwork—wicker chair seats, screens, or radiators—do you turn the spray can at an angle. Tilt to 45 degrees then, to prevent too much paint from passing through the openings. Here, spray the first coat left to right, the second top to bottom to be sure you are painting all surfaces.

Anyone who has had trouble applying lacquers by brush will appreciate the spray-can method. The thickness of each

10-6. *How to spray with aerosol paints: 1. Test the spray pattern against cardboard before starting work. Measure the distance from the target: note the spread of the sprayed pattern.*

2. *Start coverage of the surface at the left and work to the right evenly. Carry spray on past the end of the piece and then release the button to stop the spray. (Continued)*

1.   2.

3.

4.

5.

6.

(Figure 10-6 continued)

3. The second stroke overlaps the first by about one-third. Maintain equal distance from the work at all times for uniform application. 4. If the spray can is tilted at an angle while spraying, paint "piles up" and runs badly. A right-angle position is best for flat work. 5. After spraying, turn the can upside down and press the button once or twice. This frees the feeder tube and valve and prevents the can from clogging. 6. A removable trigger on some cans ensures nonclogging, since the trigger can be cleaned after use. Thinner or solvent will clean the trigger.

10-7. In spraying a finish on wickerwork, the can should be held at a 45-degree angle so that the finish is not forced through the weave openings.

coat is easily controlled. Brush marking is done away with.

If you wish to have a particularly smooth-finished product, it is helpful to sand the surface between each coat of paint. Number 400 sandpaper is best for this job, and one should apply two or three coats of spray paint for maximum coverage. Shake the container frequently throughout to ensure consistency of the paint.

Although ventilation is an important safety factor in spray painting, attempt to find a spot that is both well ventilated and yet not in a draft. Wind gusts can catch the

paint particles and deflect the spray. Work in a room where the temperature is about 70 degrees F or higher. This rule applies to all painting, but the spray can works better and won't clog at this temperature.

If you are planning a touch-up rather than a complete repainting, it's a good idea to spray a swatch of paper, let the paint dry, and then compare the spray paint with the covering that was originally used on the piece. Sometimes even a small color difference will be glaring when the job is done.

Stenciling with a spray can is fun. Make a stencil cutout and paste it to the wall or other surface with a paste made of soap flakes and water. Spray through, and when the paint is thoroughly dry, remove the stencil. It picks off easily, and the wall can be wiped down to remove the paste.

Safety Hints

Label instructions on aerosol products have safety hints as well as instructions for the user. Remember, these products have been tested by their manufacturers, and instructions are well founded and should be followed. The manufacturer knows his product, so try it his way.

Aerosol paints are flammable mixtures, so one of the most necessary safety precautions is keeping these products away from open flames, particularly during use. The nature of the container also requires the user to store the aerosols in areas that are not too sunny and warm. Absolutely *never* keep them where temperatures are warmer than 120 degrees F—even when empty. And do not incinerate these products.

If by now you are wondering how one does safely discard these products—without incinerating or puncturing—there is a way. Turn the can upside down, press the nozzle, and allow every bit of the propellant to be released. When nothing further comes out, the can is empty and you may discard it. Incineration is still a hazard, however, so let the community sanitation service deal with the empty containers.

HANDY FINISHING ITEMS

There are several items that you can make that will simplify wood finishing.

Tack Rags

A tack rag is used for the final wiping of a piece to be varnished. Dry brushing and wiping with a clean soft cloth will not remove all foreign particles and dust. A tack rag must be used for a smooth finish and will save much sanding and rubbing. These rags may usually be purchased in paint and automotive parts stores.

1. The best material for this purpose is a piece of finely woven cheesecloth about 2 feet square. This should be washed in several changes of tepid water and wrung out slightly to prevent drip. (The back panel of a man's shirt, hemmed to turn in raw edges, also can be used to make a tack rag.)

2. Apply pure turpentine to the moistened cloth and shake it out loosely. Then sprinkle varnish freely over the cloth, fold

10-8. Above: *Turn chairs upside down; first spray the inner surfaces of legs and rungs; then spray the outer edges and the upper portion.* Below: *In spraying a chest of drawers, open the drawers about ¼ inch so that all the edges are completely painted.*

all edges to the center, and twist it into a tight roll to force out the water and saturate the cloth fibers with the varnish and turpentine. Refold the cloth and wring it as tight as possible. Then unfold the cloth, wave it in the air a few moments, and refold it, being sure all raw edges are turned inward to avoid threads coming loose. Enough varnish should be used to make the cloth quite yellow. It should be sticky enough to pick up dust but dry enough so it won't deposit moisture.

3. A tack rag, when properly cared for, may be used almost indefinitely. It should never be allowed to dry out—even for a few minutes. It should occasionally be unfolded, sprinkled with a few drops of water and turpentine, refolded, and wrung out. Under this treatment a tack rag improves with age and is kept soft and flexible.

4. Store a tack rag in a mason jar, sealed tight with a rubber washer. Never store the rag in a metal container, since the water in the rag will rust the metal. Always add some turpentine and water to the rag (as mentioned earlier) before storing it. A tack rag left in the open air for some time becomes a fire hazard through spontaneous combustion.

Pick Sticks

Pick sticks are used to remove small particles from a freshly varnished surface. They can be made as follows:

1. Swab sticks used by doctors and sold by drugstores are the best for this purpose.

2. Place 1 part of liquid varnish (less than a teaspoonful) and about 6 to 8 parts of dry brown varnish (crushed) in a small, clean tin can. Place this can in a larger one, a quarter full of water, and then heat.

3. Stir and cook until a drop of the melted mixture will form a stiff pill when cooled on glass and rolled between the fingers.

4. Dip a stick end into the melted mixture and, with fingers moistened with saliva, form a small pear-shaped ball.

5. For use, tap the ball on the hand and, if the consistency is correct, the ball will become sticky. With an upward motion, lift the speck of dust, lint, etc., with the stick.

It is a difficult problem to store pick sticks for future use. They may sometimes be softened by heat but, as they are easy to make, it is best to make fresh ones for each job.

Strike Wires

Professional wood refinishers use a strike wire in a small can (or tin cup) when brushing varnish. Surplus varnish can be wiped from the brush after it has been dipped in the can, by "striking" (wiping) the brush on the wire, rather than against the side of the can.

A strike wire may be installed in a small can (or tin cup) by punching a hole in each of the opposite sides, just below the rim. A wire is then run through the holes, cut off about an inch from the outside of the can, and the ends turned down. The holes should be spaced in such a way that the wire will be off center and closer to one side of the can than the other.

It is always good practice to varnish

from a small can rather than from the container in which it was purchased. The greatest detriment to successful varnishing is small particles like dust, which must be avoided by every possible means. When the job is completed, any varnish left in the small can should be thrown away, as it may contain dust or be damaged by exposure to the air.

The greater the pains taken when varnishing, the more success will be attained in the final finish.

Rubbing Blocks

A rubbing block is best made of flexible material, like a sponge-rubber pad or a block (about ½ inch thick) of hard rubbing felt. This should be cut slightly narrower than the abrasive paper and placed over it for rubbing. Two types of rubbing blocks may be purchased. The first is of a size for an eighth cut of abrasive paper and is made of thin sheet metal, with an inverted U-shaped grip and a padded rubber bottom. It is cheaply made but good. The second is made of an aluminum casting about 2 inches by 6 inches, with springs holding a rubber padded bottom and with a coil of abrasive paper attached, which may be drawn out as needed. Naturally, this tool is more expensive. Both may usually be found in paint and hardware stores.

Rubbing Pads

A rubbing pad is used for the final smoothing or polishing of a finish, with the use of abrasive powders (pumice stone or rottenstone) and oil and water. Professional shops seem to prefer a block of hard rubbing felt about 1 inch thick (of the type recommended for a rubbing block). One may be made of several layers of an old felt hat or several pieces of felt padding sewed together, of the kind that is used under rugs and carpets, or a blackboard eraser.

STORAGE OF PAINTS

There is no necessity for the great waste of paint, enamels, varnish, lacquer, or synthetic materials used for refinishing that is so often the case. All of these may be saved for future use with a little care.

When not properly stored, the surface of the material left in the can usually thickens into a skin, even though the lid is secured tightly, but this can be prevented. The proper storage of these materials is a very simple matter and will save much money. Proceed as follows:

1. Clean most of the material from the groove in the top of the can, but leave a small amount so that the lid will seal. If the material is heavy or dried, it must be removed until the surface is clean and even. This can be done with a screwdriver, followed by a knife blade, but care should be exercised in order that none will drop into the can.

2. Clean off all dried material from the underside of the lid with the same tools and wipe it clean with a cloth.

3. Pour on the surface of the material in the can a small amount of the thinner used

with the material. Use just enough so that it will spread to a thin film. Use turpentine or painter's thinner for house paints, enamels, and all types of varnishes. Use a lacquer thinner for lacquers. Use the type of thinner directed on the can for synthetic and any other type of material.

4. Place the lid on the can and set the can on the floor. Place a rag on the lid and step on it. Move it back to the workbench, place a piece of paper over the can, and drive the lid down to a tight fit by tapping around the edges with a hammer. (The paper over the can keeps excess material from spattering.)

5. Move the can to the storage place, taking care not to rock or shake the can so that the film of thinner does not mix with the material.

The film of thinner can't evaporate in a tightly sealed can, since there is not enough air. It is lighter than the material and will remain on top almost indefinitely, thus preventing the formation of a coating or skin. When the material is needed again, remove the lid; after stirring, it will be ready to use. It must be remembered that thinners evaporate, and it is often necessary to add much thinner before storage. Materials stored in this manner may be used without being strained.

A method employed by some in storing paint materials is to cut a piece of heavy paper the size and shape of the can, placing it on top of the remaining material in the can. This is helpful, but not as satisfactory as the film of thinner.

Materials such as linseed oils, shellac, etc., need no liquid film coating for protection. Depend on the tightness of the container top for their proper storage.

Reviving Old Paints

When a can of paint has a dried skin on its top, this can best be removed by cutting around its edge with a sharp knife blade and then picking it out by taking hold of the center of the skin with two fingers. House paints and enamels should then be thinned by the addition of some commercially boiled linseed oil, turpentine, or painter's thinner, with a little japan drier to increase their drying power. They should also be strained through cheesecloth or a sheer stocking.

Varnishes and lacquers often thicken to a point where they are worthless for further use. If thin enough to use, add pure turpentine to varnish and lacquer thinner to lacquers. Paints, enamels, varnishes, and lacquers revived in this manner are seldom satisfactory. It pays to use care and store these materials in a manner that will keep them without deterioration or destruction.

THE HOME WORKSHOP

A person who enjoys tinkering with tools is indeed fortunate if he has a home workshop where creative hobbies may be practiced and minor repairs for the upkeep of the home completed. Unfortunately, many homes do not have the space in which such a shop can be set up. That should not be a discouragement. A removable bench top can be clamped to a kitchen table, or a portable cabinet bench can be designed that may be stored. The floor around such a workshop can be covered with a mass of old newspapers, over which can be spread an old piece of canvas. Many a piece of furniture has been repaired and refinished and something useful created under such conditions, without damage to the furnishings or the room.

When there is ample space in which to create a workshop, many things must be considered. There must be good air circulation to get rid of the fumes from volatile materials. The place should be dry, for dampness ruins tools. Electric current must be available for any power tools, and work can best be done in a strong light, such as that from 100- and 150-watt lamps. The place must be of adequate size for the type of work to be done, and it must be heated for winter use.

Under certain conditions a basement is an ideal place for a shop. Attics are fine so far as space is concerned, but most of them are hot in summer and cold in winter. The side or end wall of a garage may often have sufficient space, but in most climates there is a heating problem in winter. The same is true of a barn. A small service room or bedroom may often be made available for a shop, and those with light and heat often make an ideal place in which to work. Under ordinary circumstances anyone who wants to work with tools can find a place where it can be done, even if it is necessary to set up a temporary platform outdoors on sawhorses.

A shop centers around the workbench. It is needless to give directions for building one since a bench must be built to suit the available space and personal needs. A workbench for hard service must be made of sturdy material with a thick plank top. Most of the work at a bench is done while standing. A workbench with the top 36 inches from the floor is ideal for a tall person but should be made lower, to a convenient height, for shorter people. Hard maple is the best wood for workbench tops. Many plans are available in technical books for the construction of workbenches, but most of them are too elaborate in design for the needs of the hobbyist.

The following are a few practical ideas that might be helpful in the construction of a home workshop:

1. Measure space available and draw plans prior to any construction. Make a list of materials of the kind and size necessary for the complete construction program. Don't deviate from the plan unless unforeseen conditions arise. Start with the workbench construction, followed by shelves and racks, unless prior work must be done on the space or room available. Construct one thing at a time and take plenty of time.

2. When laying out this plan, there are a number of things to be taken into consideration. The workbench should be against a wood wall or one on which a sheet of plywood can be fastened to hold loops or racks for hanging tools.

3. It is convenient and makes working at a bench easier if the most frequently used tools are on the wall back of the bench. Flat strips of heavy woven cloth, called hood lacings or hood gaskets, are

available at auto supply stores at low cost. They are perfect for holding tools when nailed or screwed, in proper-sized loops, along a wall.

To hang such tools as hammers, hatchets, mallets, putty knives, etc., on the wall, drill a ³⁄₁₆-inch hole through the handle near the end, and use finishing nails (small-headed) to hang them on. It is best to countersink the holes in the handle slightly on both sides with a "rose drill," which makes it easier to match the hole with the nail when hanging up the tool.

Some workers prefer to lock up their tools and yet have them hanging on the wall back of the bench. This may be done by making two large, shallow boxes of the same size. One is secured to the wall and the other is hinged to the first, so that it may be swung around as a cover and locked. Of course, one of the most popular tool racks is made from perforated hardboard or pegboard, with matching tool holders.

4. The question of light in a shop is very important. It is best not to place a workbench directly in front of a window, since it is difficult to face the light and see the work on a bench clearly. It is better to have strong lights over the bench and near shelves for supplies. Plug outlets for power tools are handy.

5. Ample storage space on shelves is also important. Shelves 5 inches wide for storage and easy display of small items and about 10 inches wide for the larger ones are satisfactory. Vertical space will not be wasted if the heights of the various-sized containers are measured in advance of the laying out of shelf spacing. It is of great convenience if a shelf about 5 inches wide is run along the wall about 10 inches above the workbench and for its full length.

6. When there is space for a horizontal lumber rack to be placed on a side wall, it is a great convenience. When the ceiling is of rafters that are within reaching distance, as in a basement, very convenient racks may be made for the storage of dowel rods, abrasive papers, long tools, short lumber, etc., by nailing narrow cleats across the beams. Convenient triangular-shaped racks for short lumber may be built in a corner.

7. There is one method of keeping track of tools that may be missing from their space on a wall or have been borrowed and not returned. This is by painting an outline of the tool on the wall where it is customarily kept.

8. It is a good plan to keep all edged cutting tools (chisels, planes, saws, etc.) in a locked cabinet or drawer if you expect to keep them sharp, particularly if there are children in the household.

9. The storage of small items such as brads, screws, staples, corrugated nails, etc., is always a problem. Keeping them in small "jelly glasses" with tops and storing them on narrow shelves permits visibility and easy access. Likewise, nails of various sizes and types, solder, stick shellac, powdered stains, etc., which are larger in size or kept in greater quantities, may be visibly stored in "peanut butter" jars or other glass jars with tops and wide openings.

For better identification of sizes of materials thus stored, it is a good plan to make notations on small gummed-paper labels and stick them on the jars. A good light should be near the shelves.

Then there is the problem of storing various types of materials that are useful for the type of work done in the shop or for repairs about the home, such as light cords and sockets, hinges, locks, and door knobs, etc. Labeled coffee cans, both the 1- and 2-pound size with lids, make ideal containers.

Good Shop Practice

The workshop is considered by most workers as a sanctuary, with a warning to others that "Thou shall not trespass, nor touch a thing, nor use a tool, nor clean up the place." This is not because the worker is selfish, but because he doesn't like work once started to be disturbed, and tools taken without permission damaged, not returned, or lost. He likes to clean up the place himself, so that tools and materials may be put back in order where they belong and odds and ends of lumber, etc., not thrown away but put in a special place for safekeeping and future use.

All these thoughts are natural and logical, for when a person turns out work that is admired, not only are the shop, tools, and equipment held in high respect, but more credit is given to the material things than to oneself.

Experienced workers get into bad habits, so beginners will profit if they start out with good shop practice. A few examples follow:

1. Arrange the tools that are most often used on a wall or in a cabinet in a position where they may be easily reached. When a tool is used, put it back where it belongs, unless it is to be used again soon.

2. Have great respect for edged cutting tools. Always lay a plane on its side and handle a chisel or saw with care. More tools are dulled or damaged by careless handling than by normal use.

3. Prevent rust on tools before it starts by wiping them with a half-and-half mixture of kerosene and light oil.

4. Keep the workbench neat and reasonably clean while work is in progress and brush up the entire shop when required.

5. Good receptacles for the disposal of sweepings from the bench and floor are 50- and 100-pound metal lard containers, which may usually be purchased for very little from bakeshops. (They will be greasy, so they must be washed.) When disposing of trash, it is best to separate all metal things from the burnables. The 50-pound cans are a good size for the metal trash and for storing clean rags and burlap.

6. A shop is certain to get full of dust from use of tools and sanding. Shelves and workbench should be dusted and the floor well swept before using finishing materials.

7. Regardless of how clean a shop may be, always spread clean newspapers under pieces that are being worked on. The paper will catch drippings from finish removers, glue, or finish materials, and prevent dust.

8. Oil power tools at regular intervals. Stores that specialize in the sale of electric

motors sell a type of oil that is best for motors and that will not burn if the motor should become overheated.

9. Two or more jobs may often be worked at the same time by dovetailing the work on one piece in with another.

10. Teach children proper respect for tools.

11. Lending tools is a bad practice unless it is kept under control.

12. Take all possible precautions against fire. It is a good idea to have a fire extinguisher in the shop.

13. The best products and tools are the cheapest from every standpoint.

14. Standing on floors is hard on the legs and feet. Very often sufficiently large scrap pieces of thick wallboard may be bought at a most reasonable price at builders' supply stores. These may be placed on a floor like a rug before a workbench or work table and make standing easier.

15. It is difficult to do fine, close work at a bench while standing. A flat, sturdy wooden box of the proper height makes a fine seat.

Index